HEALTH MATTE

HEALTH MATTERS
AT WORK

David A. Brodie

TUDOR

© D. Brodie 1994

First published in Great Britain by Tudor Business Publishing Limited. Sole
distributors worldwide, Hodder and Stoughton (Publishers) Ltd, 338 Euston Road,
London NW1 3BH.

A CIP record for this book is available
from the British Library

ISBN 1-872807-90-9

The right of David Brodie to be identified as the author
of this work has been asserted by him in accordance with the
Copyright, Designs and Patents Act 1988.

Typeset by Deltatype Ltd, Ellesmere Port, Cheshire
Printed and bound by Athenæum Press Ltd.,
Gateshead, Tyne & Wear.

Illustrations by G. Davies

Contents

1		The Cost of Ill Health	1
	1.1	Absenteeism	1
	1.2	Trends in Health	7
	1.3	Cost Analysis	10
2		The Benefits of a Healthy Workforce	14
	2.1	Individual Benefits	14
	2.2	Industrial Benefits	16
	2.3	National Benefits	20
	2.4	Achieving Health for All	23
	2.5	A Corporate Philosophy	25
3		The Health of the Nation's Workforce	29
	3.1	Results from National Surveys	29
	3.2	The Health of a Company	44
	3.3	Government Targets	48
4		Auditing the Company's Health	55
	4.1	Health Audit Strategies	55
	4.2	What Should Be Audited	68
	4.3	Occupational Health	97
5		Examining the Individual's Health	105
	5.1	Health Screening	105
	5.2	Coronary Risk Factors	112
	5.3	Fitness Assessment	120

	5.4	Alcohol and Drug Abuse	129
	5.5	HIV/Aids	134
	5.6	Work-Related Upper Limb Disorder	138
	5.7	Back Problems	144
	5.8	Driving and Fatigue	150
	5.9	Weight Control	154
6		Work Stress – a Special Case	157
	6.1	What is Stress?	157
	6.2	The Causes of Stress	158
	6.3	The Symptoms of Stress	160
	6.4	Likely Candidates for Stress	162
	6.5	Stress and Lifestyle	164
	6.6	Stress and Organizations	169
	6.7	Coping with Stress	172
	6.8	Case Studies	184
7		Becoming a Healthy Company	188
	7.1	The Evidence	188
	7.2	Planning Principles	191
	7.3	The Well-Being Company	196
	7.4	Resources	200
	7.5	Company Size and Structure	202
	7.6	Case Studies	205
8		Look After Your Heart Workplace Initiatives	213
	8.1	Introduction	213
	8.2	The LAYH Workplace Project	214
	8.3	The Heartbeat Award	218
	8.4	Resources	219
	8.5	Case Studies	220
9		Specific Actions at Work	225
	9.1	The Fitness Centre	225
	9.2	Exercising in the Office	229
	9.3	Health Promotion Initiatives	235
10		Keeping *Health at Work* on the Agenda	243
Appendix 1		Fitness and Health in Business Questionnaire	246
Appendix 2		The University of Liverpool Manual Handling Assessment Checklist	250

Appendix 3 Wellsource Body Composition Profile   254
Appendix 4 The University of Liverpool Policy on Alcohol 256
Appendix 5 Sections from the University of Liverpool Policy
            on Drug Abuse   258
Appendix 6 Sections from the University of Liverpool
            Advice on HIV/Aids   260
Appendix 7 Other sources of helpful information   262
Index   265

Acknowledgements

My thanks to the following who kindly gave me permission to use their material.

- Dr S. E. Bishop, Glaxo Pharmaceuticals UK Ltd
- Dr R. G. Buss, University of Liverpool
- Dr C. M. Bowes, University of Liverpool
- Lesley Burn, Mersey Regional Health Authority
- Dr B. D. Cox, University of Cambridge and Health Promotion Research Trust
- Elite Training, May Road, Heswall
- Lynda Gibson, Wirral Metropolitan College
- Dr I. Gourlay, British Rail, Manchester
- Mr J. Hammond, University of Liverpool, for proofreading the draft
- Dr S. A. Robson, Cheshire County Council
- Sister E. Smith, Urenco (Capenhurst) Ltd

Also to the numerous authors and organizations whose work I read or consulted. This is not an academic textbook so it has not been appropriate to reference every contribution in the conventional style. To do so could have spoiled the continuity of the text. Some of the lists or case studies have resulted from a précis or paraphrase of other sources. Should the reader find familiar material embedded in the bullet points, I hope it will be treated as a compliment to have been the stimulus for my efforts.

I am especially indebted to Debi Leonard who typed the manuscript of this book with fortitude, constant good humour and a rare ability to decipher my handwriting. Her industry and commitment meant that the publisher's deadline could be achieved.

To my wife, Megan, and daughter, Jo-Anne, who tolerated my absence during a well-earned holiday to allow me to remain at home to complete this book. To my son, Tom, who tolerated my cooking at the same time.

Introduction

The background to this book was a concern and a perceived need for information and suggestions around health at work. The recent government strategy on health has implicated the workplace in its proposals. However, the prescription lacks the detail needed by the practitioner. This book is an attempt to:

- consider the implications of health at work
- examine the health of a company and its employees
- establish actions to become healthier

When faced with the task of eating an elephant it is advisable to do so in small chunks. The same recommendation applies to this book. It has not been designed, like an enthralling novel, to be read from cover to cover without a break. Feel free to dip in and out at random. The 'bullet point' style is to facilitate just that approach. A final recommendation: keep a yellow[1] highlighter pen to hand as you read it. Mark the points that seem important, interesting or require action. When you have finished the book, the highlighted parts represent your personal summary. You will then have produced what matters to you about health at work – and that's what matters!

[1] N.B. It need not be yellow. Studies by the RAF show that lurid pink is the most retinal-sensitive colour, but I prefer yellow.

1

The Cost of Ill Health

1.1   Absenteeism

'Officers at Canterbury prison took an average of five weeks a year off sick'.

Absenteeism and sickness are difficult terms to differentiate. The majority of absenteeism is caused by sickness so it would not be unreasonable to relate the two. If this notion is acceptable then the evidence points clearly to the fact that *Britain's workforce is getting sicker*. In 1992 certified sickness absence exceeded 500 million days for the first time. Changed reporting methods will contribute to the increasing trend, but self-certification has now been with us for over ten years so the blame cannot be placed entirely on such aspects. In the last ten years, female absenteeism has risen by 111 per cent. This is more than twice the 55 per cent increase recorded for men.

It is also interesting to compare the absenteeism rates for different sectors of the workforce. The norm for the private sector is estimated by the Confederation for British Industry to be about seven days per year. However the average local council worker, according to the Audit Commission, is losing 19.3 days per year.

Differences occur within council workforces and between geographical areas. Firemen, for example, have an average absence of 15 days per year, post office workers 14 days and policemen 12 days. Before Camden council (London) instituted major changes to reduce absenteeism, its direct labour force was losing 40 days per year and its leisure department workers (both white and blue collar) were away from work for more than ten weeks a year. This is in addition to their normal holiday entitlement.

A recent House of Commons select committee showed that ill health in the police force is costing some 1.1 million working days which is equivalent to more than £120 million in sick pay alone. Although this puts the police way above the national average (see Table 1.1), they are not as high as workers in heavy engineering and transport.

Table 1.1
Days Lost Through Sickness

EMPLOYMENT SECTOR	DAYS LOST PER YEAR
Transport	20
London Boroughs (manual workers)	19
Heavy engineering	15
Police	12
Civil Service	11
NHS administration staff	7-11
Energy and water supply	10
Coal miners	9
Chemical workers	9
NATIONAL AVERAGE	**7**
Shopworkers and distribution services	7
Catering	7
Construction	6
Financial services	5

An average of 20 days per employee each year is lost to sickness by bus crews and train drivers with heavy engineering taking second place with an average absence of 15 days.

A recent study by the Industrial Society found that the absence rates in the public sector are about one per cent higher than in the private sector. The health service is the highest level of nearly 6 per cent of the workforce and manufacturing running them close at 5.5 per cent.

Wales and London seem to be the areas with the highest levels of absenteeism. Northern Ireland and the Home Counties have the lowest levels. Small companies have a lower level of absenteeism than large companies and part-time workers are more liable to absence than full timers.

There also seems to be a relationship between a company's attitude to health and its level of absenteeism. Those companies that provide healthy food in their canteens tended to have lower rates of absentee-ism, as did organizations which had a rigorous smoking policy. Also 95 per cent of those companies who operate performance-related pay had low absence rates indicating the merits of incentives.

With the exception of the Netherlands, the United Kingdom has one of the poorest overall absenteeism records in Europe.

Table 1.2
Percentage of Working Days Lost During 1991
(absenteeism)

Netherlands	6.8
UK	5.8
Canada	4.6
Portugal	4.2
France	3.9
Spain	3.8
Italy	3.2
Germany	2.9
Belgium	1.9
USA	1.4

In terms of the percentage of days lost, the UK has nearly 50 per cent more absenteeism than the average for Europe. These percentages are not always easy to authenticate especially as it is estimated that in the private sector nearly half of all companies do not keep accurate figures on absenteeism.

Reasons for Absence

The main reasons provided by employees for absence are given in rank order as:

1. Colds and 'flu
2. Stomach upsets
3. Back problems
4. Emotional problems and stress
5. Non-work injuries
6. Medical appointments
7. Pregnancy problems
8. Ear-ache

It is difficult with self-certification to assess the authenticity of this list and it is recognized that interpretation may differ. For example the incidence of a genuine 'flu epidemic is quite rare but many people report a heavy cold as 'flu. In terms of the potential to infect other people it could be argued that in certain working environments it is preferable to stay away from work. However it is quite clear that some employees will use a heavy cold as a reason for absence whereas others will ignore the symptoms and continue to work.

Stress-related conditions appear to be on the increase with some reporting the incidence to be as high as 35–40 per cent of the total absences. A leading cause of stress-related psychological illness is divorce with companies losing £200 million a year in absences. Stress-related illnesses include heart disease, depression and hypertension and it is for this reason that a whole chapter of this book is devoted to the subject. One of the consequences of stress-related illness is that alcohol and drug dependence increases and the seven years up to 1991 have shown a major increase in this area which could have been even greater if short spells of illness lasting less than four days were taken into account.

Recent government studies have revealed that ten per cent of male employees will take sick leave as a result of drinking alcohol heavily. It has been estimated that these so called 'problem drinkers' may take up to four times as many days off work as others. This results in between eight million and 14 million additional days of absence. The cost to industry is a staggering £700 million annually. This level can be put into perspective when comparing the loss to British industry as a result of strikes. During the same period of time there were 586,000 working days lost through strikes which is a difference of about 24 times. Not only are problem drinkers likely to take more time off work but the accident statistics indicate that a quarter of the incidents reported involve workers who have been drinking. This is supported by a survey of 300 British companies showing that alcohol-related problems are common, with at least 60 per cent of employers blaming alcohol for poor performance and absenteeism. Over half of those surveyed considered alcohol to be a factor in workplace injuries. The smaller

Table 1.3
Liver Cirrhosis Mortality Among British Males

OCCUPATIONAL GROUP	RISK
(Risk compared with average)	
Publicans	10.2 times greater
Foremen of ships, lighters and other vessels	9.0 times
Deck, engine room hands, bargemen, lightermen and boatmen	8.7 times
Barmen	6.1 times
Managers of hotels, clubs etc.	5.5 times
Waiters	4.6 times
Deck, engineering and radio officers and pilots on ships	4.1 times
Electrical engineers	3.8 times
Hotel, residential club managers	3.4 times
Officers (ships and aircraft), air traffic controllers	3.3 times
Innkeepers	3.1 times
Officers, UK.armed forces	3.0 times
Catering supervisors	2.9 times
Fishermen	2.9 times
Bus conductors	2.7 times

Chefs, cooks	2.6 times
Restauranteurs	2.6 times
Authors, writers, journalists	2.6 times
General labourers	2.4 times
Travel stewards, hospital and hotel porters	2.3 times
Drivers' mates	2.2 times
Actors, musicians, entertainers, stage managers	2.2 times
Winders, reelers	2.0 times

companies of less than 200 employees were found to be less likely to have the problem than larger companies.

There also appears to be a large discrepancy between occupational groups and risk of alcohol-related illness. It appears, rather unsurprisingly, that publicans lead the table of jobs most at risk from death by cirrhosis of the liver. They are ten times more likely to suffer than the average British male.

Other high risk groups include air traffic controllers, ships' officers and airline pilots. Table 1.3 refers specifically to men and studies have not shown the same link between drinking and absence in women. This may simply reflect a lower level of alcohol consumption in women, but increasing affluence, full-time employment and stress could well see a future which shows similar relationships in women. In men the likelihood of sick leave is clearly greater in those that drank in excess of 35 units (i.e. 17 pints of beer or lager) per week. Twelve per cent of these heavy drinkers took sick leave compared with 9 per cent of those who drank five pints or less per week. There is only a very small difference between the drinking habits of manual workers and managers or junior white-collar workers. A higher proportion of heavy drinkers are to be found in construction workers compared with either service workers or manufacturers.

The total cost to the country is difficult to establish with certainty, but the Health and Safety Commission estimate that the cost of absence through sickness in Britain is £25 billion per year. It is quite clear that the cost to the health service, to the efficiency and productivity of the workplace has to be taken seriously. Companies must be prepared to given more attention to every aspect of health. This will bring immediate financial benefits in addition to improving the morale and health of all members of staff.

1.2   Trends in Health

Although section 1.1 indicated that over the last ten years, there has been a major increase in absenteeism, a recent survey by the Industrial Society has shown a somewhat different trend. In answer to the question 'How has your absence rate changed over the last five years?', 17 per cent of UK companies considered there to have been an increase overall. However 43 per cent thought that there had been a decrease and 24 per cent thought that the incidence had stayed the same. It is important to recognize that this may have been an impression as opposed to a quantified fact as 45 per cent of the UK companies surveyed could not provide the total number of days of absence within their organizations in the preceding year. This was supported by a separate research by the consultants Arthur Anderson who showed that nearly half of all companies in the private sector fail to keep proper figures on the subject.

Even allowing for uncertainty over reporting accuracy, the overall trend seems to be an improving one. The comparative figure in 1987 was 5.05 per cent which has now dropped to 3.97 per cent for the UK companies surveyed.

One of the clear trends is that when unacceptable levels of absenteeism are recognized and appropriate action is taken, then changes for the better are possible. Camden council in London was reported earlier as an example of high absenteeism at an average of 40 days lost per year but the situation has since changed dramatically. Absenteeism became a priority at monthly management meetings, procedures were put in place to dismiss persistent offenders and senior management had part of their bonuses calculated on the levels of sickness in their departments. The outcome is that Camden's employees are now slightly above the national average with white collar workers off sick about eight days per year (national average is seven) and manual workers about 11 days. This has come about by a change in the working environment but especially because workers are now monitored far more closely, a situation which was far more lax four years ago.

Any trends in absenteeism should be seen in the context of the objectives to be achieved. The Industrial Society survey showed most interestingly that only 37 per cent of UK organizations had a policy on target absence rates for the following year. This compared with 49 per cent of UK-based Japanese companies, indicating clearly that future

Table 1.4
Actual, Acceptable and Target Absenteeism Percentages
for UK and Japanese Companies

Companies	Current Actual	Acceptable	Target for Next Year
UK	3.97	3.44	3.75
Japanese (UK Based)	2.35	2.98	3.80

absence rates were a more important issue for the Japanese companies, but even then only half of them.

Table 1.4 gives a comparison of the *current* absence rates for all UK companies surveyed, what is considered to be an *acceptable* level of absence and what is the *target* for the following year. These figures, taken from the Industrial Society Report *Wish you were here* are a little strange because they suggest that Japanese companies are out-performing the levels they would find acceptable. There is a consis-tency between the levels deemed acceptable to be lower than the target for the following year. The gradual decrease in absence rates in UK companies is also what would be anticipated. Perhaps the Japanese companies have a more realistic expectation of the following year, aiming to get back on track thereafter at a level below three per cent absenteeism.

The trend in alcohol consumption has risen according to Alcohol Concern from 7.6 pints per head in 1960 to 13.3 pints in 1988. One in four men in Britain drink more than the medically recommended sensible limit of 21 units of alcohol per week with 12 per cent drinking more than 35 units per week. With the trend moving to drinks with a higher alcohol content (wines, spirits) the alcohol intake, especially in women, is likely to increase. Currently the overall cost of alcohol misuse is in excess of £2000 million per year, and although this is not all work-related it is likely to increase annually.

Stress at work is clearly on the increase. A recent report by the Greater Manchester Industrial Mission indicates that in men the number of days lost because of neurotic disorders has increased by 6.8 per cent to 22.3 million days. Among women the comparative figures for neurotic disorders is an increase of 19.8 per cent to 16 million days lost.

Table 1.5
Number of Working Days Lost

	Up by %	Days lost (m)
MEN		
Heart diseases	7.1	46.8
Hypertensive diseases	4.8	10.6
Depressive disorders	17.3	11.2
Alcohol dependence	44.3	1.9
Drug dependence	34.9	0.33
WOMEN		
Heart diseases	5.5	4.75
Hypertensive diseases	24.1	3.4
Depressive disorders	21.7	9.5
Alcohol dependence	-1.0	0.15
Drug dependence	n/a	0.16
Source: Greater Manchester Industrial Mission		

The trends in certain other disease categories are shown in Table 1.5 with an increase over a 12 month period the common trend. The consequence of these changes on productivity is significant with a direct effect on social costs at home as a result of work stresses. There will be a number of contributing factors including the uncertain economic climate, the possibility of redundancy following business failure and the additional workload caused by unreplaced staff.

Not only is there a trend for certain diseases to be on the increase, but conditions such as the so called 'yuppie 'flu' are apparently now finding victims in all sectors of employment. The disease is known medically as chronic fatigue syndrome (CFS) or myalgic encephalomyelitis (ME) and was originally thought to be concentrated in high fliers. More recent evidence from a survey of 180 GPs' practices in Scotland suggests that professionals only account for five per cent of those affected by the illness. The largest group at 25 per cent were teachers and students, 17 per cent were skilled or unskilled workers, closely followed at 16 per cent by the retired. A further 13 per cent were housewives, 11 per cent were working in the service industries, 9 per cent in secretarial or clerical work and 7 per cent were hospital workers.

1.3   Cost Analysis

It is quite reasonable to attempt to measure the cost effectiveness of investing in the health of employees. Most costs are attributed to the negative aspects of how the company may suffer as a result of ill health. Table 1.6 shows figures based on information from the British Heart Foundation.

Table 1.6
Cost of Heart Disease for a 1000 Person Company

■ 21% of male absence from work due to heart and circulatory disease
■ Major cause of premature death (45 per cent for 35-64 year-old men)

■ In a company of 1000
   Days lost per year
      Men   4270
      Women   1470
 	
   Premature deaths
      Men (35-64)   3.85
      Women (35-59)   0.80

■ Average Cost
      Men   £   210,000
      Women   £   60,000

■ Total Cost   £   270,000

The equivalent costs for any country without a free national health service is likely to be dramatically higher. It is estimated in the United States, for example, that each fatal heart attack suffered by a major corporation executive will cost above £700,000 to the firm including business, time and experience lost, recruiting, training, stock, insurance and irreplaceable business contracts and contacts lost. Each non-fatal heart attack costs the company £25,000–£30,000 in hospitalization, worker's compensation and higher insurance premiums.

The common backache alone is responsible for £1000 million in lost output annually in the USA.

One approach is to undertake a *cost-effectiveness* analysis. The company is required to establish some criterion of effectiveness such as a decrease in medical insurance or a reduction in absenteeism. Health strategies are then compared in terms of their costs for the chosen measure of effectiveness. The difficulty with this is that the full financial equation may take many years to work through. If, for example, decrease in coronary artery disease were the criterion, it will take ten to 20 years before the full impact is observed. However the principle may still be a basis for investment. It may be decided that effectiveness could be measured in terms of the average number of years of normal quality of life. A company may be prepared to invest £20,000 per year to contribute to such a criterion but may not consider that a higher figure of say £100,000 is justified. In many ways, the management of a company has easier decisions to make than in the public sector such as hospital administration. This is because it is very difficult to satisfy the ethical decisions associated with medical expenditure. Money spent on an organ transplant is no longer available for preventative medicine. It is almost impossible to balance the policy alternatives in financial terms, but this may be preferable than to respond only to emotional appeals from special interest groups.

Clearly the impact of improved health strategies at work and the consequent retention of staff in better physical condition until retirement could also result in greater pension costs. This means that the company may gain during employment but lose afterwards. Although this appears to be a harsh economic view it does at least introduce the alternative options. Ethical considerations would also apply as to which personnel should specifically benefit from health intervention. A rigid cost analysis might argue that it is more profitable to service a high-cost executive than a minimal wage earner. If risk was equal between such disparate employees the financial logic would be straightforward. However, the target group needs to be chosen with care because experience has shown that the lower paid exhibit more ill health and higher levels of absenteeism, so intervention may be better placed with them.

Once decisions have been made as to who will be offered improved health opportunities, the variation in participation rates have to be considered. Health care benefits, for example, assume that the person accepts full treatment options. Early discharge from hospital, incomplete follow up after acute surgery or simple refusal to accept the available treatment will also compromise the calculations. To give an example, every person who survives a myocardial infarction in Wirral, a borough in the north west of England, is offered cardiac rehabilitation. Some patients will not make use of the service, preferring to plan their own rehabilitation or manage with none. The compliance rates for exercise prescription classes is often disappointingly low with some sources suggesting a 20 per cent participation rate after six months. When costing the investment in health, a company needs to anticipate the compliance rates in estimating the financial return. However, it is important not to judge outcome purely on what is observed within the workplace. There is increasing evidence that a formal employee fitness programme can become a catalyst for informal exercise which continues long after workers have dropped out of structured classes at the place of employment.

Similarly, it is almost impossible to quantify the importance of the social climate in changing health behaviour. Changing the culture of an organization to have a more positive health outlook will not turn everyone into exercisers. It may, however, cause many who associate with the exercisers to alter their diet, recreation and smoking habits to become more healthy.

A further factor to consider in the cost analysis is the dead time associated with the health promotion initiative. If, for example, a smoking cessation class were held in a separate building from the normal place of work then time spent travelling is dead time. This becomes unproductive time and must incur a cost. Similarly, a company which offers sufficient staff flexibility to allow a game of squash during work time is not only paying for the perceived benefits of the exercise, but also for the changing time before and after the game. Of course not all travelling and changing time is dead time because there may be a degree of useful socialization including work-related discussion. The golf course is a notorious venue for business deals, although probably more anecdotal than real at least until the 19th hole! The fact remains that alternative exercise and other health promotion opportunities must take into account the associated dead time. This becomes even more critical in large cities when travelling time is often greater. In theory this gives an additional cost advantage to the on-site exercise facility compared with other types of employee fitness programme which may necessitate travelling to the suburbs to find suitable open spaces. Personal preferences must not be overlooked because it is recognized that many people will be prepared to travel long distances for watersports, fell-walking or even skiing rather than gain an equivalent amount of health benefit by using the stairs from the office car park.

A complete analysis of costs should take into account not just changes in health and productivity of the individual. Any change in provision for exercise has an impact on other sectors of the community. At its simplest, a company provision made available at off-peak time to others will enhance the public attitude to that company. There is also the stimulation of regional economy associated with recreation. One only has to observe the *per capita* expenditure in small towns in tourism areas such as the English Lake District to see the major economic regeneration. By the same token there will be those who object to tourists and view them as spoiling the peace and tranquillity of the area. It is possible that sectors of the economy will suffer, with cigarette manufacturing being the classic example of decline in a health conscious society. Estimates of income investment vary but one study suggested that for every £1 invested by local government in fitness promotion a further £2.50 of investment could be expected from the private sector. Figures will vary dramatically with the type of recreational provision, the region of the country, whether urban or rural settings and the current level of employment. It is, however, interesting to observe that decisions to build health-promoting facilities are increasingly being made on the basis of economic regeneration in addition to other reasons.

It is also important to recognize that health cost analysis is embedded in current society and that social change has rarely been as dramatic as today. Most western civilized societies are seeing a population shift from rural areas to towns or cities resulting in totally different recreational needs. The age demography is changing with a much higher proportion of the population being in the active elderly group requiring special recreational opportunities. The ethnic mix has altered dramatically with many countries having substantial multi-cultural and multiracial communities. All these trends including those associated with security, greater car ownership and the predominance of passive entertainment will impact on society's health and recreational needs. The cost-benefit equation has to be examined against this backcloth and decision taken after making the best predictions for future societal changes.

2

The Benefits of a Healthy Workforce

2.1 Individual Benefits

The benefits of being healthier at the individual level may appear obvious. Most people place their health as the most important aspect of their lives, much higher than satisfactory personal relationships or financial status. If health is defined purely as absence from disease, then for the majority of people, at least during their working lives, they would be healthy for most of the time. As was shown in the first chapter, if absence from work through sickness is used as a crude indicator of unhealthiness, then people are healthy 90 per cent of the time. However, as any ill health is traumatic, often causing pain or discomfort, inconvenience, irritability, and an increased dependence on others, any increase in overall healthiness would be of great benefit to the individual. Most individuals remain adequately healthy to perform their work tasks satisfactorily. However for some, quality of life is restricted by their health and fitness. They may be unwilling or unable to participate in a full range of active pursuits whether it is associated with work or home life. It is recognized that not everyone wishes to run marathons or spend their leisure hours in sporting endeavour. However, there is increasing evidence that many employees are physically unable to consider even moderate physical recreational activities because they come home from work exhausted. They will recuperate by engaging in passive recreation such as watching television. To illustrate the issue, there is one county ambulance service where the incidence of *normal* retirement is so low it can be considered negligible. By far the majority of active ambulance crew within this authority retire prematurely on ill-health grounds, often associated with low back pain or stress-related diseases. This must mean that for such individuals their quality of life has been compromised.

Quality of life is a concept which becomes a major variable in analysing the benefits an individual can gain within the working environment. Techniques to measure the quality of life are rather embryonic but this does not alter the fact that it is an important concept at an individual level. It does not always follow that a pay rise alters the quality of life for individuals any more than other actions especially as the consequence is likely to be seen outside the workplace. Quality of life may be considerably enhanced by changes in organization at work or a more acceptable working environment. Quality of life will differ substantially between a person who has sufficient energy only to meet the minimum demands of daily life compared with someone with boundless energy for all sorts of extra-curricular activities.

It is self-evident that a person who is rarely ill will be absent less often and therefore contribute more to the smooth running of a company. The problems of covering for absent staff, broken appointments, lower productivity, overtime payments etc., are all undesirable. However, even if lack of full health does not result in absenteeism, an employee not operating at full capacity can present difficulties. Lack of concentration, ill-considered decisions, accidents and injuries can all be the consequence of someone operating below par.

The individual benefits of a healthy workforce can be summarized in the following table:

Table 2.1
Benefits of a Healthy Workforce

I:	I'm less:	I'm more:
feel better	stressed	confident
look better	tired	energetic
sleep better	anxious	alert
work better	worried	decisive
cope better	irritable	in control etc.

To take one health-promoting activity alone, that of exercise, many people claim that the reason they exercise is simply to feel better. An active lifestyle can promote a number of personal benefits. They include:

- elevation of mood
- an increased range of experiences
- enhancement of self-image
- improved personal appearance
- avoidance of chronic disease
- a one to two year extension to lifespan
- greater opportunities for socialization.

2.2   Industrial Benefits

The difficulty is how to convert the individual benefits of being healthy into positive results and financial dividends for the company. There are a number of ways to achieve this, one being to examine the cost of ill health to a company. The Office of Population Censuses and Surveys at the Department of Social Security provide statistics which indicate the cost of one major source of ill health, namely heart disease. For a company of just 100 staff, the average number of working days lost per year is 631 for men and 145 for women. This will cost on average £30,364 for men and £4643 for women (1990 figures). Figures for larger or smaller companies will be in proportion, so a company of 500 staff will cost on average £175,034 in lost production combining the men and women. It must not be forgotten that these figures are for heart disease alone.

An alternative approach is to calculate the difference between participants in a company health scheme and non-participants in the same company. The annualized savings per participant is broken down into health care costs, absenteeism costs, increased productivity and staff turnover. The following table shows the range reported from a number of studies and the saving effect based on the average salary paid to the member of staff.

Inevitably the savings may include some double counting and those reporting the savings may inflate the figures to justify their involvement. Even so if the figures were to be halved, they still represent about 4 per cent of the total salary bill. Taking a company of 500 staff it will

Table 2.2
Annual Savings per Employee

Item	Reported Range	Ave Salary Paid (Saving Effect)		
		£15k	£25k	£35k
Health Care Costs	£100 to £825	£160	£160	£169
Absenteeism	£30 to £1000	£125	£200	£300
Increased Productivity	4% to 50%	£900	£1500	£2100
Labour Turnover	10% to 33%	£150	£250	£350
TOTAL		**£1335**	**£2110**	**£2910**

gross up to represent a saving of between £250,000 and £600,000 depending on the salary band of the average employee. To quote one specific example, treatment for back pain alone showed an annual saving of over £300,000 in lost working days.

There are a number of possible benefits to be gained from company-sponsored health and fitness programmes. In addition to the positive changes in health status, a company might expect:

- an improved corporate image
- greater worker satisfaction and productivity
- decreased employee turnover
- a decreased industrial injury rate
- better morale
- better teamwork
- better quality of staff recruited
- improved loyalty and motivation

Companies choose to introduce wellness programmes for a variety of reasons as stated above. The perceived benefits of one such programme are enumerated by the fitness director of Xerox. He considers the following to be relevant:

- reduction of employee stress
- improved recruitment caused by a progressive company image

- enhanced physical and mental work capacity as a consequence of improved health
- employees' work and personal lifestyle more in harmony
- a more positive and productive perception of the workplace
- a strategic advantage by considering staff to be an asset to the company

These largely altruistic benefits may be masking the two major motivations: the reduction of health care costs and increased productivity. The former benefit is based on the experience of countries such as the USA where companies invest extensively in the medical care for their employees. In the UK, and other countries with a well-developed free health service, this will be less important. The North Americans often look at the introduction of health promotion activities as simple economics. Healthy employees are not only less expensive to maintain but they are more productive. This may account for a much greater predominance of such programmes in the USA.

The success of an employee health and fitness programme in terms of corporate image may depend on the product being manufactured or sold. Insurance companies and food manufacturers seem especially interested in promoting an image associated with good health. Within the hierarchy of a company a health and fitness programme may increase worker satisfaction related to the improved image of managers. Any changes in levels of satisfaction will be related to the initial level. It may be more difficult to show a positive change if the workers are well-satisfied with the *status quo*. In an organization where working relationships are at a low ebb a greater improvement might be expected, although the implementation of such a scheme could be problematic.

There have been a number of studies to assess the impact of fitness and lifestyle programmes on productivity. One such study was the result of introducing an employee fitness programme at the Canada Life Assurance Company. One year after the programme was introduced productivity had increased by 7 per cent. However this was not the whole story because another company that acted as a matched control increased its productivity by 4.3 per cent. Even so, a net difference of 2.7 per cent represents a major saving in costs.

The following table shows some of the productivity benefits as a result of fitness and lifestyle programmes gleaned from over 20 different studies.

Table 2.3
Impact on Productivity of Fitness and Lifestyle Programmes

▪	2.7% - 25% gain in productivity.
▪	25% - 35% loss in productivity if programme withdrawn
▪	76% of participants more productive
▪	Improved memory
▪	Improved muscle control and strength
▪	Improved work performance
▪	39% increase in commendations for police officers
▪	No effect on promotions, merit pay or supervisor assessments
▪	No benefit in middle managers
▪	Greater self-reported productivity
▪	Less fatigue
▪	Greater creativity
▪	31% decrease in errors
▪	No effect on teaching or research output
▪	No benefit from recreational programmes.

It can be seen that not all studies yield positive results. The intensity of the fitness programmes differs as to the types of personnel involved. In general however, more studies show an improvement than not. Those that did not show a benefit showed no decrease in productivity so at least the company's output did not suffer.

Absenteeism was also examined at Canada Life as a result of the programme. Although there was not seen to be an overall difference, when the data were examined more closely they showed that the people who had adhered most strictly to the exercise programme had decreased absenteeism by 22 per cent compared with others.

Studies on the effect of exercise on absenteeism ranged from no reduction at all to a 50 per cent drop in days off work. Out of 20 studies reviewed the average percentage change was a 30 per cent reduction in absenteeism.

A further aspect of the Canada Life study was the annual turnover rate for new staff. The average cost of training a new employee was estimated at £4000 so any decrease would create useful savings. The average turnover rate was previously 18 per cent and for those who adhered closely to the fitness programme the level dropped to only 1.8 per cent. In monetary terms this is equivalent to about 2.2 per cent of payroll costs and clearly a great benefit.

Most of the studies reporting absenteeism, productivity and turn-over of staff have been conducted on white collar workers. This means that industrial injuries are unlikely to feature very commonly. Even so, several studies have indicated that in certain 'at risk' groups such as the police, fire and ambulance services fitness programmes have reduced the number of specific claims such as low back injuries.

There will always be those sceptical of the industrial benefits of health and fitness programmes. Some will argue that sufficient longitudinal studies have not been conducted. Others claim that participants are self-selected which causes bias. There is some justification for the criticism that those investing in wellness pro-grammes will not wish to admit their errors and report success selectively. Although in strict scientific terms some of these criticisms are accepted, the overriding evidence points in favour of the benefits of a good-quality lifestyle programme. Employers should at least consider with an open mind the industrial benfits of improving the health of their workforce.

2.3   National Benefits

The expenditure from the National Health Service budget of £26 billion (1989 figures) on the Health Education Authority was only £26 million. This indicates the emphasis given to health promotion compared with general health care. The disparity in the treatment of established disease and the prevention of disease has at last been recognized and the UK government's strategy has more recently been to give greater emphasis to primary health care. However, unless major financial resources are found to fund new initiatives in preventative medicine the service will still be regarded by many as a National Disease Service.

Diseases such as tuberculosis, typhoid and others associated with poverty have largely been replaced with an alternative group of disease associated with affluence and modern lifestyle. Heart disease, cancer and alcoholism are seen by some as the inevitable consequence of prosperity and economic development. An especially alarming feature of such diseases is the impact it has on relatively young people – those that are productive in employment terms and still active. The consequence of premature death and disability is personal misery for many and a massive change in lifestyle for either the sufferer or those left behind. The economic consequences for such individuals on their companies and the nation as a whole are enormous. To take one preventable activity alone, that of smoking, it has been estimated by the Royal College of Physicians that, out of a total of 350 million working days lost in the UK each year from sickness, 50 million are lost directly as a result of cigarette smoking. This results in over 100,000 premature deaths per year as a result of smoking. This is more than all the civilian casualties in Britain throughout the second world war, or equivalent to at least one full jumbo jet crash killing all passengers and crew daily.

It is clear from the way governments are starting to appreciate the value of preventative medicine that national benefits are recognized. An increase in personal fitness, for example, has anticipated national benefits in both the direct and indirect costs of illness, an improvement of overall lifestyle and a reduction in the funding for geriatric care. The latter is beneficial as greater independence and a more active lifestyle for the elderly will make a major impact on costs. Keeping an elderly person as an active and independent member of the community is a far more preferable option than providing resources for geriatric care in hospitals or nursing homes.

There are numerous direct costs of real or perceived illness which include the patient services of the doctors, nurses and auxiliary staff in hospitals, and the drugs and supplies to support the patients. The non-personal items such as medical training, medical research, the health service infrastructure, the capital building costs and even private insurance schemes are all a drain on national resources. The indirect costs to the nation are those already mentioned including losses to production, premature death and the grief associated with it.

There is increasing evidence that those people engaged in fitness programmes make fewer visits to the doctor and require less medical attention overall. Many of the studies have been undertaken in the USA and Canada where the cost of medicine is borne by insurance companies. In countries such as the UK where the cost is attributed to the state, it has even more national significance. Three studies showed a reduction in medical claims; one showed a fourfold reduction in medical consultations; another showed a reduced use of hospital beds; a further study demonstrated that those who continued to attend fitness classes claimed less on health insurance than those who dropped out and a study on industrial injuries showed that the fitness enthusiasts reduced their compensable injury rate to zero. If such studies were extrapolated to larger populations it is clear that fitness and lifestyle programmes would have a major impact on medical services and subsequent national benefits.

Lifestyle is often improved by physical activity both in general terms and in specific health benefits such as decreased use of alcohol and tobacco. People seem to develop a health culture by associating more commonly with healthier individuals. Although general lifestyle factors are difficult to measure one study suggests that 'appraised age' – an indication of how people feel relative to chronological age – was reduced by over two years on average for people who followed a fitness programme.

Smoking, apart from the direct health aspects, can also influence society. Employees who stop or decrease smoking will spend less time in the purchase and ritual of cigarettes. There will be a reduction in damage caused to furnishings, less co-workers will be irritated by smokers, more money will be saved on heating and ventilation and less damage will occur as a result of fire. This could in turn reduce insurance premiums.

As people age they tend to lose aerobic power, flexibility and muscular strength. The rates of decrease are often linked to external factors such as increased affluence and decrease in activity. The decline need not proceed at the rate of the average for a given society. There are plenty of examples of individuals who retain an activity level belying their years and those same people will have nothing like the same rate of decline of physical features. The unfortunate aspect of any decline is that eventually it reaches a threshold where the normal minimum activities of daily living become impossible or difficult without assistance. Regular physical training can restore aerobic power and defer aspects of the ageing process, especially mobility, by ten years or more. This has been shown in those who regularly engage in indoor sports with respect to body fat levels. The regular exerciser has on average a body fat level equivalent to someone 10 to 15 years younger. Of course, if an active person then becomes dependent on others for a similar amount of time as a previously inactive person there would be relatively little fiscal gain. People are living longer but the key to the argument is the quality of life during its length. It is this difference which will substantially benefit the nation. As the old adage states, 'It is not the years of life, but the life in the years that counts'.

2.4   Achieving Health for All

Most countries and indeed most employers would wish to achieve a level of health care of which they could be proud. Although in many ways there is evidence of improvement in health care, the notion of 'health for all' is still a long way off. Health policies and practices need to address a number of major challenges before we make significant claims of success:

- *inequity*: significantly lower life expectancy, poorer health and a higher level of disability is found among disadvantaged groups.
- *preventable diseases*: the health and quality of life is undermined by various forms of preventable diseases.
- *community support*: chronic diseases, emotional stress and disability are suffered by many without adequate support from the work and local community. People could cope better and subsequently lead more productive, meaningful and dignified lives if more support were provided.

It is impossible to consider health at work out of context from society at large. We live in times of rapid and irreversible social change. Demographic changes, family structures, and greater numbers of women in the workforce are all creating different requirements for social support. The attendant health problems require new approaches to deal effectively with the current situation and the health concerns of the future.

Health for all has moved from the simplistic definition of absence of disease to the World Health Organization's definition of a *state of complete physical, mental and social well-being*. This intimates that health is influenced by many factors including genetics, human and social biology, lifestyle, the physical and social environment and the way health care is organized and delivered. This book examines the thesis that health is an integral part of everyday life, especially working life. If health becomes a major ingredient of our quality of life, it must be a manageable resource and we must respect the opportunity to make informed choices concerning health. This approach to health accepts freedom of choice for individuals, companies and communities, especially in defining what health means to them. The achievement of health for all thus becomes a dynamic issue in life influenced by our beliefs, customs, culture and total environment. This is not a new philosophy, but one that in the working environment has rarely been placed high on the agenda. It should now be recognized that by giving health more dominance, then work, individuals and society can benefit.

The mechanism for tackling the challenges of health in general or health at work in particular seem best answered by *a wider application of health promotion*. This is not being in any way critical of what exists, the merits of which are self-evident. No person suffering from disease, injury or infirmity should be denied health resources. A health promotion approach should integrate comfortably with the existing health system.

The danger with a general term like health promotion is that it can be associated with a style or stereotype which does it an injustice. Health promotion tends to be associated with posters and pamphlets. It is much more a strategy to enable people to have greater control over their health by integrating personal choice, their environment and their social responsibility. It is now recognized that health promotion has to be multi-faceted. It must include education, research, training, community development, legislation and integrating policies. Although this might be seen as a general approach it can equally be specified for the workplace.

To achieve health for all, certain health promotion mechanisms may be worth considering:

- *personal action*: the decision followed by action of individuals to take an interest in and to change their own health
- *support*: the actions by people to help others cope with health problems
- *environment*: the creation of healthy conditions and surroundings for work and leisure

Personal action involves all the decisions and actions taken by an individual which contribute to health. These will vary from life-threatening decisions such as appropriate use of inhalers by asthmatics or decisions never to drink and drive to modest health-promoting decisions such as eating more fibre. There will be a continuum of personal actions such as use of appropriate footwear in icy conditions, undertaking regular exercise or limiting high cholesterol foods. A positive personal action plan means making healthy choices. This requires developing the appropriate beliefs, gaining access easily to accurate information and operating in a supportive environment.

Support involves dealing with health concerns by working cooperatively. It will require people supporting each other emotionally and actively. Experiences, information and ideas will need to be shared. Social support will occur at an individual, family, community, work or national level. It will include voluntary organizations, churches, self-help groups and national societies. People with strong social support are generally healthier than those without. It is often a combination of emotional and practical involvement. This enables the parent supporting a handicapped child, the worker with a drug dependency problem, or the operative with arthritis not only receiving professional advice but also getting support from colleagues and employers. There are a number of self-help organizations at both national and local level. Understanding of individual need and a company policy which allows access to these is important. Larger companies may provide their own whereas smaller companies may need to be better aware of situations where support is needed.

Environment involves creating a total situation which is conducive to health. Policies and practices at home, in travelling to work, at work and elsewhere have to be established to maximise the impact of health. Health workers are in danger of operating within specific boundaries and this can be counter-productive. In a local council, for example, it is normal to have departments of education, housing, public works, leisure and social services. Each will have their own mission statement and objectives which may or may not include health. To manage the council's total health environment, it would be necessary for individual groups to meet regularly to discuss common health issues and policies. In most cases the notion of a healthy environment at work tends to be implicit. Achieving health for all will require this to become more explicit and strategies for health promotion to be agreed and acted upon.

2.5   A Corporate Philosophy

The earlier part of this chapter has established that good health is a major resource for economic development. Health promotion requires a co-ordinated action by a range of economic sectors, particularly industry. Work should become a source of health for people. The changing patterns of work from physical to mental tasks will have a significant impact on health. There is no better time to develop a corporate philosophy which integrates broader social, political and environmental components of health services.

A depressed national and local economy with high unemployment and poor living conditions will affect health adversely. A progressive self-generating local economy can produce improved resources for health and also provide an environment which stimulates personal health. Thus a company which is financially healthy may directly promote the health of the local community and individuals which make up that community. During recessionary times it is often difficult to appreciate the benefits of investing in a healthy workforce. In many ways this is exactly the time to do so because, when difficult financial decisions are being made, staff are under considerable stress and need to be especially healthy to cope satisfactorily. Every industry is set within a community with the larger company being a community of its own. Employers are increasingly accepting their responsibility to the community. This is not being philanthropic; it is a recognition that for long-term survival of business there needs to be total interdependence between business, its workforce, the environment and the local community.

A corporate philosophy could be based on a number of dimensions such as fairness in trading, in working conditions, in attitudes to others and in improving broader aspects of society. *Attitudes to others*, for example, will involve a concern for public health and safety, a respect for the appearance of the company in its industrial setting and a protection of the environment. Recent examples of oil leakage and chemical effluent being discharged into rivers shows scant regard by those companies for others. *Fairness in trading* is a dimension of corporate philosophy which requires the highest standard when dealing with suppliers, customers, dealers and investors. Some would argue that the realism of business is such that these are impossible ideals. However, if issues of health and wishing to take into account health matters, are part of such relationships and are kept firmly on the agenda, then the philosophy of fairness in trading may be enhanced. *Fairness in working conditions* requires the provision of good communications between employees, high standards of health and safety, equal opportunities, reasonable remuneration and satisfactory training opportunities.

The health service in most urban settings is one of the major employers. This means that it will have a major impact on local economy. It can interact with businesses in a number of ways by such aspects as providing health authority support for the local economy and by giving advice on health at the workplace. The businesses will provide services to the local health services thus making the relationship mutually supportive.

The initiative of operating a *health at the workplace* programme (see Chapters 7 and 8) can utilize the resources of the health authority. Many authorities have a health promotion unit which is mandated to support all aspects of the community including businesses. The physical and human resources, access to literature and expertise would be invaluable in assisting local businesses to develop their own health promotion scheme.

Businesses in turn may be in a position to assist the local health services. In the same way that businesses have seconded managers to the Prince's Trust, particular projects could benefit from staff time and management acumen offered by business. Examples might be quality assurance programmes, fund raising and sponsorship. The more the business community understands the health service the greater the possibility of advocacy.

The manner in which a health authority can support the local economy includes such aspects as having a local purchasing policy. This is less easy as authorities become larger and central purchasing predominates. However, the identification of local suppliers and ensuring that they are aware of the business needs of the authority will help to support the local economy. A health authority can also stimulate local economy by ensuring that policies and practices for equal opportunities, for work experience and for training schemes all reflect the needs of the local community . Links can also be established between local educational institutions to ensure that the training and skills match the requirements of the health authority.

A corporate philosophy which takes into account the health of the employees is espoused indirectly in a quote from Sir John Harvey-Jones. He states,

> Increasingly companies will only survive if they meet the needs of the individuals who serve in them; not just the question of payment, important as this may be, but people's true minor needs, which they may even be reluctant to express themselves.

A similar philosophy is stated by Sir Hector Laing, Chairman of United Biscuits, who states,

> In the last few years there has been a strong feeling behind the whole philosophy of corporate social responsibility. Attitudes in the private sector have changed from rather dismissive detachment to an acknowledgement of constructive self-interest.

Although these quotes are not specifically making reference to health matters, the importance of employee health is becoming an issue of corporate philosophy. The recognition of health on the business agenda, along with other issues, is the decision which so closely reflects the new emphasis of the needs of the individual. This, of course, is nothing new. The great social reformer and businessman the first Lord Leverhulme established working conditions and supportive health structures such as good housing, swimming baths, annual holidays, opportunities for entertainment and reduced working hours unheard of at the time. It is now time to re-establish individual health, based on a pleasant working environment as one of the fundamental policies of business. This is the basis of a corporate philosophy where health matters. The methods of achieving this will be examined in detail in Chapters 4–6.

3

The Health of the Nation's Workforce

3.1   Results from National Surveys

The government through agencies such as the Office of Population Censuses and Surveys produces annual reports on the state of the public health. Other independent organizations such as the Kings Fund, the Health Promotion Research Trust and Allied Dunbar have also undertaken recent national surveys of the health of the nation. Although none of these are specifically targeted at the workplace, they provide a backcloth to the working environment. From the mass of data available, this book concentrates on those issues which can be influenced within work. These will include accidents, respiratory diseases, cardiovascular diseases, alcoholism and other drug abuse, obesity and conditions influenced by the environment.

Mortality

The overall trend in death rates for the last 10 years is for a decrease in most age and sex groups. Death rates for men aged 15–44 years rose from 1985 to 1990 by 8 per cent, but a decrease in that age group has been seen since then. In men there has been a steady decline in deaths from cancer, circulatory diseases and accidents. However, these reductions have been offset by increases in deaths from suicides, open verdicts and AIDS. Another area of increase in men is from diseases of the digestive system. Most of these are accounted for by chronic liver diseases often associated with alcoholism. In women breast and cervical cancers are causing fewer deaths than in recent years. Yet the same male pattern of chronic liver disease is being followed, with an increase being the main cause of digestive system deaths.

Suicide rates have increased in males aged 15–44 over the last ten years, whereas in females the overall rate has declined, though less sharply in the 15–44 year age group. A particularly vulnerable group is single, or widowed or divorced man over the age of 24.

The general household survey which collects information continuously on about 20,000 adults asks basic questions on chronic and acute sickness. Levels of acute sickness have changed very little over the last decade whereas long-standing illnesses have increased during the 1980s with a slight fall in the early 1990s. In 1991, for example, 31 per cent of people surveyed reported a long-standing illness with 18 per cent having a condition that limited their activities in some way. Acute illness was based on whether activity had been restricted in the two weeks prior to the interview and some 12 per cent reported that this was the case.

Cancer is one long-standing illness which is reported by about one per cent of the population. Although grouping all cancers together shows little change in trends, malignant melanomas of the skin appear to be on the increase, whereas stomach cancers are decreasing. In men there is now a fall in the rate of lung cancer, whereas in women there is unfortunately a steady rise.

In targeting health promotion at work it is useful to know what are the causes of death by age groups. In younger men aged 15–34 the most common cause of death is from road vehicle accidents (21 per cent), followed by other causes of injury and poisoning (20 per cent) and then suicide and self-inflicted injury (17 per cent). In younger women the same pattern emerges with about a 9 per cent lower rate for each cause of death. In the age group 35–54 years the situation changes dramatically with ischaemic heart disease being the main killer in men at about 28 per cent, followed by cancer of the digestive organs (9 per cent) and internal organs (8 per cent). With women 22 per cent of those that die in this age group do so from cancers of the bone, connective tissue, skin and breast, followed by cancers of the genito-urinary organs (10 per cent) and the digestive organs (9 per cent). Heart disease, the major cause of death in males, still only accounts for 8 per cent of death in pre-menopausal women. The older age group (55–74 years) is now predominated in both sexes by ischaemic heart disease (34 per cent in males, 24 per cent in females). Strokes at this age group start to become a cause of death at about 8 per cent, getting more common as people get older.

It is possible to express this information in terms of working life lost, which is highly relevant to health in employment. Thus a death occurring at age 15 would cause the full 50 year period of loss, whereas a death at age 60 only contributes to a five-year loss of working life. Table 3.1 shows the percentage contribution for both males and females for the major causes of death.

Table 3.1
Percentages of 'Working Life' Lost in England and
Wales for Various Causes of Death

Cause	Males Percentage	Females Percentage
Circulatory diseases	24	15
Cancers	22	41
Accidental deaths	16	8
Suicides	8	3
Respiratory diseases	4	4
Source: OPCS		

It can be seen that only in respiratory disease, which includes pneumonia, bronchitis, emphysema and asthma, is there much similarity between male and female percentages. Cancers have the greatest impact on working life for women, whereas circulatory diseases still predominate in men. The effect of accidental death on working life is twice as great in men as women. Percentage figures tend to mask the total impact of death on 'working life'. Although the total number of deaths is similar between males and females, the total years of *future working life* lost is much higher in males. This reflects the much higher figure of premature deaths occurring in males. Thus in terms of impact on working life, male ill health is far more damaging.

Some deaths are clearly unavoidable with our present preventative and clinical knowledge. However, it may be useful to consider certain conditions which are potentially avoidable. These are the sorts of causes of death in which intervention may reduce the levels. If we consider the years between 1979 and 1992 the predominant trend in all the diseases listed in Table 3.2 has been downwards. The only exception is asthma which increased to a peak in 1985, decreasing since then. The figures given in Table 3.2 represent the percentages of the 1979 value. Thus in 1992, the percentage of deaths from asthma is 68 per cent of the 1979 value. It can be seen that chronic rheumatic heart disease has reduced most, largely as a result of the major reduction of rheumatic fever in childhood.

Table 3.2
Percentage of potentially avoidable deaths in 1992
in comparison with the 1979 baseline

Condition	1992 per cent
Asthma	68
Cervical cancer	68
Surgical diseases	60
Hypertension/cerebrovascular	55
Tuberculosis	47
Chronic rheumatic heart disease	14
Source: OPCS	

Of all the potentially avoidable diseases, the one most subject to intervention is lung cancer. The trend in cigarette smoking in England since 1974 is a steady fall in men from 51 per cent to a 1990 figure of 31 per cent. In women the trend is similar with a drop from 40 per cent to 28 per cent. Although the health message is clearly being translated into action with adults the same cannot be said for teenagers. In the decade up to 1992 there has barely been any change in children aged 11–15 who smoke. The figures have been static at around 10 per cent and if anything the evidence suggests that teenage girls are smoking more and continuing into young adulthood.

Alcohol Consumption

The recommended sensible limit for alcohol consumption is 21 units per week for men and 14 for women. A unit is equivalent to a half pint of ordinary strength beer or lager, a glass of wine, or a pub measure of spirits. Recent surveys have shown that 27 per cent of men and 11 per cent of women drink more than the recommended sensible limit. Of these some 6 per cent of the men consume over 50 units per week and 1 per cent of the women consume over 35 units per week, a level which is considered dangerous. There is some recent evidence that high-earning professional women drink more heavily than female manual workers. Only 8 per cent of unskilled manual workers drink more than the recommended 14 units of alcohol per week, whereas in professional and management jobs the percentage is as high as 30. In men the number exceeding the recommended maximum of 21 units has remained fairly constant over the last six years. In women during a similar time there has been an increase of 2–3 percentage points exceeding their recommended levels. Total alcohol consumption has increased from a *per capita* volume of 6.88 litres in 1970 to 8.95 litres in 1991. At the same time there has been a change in drinking habits with British people drinking larger quantities of wine and spirits and less beer and lager.

GP Consultations

One way of understanding the health of the nation's workforce is to examine the pattern in which people consult their general practitioner. In the 25–44 year old age group the most common reason for men to consult their GP is diseases of the respiratory system, followed by musculo-skeletal conditions, injury and poisoning, and skin diseases. In women the rank order for the same age group (25–44 years) is similar except mental disorders cause about the same number of consultations as musculo-skeletal disorders. In the older age group of 45–64 years, both men and women visit the doctor most for respiratory and musculo-skeletal diseases. The next most common reason for visits for men is circulatory diseases but for women mental disorders. A contribution to cardiovascular and respiratory disease will be lifestyle habits such as smoking, poor diet and nutrition, alcohol abuse and inadequate exercise. Unhealthy lifestyles will provide part of the explanation for the prevalence of those diseases most common in men. Men exceed the recommended weekly level for alcohol consumption more than women at every age group. A lower proportion of men at every age group fall within the recommended level of fat in their diet (35 per cent). There is little difference between men and women at each age group for total cholesterol levels, although once people become older than 35 the average values exceed the recommended level of 5.2mmol/l.

Physical Activity

A survey question on the amount of physical activities undertaken during the previous four weeks revealed that for women the range of total non-participants was from 7–20 per cent depending on age group. For men the equivalent range was 8–28 per cent.

One of the more recent fitness surveys conducted within the UK was the Allied Dunbar National Fitness Survey. About 70 per cent of the 4316 people surveyed undertook physical appraisal tests which included measures of body fat, blood pressure, muscle function, shoulder flexibility and aerobic fitness. Each person was asked about current activity levels (last four weeks) and the duration, frequency and intensity of any activities were combined to produce an activity level for each person. It has been established that to reduce the risk of heart disease or stroke the optimal activity pattern should be three times a week at a vigorous or moderate level for at least 20 minutes on each occasion. The length of time per occasion is currently being challenged

Table 3.3
Activity Level scale

Level	Activity of 20 minutes duration in the previous 4 weeks
Activity Level 5	12 or more occasions of vigorous activity
Activity Level 4	12 or more occasions of a mix of moderate and vigorous activity
Activity Level 3	12 or more occasions of moderate activity
Activity Level 2	5 to 11 occasions of a mix of moderate and vigorous activity
Activity Level 1	1 to 4 occasions of a mix of moderate and vigorous activity
Activity Level 0	None
Source: Allied Dunbar National Fitness Survey	

as some researchers suggest that a cumulative 30 minutes made up of short bursts of activity may be sufficient. However, based on continuous exercise an activity level scale was proposed as in Table 3.3.

It is now possible to assign people to one of these activity levels. However, it is reasonable to take age into account because it is quite unrealistic to expect older people to be taking part in vigorous activities such as squash, aerobics and running. Thus each age group was given a target level. Young people aged 16–34 have a target of activity level 5, people aged 35–54 should be able to achieve activity level 4 and older people, aged 55–74 would benefit from activity level 3. The moderate activities in activity level 3 would include long walks at a brisk pace, swimming, tennis, social dancing and heavy gardening. The overall results are shown in Table 3.4, not taking age into account.

Table 3.4
Activity levels for men and women

Activity Level	MEN per cent	WOMEN per cent
▪ Level 5	14	4
▪ Level 4	12	10
▪ Level 3	23	27
▪ Level 2	18	25
▪ Level 1	16	18
▪ Level 0	17	16
Total	100	100
Source: Allied Dunbar National Fitness Survey		

It can be seen that one out of every six people fail even to take any moderate or vigorous activity. Table 3.4 does not take the target levels into account and when this is done the pattern of activity in Britain is even more worrying. For each age group by far the majority failed to exercise sufficiently to gain health benefits. Even in the youngest age group of 16–24 year olds, 70 per cent of the men and 91 per cent of the women were not as active as their target levels. As premature death from heart disease is commonly associated with the 45–54 year old male age group, it was especially worrying to find that 81 per cent of the men exercised below their target level. It was interesting to note that activity at work has declined to a level that only 20 per cent of men and 10 per cent of women were in jobs that demanded any vigorous or moderate physical activity. Seventy per cent of women and 60 per cent of men get their moderate activity from home-based pursuits. Sport and recreation is, as we might expect, the way most people exercise vigorously, with 40 per cent of women and 44 per cent of men taking part in sport at a vigorous or moderate activity level. A number of studies have shown that people who are active at a young age will tend to continue into later life. It is especially important for employers to promote physical activity amongst young staff so that the 'exercise culture' is established early. One of the most striking findings of the Allied Dunbar National Fitness Survey was the relationship between past participation in physical activities and the extent of heart disease, breathlessness and angina. Twenty-one per cent of men and 15 per cent of women over the age of 55 *who had not taken part in sport regularly in adult life* suffered from one of these chronic conditions. The figures for the regular participants dropped to 14 per cent for men and 3 per cent for women.

Body Fat, Muscle Strength and Aerobic Fitness

Body weight showed some worrying trends with 48 per cent of the men being overweight and 40 per cent of the women. This represents an increase of nine and eight per cent respectively over the last 10 years. The number of obese people has also increased in the last 10 years with the current levels being eight per cent for men and 13 per cent for women. The ratio of hip to waist measurements is considered to relate to the incidence of coronary heart disease and stroke. The waist circumference should not exceed the hip circumference in middle aged men. About 11 per cent of those surveyed fall into this category; another indication of lack of health. The general level of aerobic fitness was low with about one third of the men and two thirds of the women unable to walk up a 1 in 20 slope at a steady pace of about 3 mph. Although there were a few exceptionally fit people at older ages, the general trend was for fitness to decline as people get older. Muscle strength showed a similar pattern with 30 per cent of the older men and 50 per cent of the older women being unable to lift half of their body weight. The consequence of this would probably be an inability to rise from a low chair without using their arms. A reduction in body weight would have an enormous impact on tasks requiring muscle strength and walking with many people finding life much easier if body fat were reduced.

Fitness Beliefs

One of the most interesting findings from the Allied Dunbar Survey was that the majority of people believed themselves to be fitter than they really were. Eighty per cent of men and women considered that they were fit, whereas the more objective evidence showed that this was not the case. Even half the people who came into activity level 0 thought they were very or fairly active. It is clear that people's perceptions are very different from what is necessary to gain health benefits. It is somewhat comforting to find that most people (80 per cent) recognized the value of exercise, but the disparity still exists between appreciation and action.

Accidents

About three-quarters of accidental injuries at all ages involve men. Motor traffic accidents account for 46 per cent of all male deaths, largely reflecting the greater mileage driven by men. The most common cause of accidental death for women is accidental falls. Table 3.5 shows the number of fatal and major injuries per 100,000 employees for different industries.

It can be seen that the high-risk industries such as construction have twice as many fatal and major injuries as the middle-ranked group. This indicates the extra efforts that should be made in those industries to ensure health and safety of their employees.

Lifestyle

A major survey supported by the Health Promotion Research Trust was conducted in 1984–5 and repeated seven years later. It provides an insight into the health and lifestyle trends and gives a context to consider health issues at work.

With permission from the Health Promotion Research Trust the following bullet points are reproduced from the summary document: 'The Health and Lifestyle Survey: Seven Years On' based on the work edited by B. D. Cox, F. A. Huppert and M. J. Whichelow. The full text of

Table 3.5
Injuries Reported in 1990 per 100,000 Employees

Industry	Fatal and major injuries	All reported injuries
Construction	316	1971
Energy and water supply (excluding offshore)	256	2792
Extraction of minerals and ores	232	1939
Agriculture, forestry and fishing (excluding sea fishing)	148	674
Other manufacturing industries	146	1392
Metal goods, engineering and vehicle industries	115	1025
Transport and communication	92	1113
Total service industries	51	514
Banking, finance and business	10	60
Average	**152**	**1275**
Source: Health and Safety Commission		

the same title is published by Dartmouth and is available from all good
bookshops.

Patterns of Mortality

- the death rate for men in the north and west of the country was much
  higher than that of men in the south and east
- the higher mortality of manual workers over those in non-manual
  work was largely due to the well-known fact that they have higher
  rates of heart disease
- up to age 55, married men and those living with a partner had a
  lower mortality rate than men of the same age who lived alone, but
  this association was not as strong for women
- people who said originally that their health was 'fair to poor', even

if they had no known disease, were almost twice as likely to have died seven years later as those in the same age band who said it was 'excellent to good'

- being underweight or overweight for one's height, even when not due to known underlying disease, was associated with a higher rate of mortality
- sleeping less than the 'standard' six to eight hours a night was associated with excess mortality, especially among older men, and so was sleeping more than eight hours, especially in older women

Self-reported Health

Respondents were asked to assess their own health by answering questions such as 'Would you say that for someone of your own age your health in general is excellent/good/fair/poor?'

- in 1991–2 more young manual workers said they were in good or excellent health than had done so at the same age in 1984–5; for older men – above 60 – those in non-manual occupations were more likely to report better health
- women were twice as likely as men to say they had ever suffered from ME (post-viral fatigue syndrome)
- fewer people had suffered from colds or 'flu in the month before interview in 1991–2 than had done so in 1984–5; hay fever was more common; asthma had increased in men and women in all age groups; the rate of constipation reported by middle-aged men had doubled

Blood Pressure and Respiratory Function

Blood pressure is usually found to rise with age and respiratory function to decline.

- the blood pressure of the population had risen less than expected with age over the seven years, maybe because of the increased use of anti-hypertensive drugs in the older age groups (more than 30 per cent of people over 60 took them). There was a strong association between obesity and raised blood pressure
- there was a great increase in the overall use of drugs with anti-hypertensive effects, though not necessarily to treat high blood pressure

- more people in the north than in the south of the country had raised blood pressure
- in those who continued to smoke, lung function had deteriorated more than in the non-smokers or those who had given up smoking

Body Size

The population has increased in weight more than expected for the seven year increase in age. The proportion of men classified as overweight (body mass index 25–30) or obese (index above 30) has risen from 47 per cent to 53 per cent and of women from 50 per cent to 57 per cent.

Diet

Diets have changed over the seven years between the two surveys.

- more people were on medical diets in 1991–2 than were in 1984–5
- there was a marked fall in the frequent consumption of high fat foods, and butter and margarine had been largely replaced by polyunsaturated and low fat spread
- more respondents drank tea and coffee without sugar
- there was a modest increase in the consumption of cereals and brown bread but no change in the consumption of fresh fruit and vegetables
- knowledge that certain foods did not contain dietary fibre was no better by 1991–2 than it was in 1984–5 when it was poor; there was improved knowledge of the fibre content of fibre-rich foods (i.e. food of plant origin)

Mental State and Personality Measures

The surveys collected answers to questions about symptoms of depression, anxiety and general satisfaction with life; it measured emotional stability and how outgoing and gregarious people were; it also explored how much time pressure they were under in their jobs, and how ambitious.

- women reported more mental health symptoms than men maybe because they were more ready to admit to emotional difficulties
- on the whole, men aged 25 to 34 in 1984–5 had fewer symptoms by

1991–2 than other groups perhaps because more of them were now living with partners

- the mentally healthiest women (fewest symptoms) were those aged above 65 years and in the highest socio-economic groups; older men in the second highest socio-economic group, on the other hand, were among the least mentally healthy
- on the measures used, people become less extravert over the seven years, supporting the belief that young people are more extravert than their elders
- changes in physical illness symptoms reported were associated with changes in the number of mental health symptoms

Cognitive Function

Changes in the ability to think and to react have an important bearing on health.

- young people were fastest, but least accurate in reacting to stimuli; men tend to maximise speed of reaction and women accuracy
- the time it took to react to a stimulus increased with age, and people's memories got worse, particularly over 55; the peak performance was at 25 to 44 years of age
- those with no educational qualifications tended to have slower reaction times than the well-educated

Life Events

Subjects were asked if they had experienced each of a series of 25 life events (e.g. job change, illness, death of relatives, divorce, moving house, etc.) over the course of the previous year, and how disruptive or stressful the adverse life events had been. The replies were then related to their actual health experience, recorded at the interview.

- more women than men reported a great deal of disruption to their lives, and more worry and stress when they had experienced an adverse life event
- for all age groups and both sexes, people registering four or more symptoms of physical illness during the month before the survey or developing a health condition since 1984–5 had also experienced more adverse life events in the previous year

- a reported high level of social support or a pleasant event mitigated the effect of an adverse life event, measured by the number of mental health symptoms
- when they were asked about pleasant events, only half the respondents volunteered any; the most frequently mentioned were the birth of a child, a holiday or special anniversary

Smoking

In the past few years health professionals have worked to make people aware of the relationship between smoking and respiratory and circulatory disease and to discourage smoking. The second survey confirmed that mortality rates for smokers were higher than for non-smokers. It was also found that changes in smoking habits have occurred since 1984–5 – there are now very few occasional smokers (fewer than one cigarette per day).

- the proportion of regular smokers has fallen, particularly among the middle aged
- among regular smokers of all ages there was no decrease in the cigarettes smoked per day
- fear of illness and current ill-health were the main reasons for stopping smoking, but social pressures and the health of others were given as reasons more often in the second survey
- among young women 41 per cent of those who had been occasional smokers in 1984–5 had become regular smokers seven years later
- many who said in 1984–5 that they were ex-smokers claimed they had never smoked when the were asked seven years later

Prescribed Medicines

Both in 1984–5 and 1991–2 people were asked if they were taking prescribed medicines.

- there was a more than 30 per cent increase in the proportion taking medicines
- more respondents were using broncho-dilators and anti-asthmatic preparations
- some people, particularly the elderly, were unsure why they were taking the medicines

- by 1991–2 over 15 per cent of women aged from 50 to 59 were receiving hormone replacement therapy
- it was especially noticeable that regular smoker and ex-smokers were taking drugs for respiratory problems more frequently than were non-smokers; more surprisingly, they were more likely to be taking pain killers
- there had been an increase of 53 per cent of men and 56 per cent of women taking tonics and vitamin supplements over the seven year period.

Sport

There was a change in the pattern of exercise between 1984–5 and 1991–2.

- there has been an increase in reported sports participation, especially keep-fit and yoga for women
- more men said they played golf and football in 1991–2 than did so in the mid-eighties
- fewer people reported going for long walks at weekends in 1991–2 compared with seven years earlier
- in 1991–2 there was an increase in the number of people who said they felt they did not get enough exercise
- many people who were under 25 years old in 1984–5 and were joggers had stopped by the time they were asked seven years later. There were more middle-aged men jogging in 1991–2 than there were earlier; overall, fewer people jogged in 1991–2 than in the mid-eighties

Alcohol

Overall consumption of alcohol has changed very little in the seven years between the surveys.

- at all ages, women drank less than men in both surveys, but there was an increase in the proportion of women in the professions who were regular drinkers by 1991–2
- for men there was a steady fall in alcohol consumption with age at both surveys, but for men under 45 the average consumption was above the level defined by health professionals as prudent. There

was a worrying number of young male drinkers who drank above the prudent level – 30 per cent

3.2   The Health of a Company

A recent survey which concentrated exclusively on people in a large company/organization produced some interesting findings not only on the health of the employees but also on aspects more closely associated with occupational safety. Once again, the responses provide a useful background to the subsequent chapters which discuss the actions to be taken in improving health at work. Rather like the previous section the results will be presented as bullet points, partly on the basis of brevity, but also to maintain confidentiality.

Health and Safety Material

- the majority of workers (58 per cent) have seen health and safety information relevant to their job
- knowledge on health and safety matters was gained from their employers (23 per cent), the trade unions (22 per cent) and from safety officers (19 per cent)
- most health and safety knowledge (in rank order) was on protective equipment, safe lifting practices, dust hazards, fire hazards and safe noise levels
- health and safety was rated as very important by 89 per cent of the staff and reasonably important by the rest
- the majority of staff thought that the supply of protective equipment/clothing, supply of materials, washroom facilities, the canteen and communication with the employer was adequate
- however, the majority of employees thought that first aid facilities, health and safety practices, supply of office equipment and sick room facilities were inadequate
- staff admitted to cutting corners on health and safety to obtain bonuses, to reach set targets, because of pressure from employees, the public and work colleagues

Working Conditions

- the most common activities during the working day were lifting

tasks, repetitive movements, bending and stretching, walking/standing and driving
- Employers were subjected to a variety of environmental conditions including draughts, cold, inadequate lighting and stuffy conditions
- the most common exposure to hazards included dust, verbal assault, fumes, high noise levels, and vibrating tools and machinery
- few of these resulted in a health problem, but dust was easily the one most likely to do so with 10 per cent reporting the relationship
- safety measures were used by approximately half the people who reported any exposure to hazards
- half the employees reported no accidents causing personal injury to themselves in the last 12 months. Most of the remainder (38 per cent) reported up to three personal accidents, with 8 per cent more than three accidents
- almost all the accidents were reported
- there was a wider distribution of accidents without injury or 'near misses'. Less than half said none, with 28 per cent claiming 1–3 near misses and 21 per cent above three accidents without injury

Health Complaints

- the most common health complaint *that was thought to be work related* was back problems
- this was followed in order by tiredness, worry/anxiety, stress, aching limbs, eye strain, frequent headaches and skin problems
- the way in which most people would like to make changes at work was by re-thinking bonus schemes
- the other popular methods were: improving communication with employer, improving health and safety and improving the physical environment
- ninety-one per cent of employees attended work at some time when ill
- the main reasons for doing this were because of a sickness points system and potential loss of earnings

General Health

- there are striking differences in the way that men *perceive their health* compared with women. A larger proportion of men fall into the *excellent* or *fair* category, whereas more women respond with *good*
- a similar *pattern* was observed for self-perceived fitness, although

more people considered themselves to be in the *fair* category and subsequently less in the *good* and *excellent* categories

- the most common health disorder was high blood pressure (14.1 per cent overall) followed by high cholesterol (3.6 per cent overall)
- the age group 31–45 years considered themselves to be suffering most from stress, both at work (70 per cent) and at home (41 per cent). All age groups and sexes reported approximately twice as much stress at work than at home

Exercise

- compared with people of their own age, 36 per cent considered that they were physically more active. Half thought they were about the same and only 7 per cent thought they were less active
- the most common physical activity for men was walking followed by gardening. For women, it was housework, followed by aerobics
- other reasonably popular activities were running/jogging, soccer/rugby, weight training and swimming
- the activity undertaken most often was housework/gardening (most days) followed by martial arts (six times in two weeks)
- weight training was undertaken four times in the previous two weeks, but no other activity was completed more than once per week on average
- golf and backpacking/hiking were the recreational activities that took the longest (four hours). Martial arts, dancing and windsurfing/sailing took two hours on average whereas all others took one hour or less
- improvement in health and fitness was by far the most popular *reason given for exercising* in the 16–30 and 31–45 year age groups. It exceeded socialising as the next most popular reason given by about 40 per cent. However, in the 46–65 year age group, the number of respondents who did not exercise was almost as high at about 43 per cent
- the most common *reason for not exercising more frequently* was time (70 per cent overall) followed by family commitments (43 per cent). It was clear that a much higher percentage of men (20 per cent) exercised whenever they liked compared with women (10 per cent). Medical conditions were only reported by 4 per cent as a reason for not exercising more frequently
- it was interesting to observe that when the results were broken down

by age groups, the number who claimed to exercise whenever they liked went from 19 per cent in the 16–30 year age groups, *down* to 11 per cent in the 31–45 year age group and *up* to 37 per cent in the 46–65 year age group
- ninety per cent of the employees would welcome better opportunities for health and fitness at work
- when asked which health promoting activities they would like to have at work the most popular was exercise facilities (e.g. a gymnasium)
- the next most popular request was changing facilities (e.g. showers), followed by availability of healthier foods, general health advice, stress-relief classes, a back clinic and stop smoking classes
- when asked what the employees would like to do to improve their health and fitness, the most popular choice was more sport (61 per cent) followed by diet and nutrition (43 per cent). People seemed resistant to reducing alcohol consumption with only 15 per cent selecting that option

Food and Drink

- over half of the respondents used skimmed or semi-skimmed milk, with 42 per cent of the remainder drinking whole milk
- thirty-six per cent usually used soft margarine on bread, with 34 per cent using a low fat spread and 23 per cent preferring butter
- fried food (excluding chips) was eaten by half of the employees once or twice a week. Fourteen per cent ate fried food most days and 11 per cent at least daily
- white bread was eaten by most people (56 per cent) with brown or wholemeal eaten by about 20 per cent each
- one-third of those interviewed ate vegetables with their main meal daily. Twenty per cent ate vegetables five or six days per week and 30 per cent ate vegetables three or four days per week
- over a third took sugar in both tea and coffee with a similar amount in neither
- the majority (82 per cent) considered that their diet could be improved
- the number of days per week that people drank alcohol varied considerably. Twenty seven per cent drank twice per week with about 15 per cent drinking either once, three times or four times per week. Five per cent drank daily

- there was a similar range of values for the average number of standard units of alcohol consumed on the days the people drank. The cumulative average was eight units
- the total average weekly consumption of alcohol varied with the types of job undertaken. It ranged from 23 units per week for white collar positions to 38 units per week for manual occupations. Even the lower limits of this range exceeds the recommended levels of drinking, bringing most employees into the area of increasing risk

Smoking

- smoking was slightly heavier in males (38 per cent) than in females (28 per cent). When examined by age group and overall, it was close to the national average of 30 per cent
- the average amount smoked by the smokers was 18 cigarettes or five cigars per day
- passive smoking at home ran at about two-thirds for both sexes, yet at work men reported 78 per cent compared with only 53 per cent of the women. Care must be taken in interpreting these data as the female sample was only 10 per cent of the males in absolute numbers

3.3   Government Targets

In July 1992, Virginia Bottomley, the Secretary of State for Health, introduced a strategy for health in England in the form of a white paper entitled *The Health of the Nation*. This was based on a green paper published in 1991 which stimulated broad public debate. The green paper acknowledged the World Health Organization (WHO) 'Health for All' strategy which had been in place for several years and formed the basis of numerous Healthy City initiatives.

The Health of the Nation document recognizes the value of the workplace as an area of influence with people spending about one quarter of their working lives at work. It is a requirement of employers to provide a safe and healthy working environment. Trade unions and other staff associations are seeking ways to improve the health of their members. More importantly there is a recognition by employees of the benefits of general good health. The 'Look After Your Heart' workplace initiative (see Chapter 8) has been welcomed by well over 500 companies and organizations, covering over four million employees. It is intended to establish a government task force to examine and develop health promotion at work. This will involve a number of organizations including the CBI, the TUC, the Health and Safety Executive, the Health Education Authority and the Departments of Health and Employment. This task force will provide an advisory body for new health promotion initiatives and campaigns including materials which can be used in the workplace.

The Health of the Nation main targets are concerned with:

- coronary heart disease and stroke
- cancers
- mental illness
- HIV/Aids and sexual health
- accidents

Some might argue that employers can have relatively little influence over cancers, mental illness and HIV/Aids. It is true that health promotion activities may have greatest impact on coronary heart disease and accidents. However, the mortality associated with suicides and HIV/Aids suggests that it should not be ignored and the morbidity and eventual mortality associated with smoking-related diseases makes certain cancers a topic of particular importance in the workplace.

The government's main targets will be cited for each of the five areas listed above for those that apply to employment. Each target will be followed by a brief comment on the overall methodology to achieve it. Specific strategies at work will be developed in later chapters.

Coronary Heart Disease (CHD) and Stroke

- to reduce death rates for both CHD and stroke in people under 65 by at least 40 per cent by the year 2000 (from 58 per 100,000 population in 1990 to no more than 35 per 100,000 for CHD, and from 12.5 per 100,000 population in 1990 to no more than 7.5 per 100,000 for stroke)

The major risk factors for CHD and stroke include smoking, elevated blood pressure and cholesterol and a lack of physical activities. Activities which change these will reduce the risk factors and subsequently should impact on CHD and stroke.

- to reduce the prevalence of cigarette smoking in men and women

aged 16 and over to no more than 20 per cent by the year 2000 (a
reduction of at least 35 per cent in men and 29 per cent in women,
from a prevalence in 1990 of 31 per cent and 28 per cent respectively)

With 18 per cent of deaths from CHD and 11 per cent of deaths from
stroke attributable to smoking, the benefits of smoking reduction are
self-evident. This is especially relevant with the current trend in young
women for smoking to be on the increase.

- to reduce the average percentage of food energy derived by the
  population from saturated fatty acids by at least 35 per cent by 2005
  (from 17 per cent in 1990 to no more than 11 per cent)
- to reduce the average percentage of food energy derived by the
  population from total fats by at least 12 per cent by 2005 (from about
  40 per cent in 1990 to no more than 35 per cent)

A balanced diet is essential to supply the range of nutrients required for
growth, development and maintenance of life. Dietary and nutritional
advice ranges from sensible to quackery and sometimes dangerous.
The diet of many western civilized countries tends to be associated still
with high fat levels. This, usually through cholesterol, is a major risk
factor in the population and many people will benefit from reducing the
overall fat content in their food.

- to reduce the percentages of men and women aged 16–64 who are
  obese by at least 25 per cent for men and at least 33 per cent for
  women by 2005 (from 8 per cent for men and 12 per cent for women
  in 1986–87 to no more than 5 per cent and 8 per cent respectively)

Obesity is defined as a body mass index of over 30. Body mass index is
the ratio of mass in kilograms divided by height in metres squared.
Thus a 75 kg man with a height of 1.8 metres will have a body mass
index of $75 \div (1.8)^2 = 23.1$. Obesity is related to raised blood pressure
and cholesterol. Blood cholesterol itself is not specifically listed by *The
Health of the Nation* as a target although concern is expressed about the
number of people exceeding the desirable level of 5.2 mmol/l. Perhaps
there is concern that as an individual measure, without regard to other
risk factors, it may be less predictive. It is conceded however that
careful monitoring of the national picture on cholesterol is necessary.

- to reduce mean systolic blood pressure in the adult population by at least 5mm Hg by 2005

There is a linear and positive relationship between elevated blood pressure and CHD. In addition to obesity, the associated factors are high sodium (usually from common salt), low potassium intakes and excessive alcohol consumption. The link between stroke and blood pressure is even higher than CHD. If the target above is achieved it could result in a 10 per cent reduction in deaths from stroke and CHD.

- to reduce the proportion of men drinking more than 21 units of alcohol per week from 28 per cent in 1990 to 18 per cent by 2005, and the proportion of women drinking more than 14 units of alcohol per week from 11 per cent in 1990 to 7 per cent by 2005

Regular drinking at the levels well in excess of the so called 'sensible' levels of 21 units for men and 14 units for women is a cause of increased risks of raised blood pressure, stroke and even CHD. Liver cirrhosis is another possible consequence of excessive drinking as are accidents at or away from work.

Cancers

- to reduce the death rate for breast cancer in the population invited for screening by at least 25 per cent by the year 2000 (from 95.1 per 100,000 population in 1990 to no more than 71.3 per 100,000)

Cancer is one of the government's main targets because it is a major cause of avoidable ill health. It accounts for about 25 per cent of deaths as shown in the earlier section of this chapter. Breast cancer is the form that kills most women and nationwide screening for over 50s should save over 1000 lives annually.

- to reduce the incidence of invasive cervical cancer by at least 20 per cent by the year 2000 (from 15 per 100,000 population in 1986 to no more than 12 per 100,000)

Cervical cancer can often be detected at a very early stage by examining the cells scraped from the surface of the cervix. If women are examined regularly and correctly with the analysis of the cells reported accurately, there should be a major improvement in outcome.

- to halt the year-on-year increase in the incidence of skin cancer by 2005

There is currently an upward trend in skin cancer, largely caused by exposure to ultraviolet radiation. Efforts will be concentrated on reducing the risk by educating the public to less exposure to the sun's ultraviolet rays.

- to reduce the death rate for lung cancer by at least 30 per cent in men under 75 and 15 per cent in women under 75 by 2010 (from 60 per 100,000 for men and 24.1 per 100,000 for women in 1990 to no more than 42 and 20.5 respectively)
- to reduce the prevalence of cigarette smoking in men and women aged 16 and over to no more than 20 per cent by the year 2000 (a reduction of at least 35 per cent in men and 29 per cent in women, from a prevalence in 1990 of 31 per cent and 28 per cent respectively)
- in addition to the overall reduction in prevalence, at least a third of women smokers to stop smoking at the start of their pregnancy by the year 2000
- to reduce the consumption of cigarettes by at least 40 per cent by the year 2000 (from 98 billion manufactured cigarettes per year in 1990 to 59 billion)

At least 80 per cent of lung cancers can be linked to cigarette smoking. With such a poor prognosis (a death rate of 95 per cent within 5 years) once diagnosed, the importance to health of non-smoking becomes obvious. Although almost everyone is aware of the dangers of smoking, the attitudes to the habit clearly do not reflect this knowledge. Action will need to be taken on a number of fronts to achieve these targets and the workplace provides one of the best venues for intervention.

Mental Illness

- to improve significantly the health and social functioning of mentally ill people
- to reduce the overall suicide rate by at least 15 per cent by the year 2000 (from 11.1 per 100,000 population in 1990 to no more than 9.4)

- to reduce the suicide rate of severely mentally ill people by at least 33 per cent by the year 2000 (from the estimate of 15 per cent in 1990 to no more than 10 per cent)

Mental illness in its various forms such as depression, psychosis, schizophrenia and anxiety is as common as heart disease and much more common than cancer. It tends not to have the recognition in the workplace given to other conditions, but the impact can be as severe on industry as many other diseases. It is not understood as clearly by the lay public as other conditions so the workplace can become an ideal venue for education and information. As much care is now switching from special hospitals to the community, it may cause healthy employees to become carers and thus making greater demands on their recreational time.

HIV/Aids and Sexual Health

- to reduce the incidence of gonorrhoea among men and women aged 15–64 by at least 20 per cent by 1995 (from 62 new cases per 100,000 population in 1990 to no more than 49 new cases per 100,000)
- to reduce the percentage of injecting drug misusers who report sharing injecting equipment in the previous four weeks by at least 50 per cent by 1997, and by at least a further 50 per cent by the year 2000 (from 20 per cent in 1990 to no more than 10 per cent by 1997 and no more than 5 per cent by the year 2000)
- to reduce the incidence of HIV infection

Unprotected sexual intercourse is the main method by which HIV is transmitted. Safer patterns of sexual behaviour are therefore essential to reduce the incidence. This should also have an effect on other sexually transmitted diseases and unwanted pregnancies. HIV is also transmitted by sharing needles to inject drugs which is why the government schemes for needle exchange should be encouraged.

Accidents

- to reduce the death rate for accidents among young people aged 15–24 by at least 25 per cent by 2005 (from 23.2 per 100,000 population in 1990 to no more than 17.4 per 100,000)

Although the main government targets for accidents concentrate on the under 15s and the over 65 year olds, there is still concern for those young people of employment age. It can be seen that the target above concentrates on mortality, but morbidity resulting in long-term absence can be very costly for industry.

4

Auditing the Company's Health

4.1   Health Audit Strategies

Context

It is important from the outset to establish the reasons for undertaking a health audit. The company may be suffering an unacceptably high sickness and absence rate and further information may be useful before action is taken. The company may draw its employees from an area with a poor health record and this will be made considerably worse if the company employs a high proportion of manual workers. The company may have a purely altruistic reason for improving health or it may recognize the benefits discussed in Chapter 2 and wish to capitalize on this for the overall benefit of the company. It is likely that the justification for a health audit will be to provide evidence of the health and welfare of the workforce. This will give a basis for action which should result in specific benefits such as:

- better quality of life
- improved health and safety practice
- increased job satisfaction and greater job security
- increased productivity
- better quality of service for users
- increased opportunities for participation in recreational activities
- better organization and management of the occupational health service and more efficient use of resources

Objectives can then be set which summarize the procedure and outcome. The following illustrates very simply some typical objectives.

1. To carry out a company health audit by examining the health and welfare of the workforce including working conditions, fitness and lifestyles, and departmental organization.
2. To involve fully the workforce, trade unions and company management in carrying out the audit.
3. To involve the various health resources in the area to achieve substantive improvements. These improvements may also serve as a model for other companies.
4. To make recommendations which are directed at changing procedures, the organization of work, and management practice to improve health and welfare policies as well as the health and fitness of the workforce.

It is recognized that few changes will be achieved rapidly and that a *positive health culture* will need time to be adopted. It is also important to make valid comparisons. The sickness and absenteeism rates, for example, should be compared at the same time of year to eliminate seasonal effects. Thus it may be several months before the merits of an intervention programme can be evaluated.

There is also the danger that a health audit becomes a paper exercise. It is essential that all recommendations are thoroughly practical and properly budgeted. There will inevitably be a cost, but that cost should soon be self-financing as the health benefits accrue. It is important to guarantee confidentiality, especially as information obtained may indicate a previously unknown medical condition. It is also recognized that trade unions could be concerned that health information may be the basis for redundancy and this fear needs to be dispelled.

Methodology

The method of conducting a health audit will depend on the human and physical resources, time availability, the objectives and the commitment of those involved. With a small company it may be possible to examine numerous aspects and interview every employee. With a large company, selected issues such as passive smoking, back pain and solvent hazards may be the only ones to be considered initially, moving on to others as resources permit. Alternatively with a large company, it may be prudent to concentrate on a few departments or sections. If such a selection is made it is important to decide whether the policy is to be truly random, to be selective or to ensure that contrasting types of departments are involved. The random approach is the more acceptable scientifically but in doing that opportunities may be missed. Random inclusion will inevitably involve a proportion of individuals or practices which in health terms are well above average. This may not be the best use of valuable resources. It may be preferable to target individuals at greatest risk or health practices greatest in need of change. This selectivity is perfectly acceptable if it meets the health audit objectives. The other approach is to involve areas of the workforce which are initially seen as different. The common comparison would be manual compared with white collar workers. Alternatively you may wish to audit a section with an exemplary accident record in comparison with one having a poor accident record. The audit may reveal the working practices which contribute to the different accident statistics. If the audit is to deal with large numbers of staff in which the objective is to obtain an overall picture then some form of sampling is likely to be necessary. Ideally it should be random because this should eliminate any bias. However, to obtain a true random sample can prove difficult. You may, for example, wish to establish health attitudes of the workforce and relate that to sickness and absenteeism. The most important category of respondents – those that are regularly off sick – are unlikely to be at work when the survey is being undertaken so it provides immediate bias. Some effort will be required to include their responses in any survey.

The questionnaire is probably the most common method to undertake a health audit. The advantage of the questionnaire is that it can be very specific and obtains responses at a very personal level. It also gives the opportunity for individual employees to have some 'ownership' of health issues in their company. A questionnaire can be used to obtain facts, to obtain attitudes and to obtain information on employees' needs, concerns and expectations. Most questionnaires can be repeated over a period of time so changes or trends as a result of health promotion can be measured. The length of a questionnaire is important because employees may tire of completing a lengthy questionnaire and fail to provide accurate or well-considered answers. It is generally considered that a health questionnaire should not exceed 11 pages in length and should be completed within 20 minutes. To obtain a reasonable response rate it is ideal to arrange its completion during work time, so this may require negotiation between management and trade unions.

It is essential to pilot a questionnaire to establish its suitability. Ideally a sample of the intended respondents should be given the questionnaire in advance to make sure it is clear, understandable, and the questions appear relevant. If there are contentious issues it is worth checking the response rate of specific questions because if there is a high refusal rate, that question may need to be eliminated from the final survey. In a multi-cultural workforce, there may be a need to translate the questionnaire into a foreign language.

The style of questions can vary to include 'closed' questions when either one (e.g. yes or no) or a limited number of responses are required. Alternatively 'open' questions, where the respondent can provide any answer, can be used. Closed questions are much easier to evaluate. They can usually be coded for input to a computer. Open questions, on the other hand, can provide a broader range of information (often not previously considered by the questioner) but will be more difficult to analyse. An example of a closed question would be:

```
Have you at any time attended work when you have been ill?

                    [ ]    Yes
                    [ ]    No
```

An example of an open question would be:

```
Please provide comments on the safety procedures in your section?




```

A common habit when constructing health and lifestyle question-naires is to add questions purely because the opportunity should not be missed. The danger is that the questionnaire becomes tedious. It is important to be convinced that every question is necessary, will be used to meet the objectives of the health audit and could not be misinterpreted. If confidentiality is to be maintained it is important not to include questions which could identify individuals. If it is planned to make comparisons between sections of the workforce, different genders, different age groups, etc., it will be necessary to collect demographic information. Appendix 1 gives an example of a questionnaire sent by the Canadian Chamber of Commerce to over 1000 companies in Canada to establish:

- the prevalence of fitness, recreation and sport and health and lifestyle programmes in Canadian business
- the nature of existing fitness programmes
- the interest among companies not offering such programmes to start activities in these areas

It can be seen from the questionnaire in Appendix 1 that the survey asked about three types of provision. These were:
(a) fitness programmes which include aerobics, jogging, exercise breaks, etc.,
(b) health education and lifestyle programmes which include smoking cessation, preventative back care, weight control, etc
(c) sport and recreation programmes including team or outdoor sports, golf tournaments, etc

It was found that:

- 13 per cent provided some type of fitness programme activities
- 25 per cent provided health education and lifestyle programmes
- 44 per cent offered sport and recreation programmes
- 11 per cent of those not currently offering a fitness programme wished to do so in the near future

Of those that do offer *fitness* programmes:

- 52 per cent have either aerobic or group exercise classes (jogging or running programmes and individual exercise programmes are also popular, but less frequent offerings)
- 81 per cent make the fitness programmes available to all employees

- 41 per cent subsidise employee membership in off-site facilities
- 60 per cent make facilities for activities available on company premises (in most cases, consisting of changing areas, showers, and group exercise areas)
- 20 per cent permit employees to participate in activities during working hours (although lunch-time or 'after work' are the most common times for fitness activity)

As far as *sport* and *health* is concerned:

- team sports and recreational events (e.g. tournaments) are offered more frequently than individual sports
- the most prevalent types of 'health education and lifestyle programmes' provided to employees by businesses are: (a) occupational health and safety; and (b) back-care programmes. Other, less widely-used programmes, deal with stress-management, nutrition, weight control and smoking cessation

It is interesting to see in Table 4.1 how facilities vary for companies of different sizes.

Table 4.1
Type of On-Site Fitness Facilities Provided in Canadian Business

FACILITY AREA	COMPANY SIZE	
	100 to 499 employees	500 or more employees
	Per cent providing	Per cent providing
Changing area	89	77
Showers	80	80
Group exercise area	80	69
Individual exercise area	45	43
Jogging/running area	36	30
Other	14	11

There is limited comparable information on UK businesses although a recent survey undertaken by the Industrial Society did compare UK organizations and UK-based Japanese companies in terms of health provision. Each company was asked whether it catered for the health of its employees by providing (a) healthy screening for all or some of its employees, (b) 'healthy' meals in the staff canteen, and (c) access to sports facilities. A review of the results reveals that:

- there is wide regional variation in health screening with the north west and north east providing a better service
- health service respondents overall provide the best screening
- there is great variation with the type of company. Those involved with hazardous processes (e.g. extraction and chemical organizations) provide the best screening, whereas construction and catering sectors are the worst
- About two-thirds of all companies with a staff canteen or restaurant provide 'healthy' meals
- the north east is the best region for 'healthy' meals with London the worst
- the utility industries have the greatest number of respondents providing 'healthy' meals with the construction industry the fewest
- the utility industry also provides the best access to sporting facilities with the housing industry rarely making such a provision
- only about one third of the companies reviewed provide sports facilities. This is the only lifestyle issue where there is a noticeable difference between the Japanese and British companies, with 39 per cent of the British providing facilities and only 29 per cent of the Japanese
- East Anglia is the best region with 53 per cent provision, surprisingly followed by London with 47 per cent of the respondents reporting access to sports facilities

However, one suspects that the provision is likely to be considerably worse as most sport and recreation facilities tend to be off-site at sport and social clubs based at outdoor playing fields. It is dangerous to report anecdotal information as being in any way representative, but the only shower facility in one local authority administrative centre employing several hundred staff is the one provided for the rat catcher in the pest control service!

Table 4.2 shows the percentage differences between small and large companies for a wide range of health-promoting activities.

Overall the pattern is very similar when comparing companies of different sizes. The major differences are in provision of retirement planning, back-care services, occupational health and safety and recreational events. The differences will largely be explained by the

Table 4.2
*Prevalence of Selected Sport/Recreation,
Health Education/Lifestyle and Fitness Programmes*

PROGRAMME AREA	COMPANY SIZE	
	100 to 499 employees	500 or more employees
	Percentage with programmes	Percentage with programmes
SPORTS & RECREATION ACTIVITIES		
Team Sports	86	89
Recreation Events, Tournaments, etc.	65	75
Individual Sports	12	18
Others	6	5
HEALTH EDUCATION & LIFESTYLE ACTIVITIES		
Occupational Health and Safety	70	83
Back-Care	43	68
Retirement Planning	35	76
Employee Assistance	35	36
Stress Management	32	26
Alcohol Education	31	26
Smoking Education	29	23
Nutrition Education	29	23
Health Education	28	24
Drug Education	26	24
Weight control	23	17
Other	9	4

FITNESS ACTIVITIES		
Aerobic or Group Exercise Classes	52	54
Jogging/Running Opportunities	40	30
Individual Exercise Programmes	37	29
Fitness Testing Counselling	33	33
Exercise Breaks	10	5
Other	12	20
Financial Subsidy to Use Local Facilities	41	47

threshold effect where it becomes viable for a larger company to provide such opportunities. A small company may find it difficult to provide the minimum infrastructure for a provision such as occupational health or may find that a tournament such as a golf day would be too disruptive.

This type of survey provides information of a national perspective and will therefore be of limited value for a specific company. However it does provide a useful benchmark for any business to use as a comparison. Table 4.2 shows, for example, that about half of the companies surveyed provide back-care education. Is this true of your company? If not, is this an aspect that employers and employees should be discussing?

One very effective way of establishing employee needs and concerns is to use a questionnaire to survey their interests. The following simple questionnaire illustrates how this information could be collected.

The information provided in this type of survey will give an objective basis for deciding which activities should be offered by the company. Without the survey inappropriate decisions could have been made, reflecting more the expectations or preferences of the health promotion team than the staff.

A recent survey by *Hi-Care Health Products* targeted occupational health managers and health promotion managers within the NHS. In addition to a range of questions on attitudes to health care provision, respondents were invited to suggest improvements.

EMPLOYEE INTEREST SURVEY

Our company is considering providing a health and fitness programme for employees. The programme will enable you to improve your health and fitness at a convenient time and location and will, of course, be on a voluntary basis.

A working party has now been formed from various departments within the company. We have developed a questionnaire to identify your interest in such a programme. The results of the questionnaire will be used to recommend a programme to management.

The survey is confidential and anonymous. Please answer these questions and return your survey to the box in the (specify a convenient location).

Q1.   Are you male? ☐   female ☐

Q2.   What is your age?_____yrs

Q3.   Which activities would you consider participating in?

Smoking control	☐	Asthma	☐
Nutrition and Weight Control	☐	Stress Management	☐
Cooking for Health	☐	Heart Health including blood	
Gymnasium Activities	☐	pressure and cholesterol	
Aerobic Exercise Classes	☐	measurements	☐
Sporting Teams/Games	☐	Heart-lung Resuscitation/First Aid	☐
Stretch and Relax Classes	☐	Fitness Assessment	☐
Reproductive Health	☐	Diabetes	☐
Womens Health	☐	Aids	☐
Cancer and cancer control	☐	Drugs including alcohol	☐

I would be interested in the following activities here at work: (Please tick as many of the following as you wish).

☐   workshops or classes on any of the topics in the preceding list
☐   films, videos and lunchtime talks on the topic in the preceding list
☐   an employee committee to organise health-related activities
☐   special events, like a picnic, health fair, or family fun run
☐   having accurate information available to me about health topics
☐   having my family join me in health-related activities here at work

Q4 Would you consider participating in such programmes if they were provided at or through work? Yes ☐ No ☐

Q5 When would you be most likely to participate?
Before work ☐ After Work ☐ Lunch Time ☐

Q6 Do you work shift work? Yes ☐ No ☐

Q7 What are your normal working hours?_____

Q8 Do you require child care to participate? Yes ☐ No ☐

Q9 Would you like to become involved as part of a health and lifestyle committee if this was established at work and met during work time?
Yes ☐ No ☐

Q10 What suggestions/comments do you have to make regarding these sorts of activities at work?

THANK YOU FOR YOUR CO-OPERATION

================

Occupational health managers made the following suggestions and requirements:

- provide seminars for occupational health managers on the provision and value of health promotion
- cost/benefit analysis of health-promotion provision
- ensure adequate funding for resources (personnel and equipment) before embarking on a programme
- identify main target groups
- improve food choices in the canteen
- ensure that existing health-promoting facilities are made known to all employees
- fewer platitudes and more supportive action from government, e.g. tax incentives
- provide incentives to keep fit and healthy
- provide more sport and recreation facilities
- more imaginative promotion of the benefits of good health

Health promotion managers came up with a slightly different list:

- government subsidy for workplace health promotion
- cost/benefit analysis of health promotion
- more resources (personnel/equipment)
- no-smoking policies
- provide exercise facilities suitable and accessible to all personnel
- need for a comprehensive approach by coordinating catering/ occupational health/health promotion/management
- large programmes are too time/money consuming. A variety of frequent small programmes are more effective
- subsidized membership of local health clubs
- more senior management commitment needed

It is quite clear that within the specific context of the NHS (one of the UK's largest employers) there is a general feeling that more can be achieved in terms of health promotion, especially if resources are improved and senior management becomes more committed.

The employee-interest questionnaire shown earlier could be the basis for meetings between employers and employees, between health care teams if they exist in a company, between trade unions and management or indeed between any party interested in promoting health at work. Even without the objective data a questionnaire provides, meetings of various types from the formal committee to the *ad hoc* informal group could be the basis of a strategy to undertake a health audit. 'Brainstorming' sessions on the needs to be achieved within a company for improving health will start to review the current health situation. This will often result in a further series of questions which need to be answered. The prospect of company support for private medical insurance, for example, would need to be discussed with management. The provision of healthier eating options on the other hand, may be more the province of the caterers.

A health audit does not necessarily have to be undertaken in a formal, highly structured manner. It can arise as a series of initiatives from individuals or groups. Providing the outcome is a much more thorough knowledge of health practices, needs and intentions within a company, it will serve its purpose. As management is likely to become involved in implementation, the provision of hard facts will be an advantage. Anecdotal observations can sometimes be useful for illustrative purposes, but managers are more likely to be convinced by objective evidence. It could be shown, for example, that levels of obesity in the company exceeded the national norm and were likely to influence output by greater related ill-health. This may then be a convincing argument to provide weight-watching classes at work.

The health culture of a whole organization can be influenced by a decision to include health as part of its mission statement and to ensure that it is part of every company policy. This has recently been implemented by a major city council and senior staff are required to consider the health impact of departmental policy. Thus the housing department has to consider aspects of health in its building pro-gramme. Likewise the departments of social services, education, information technology and estates all need to ensure that every action is considered from a health perspective. If all companies, big or small, were mandated to consider the health implications of their actions they would need to undertake some type of review or audit to assess current practice. This may involve questionnaires as indicated above but at the other end of the scale astute observation may reveal scope for improvement. A careful and focused examination of premises, of employees' habits, of safety practices, etc., can be a very effective audit. Many safety inspections concentrate on electrical equipment, emer-gency procedures and maintenance. Far less often is the operator observed at work. Assessments are rarely made of personal fatigue levels, discomfort and such things as working relationships with colleagues. Systematic observation of employees at all levels may reveal facets which indicate where changes would dramatically improve health. The major responsibility for such 'observational audit' is traditionally given to the health professionals such as the occupational health nurse or safety officer. A different and more logical approach would be to give this responsibility to everyone. In many cases the person most familiar with the specific working environment will be best suited to act. The supervisor of a typing pool will be constantly aware of poor performance from his/her team caused by poor lighting and inadequate ventilation. Similarly the person using corrosive chemicals will be more likely to notice the health implications of inadequate protective clothing. In many cases, however, the employee may need training or advice to recognize health aspects and to see how things could be improved. The combination of each employee being encouraged to consider health issues and individuals with special responsibilities for health in the company could result in a regular observational audit. To assist in this process each company should develop a checklist of health issues which are regularly audited and examples of these are given in the next section of this chapter.

4.2   What Should Be Audited

There are many aspects which could be audited within a company and overlap between individual health and company aspects are inevitable. This is because a company is the product of individual employees. This section, although recognizing that the members of the workforce will be closely involved in all aspects, will concentrate on broader working practices.

Environmental Aspects

Many companies are becoming more responsible towards the environment and show a greater concern for a sustainable planet. This in part follows government legislation but coverage by the media and greater consumer awareness is making a major impact on the attitudes of companies.

Lever Brothers have undertaken an obligation to minimize and eventually to eliminate any adverse impact their products may have on the environment. One of Levers detergents was 100 per cent phosphate free in advance of all other national brands. Its packages are now recyclable or contain recycled materials. In their Canadian offices, 90 per cent of used paper is sold for recycling with the proceeds helping local environmental projects. Disposable cups have been replaced for each employee by ceramic mugs. On the manufacturing side, the air and water emissions are set well below government levels and the company is constantly examining new ways to re-use previously wasted packaging material and chemicals.

Manufacturers of whisky produce millions of bottles of spirit every year. As whisky is primarily sold in bottles made of glass, they are recyclable. However many manufacturers also package the bottle in a canister. Some companies are withdrawing the presentation canister as it is now recognized that it will end up as landfill.

A major oil company has developed an ethanol-enriched unleaded petrol to reduce harmful emissions significantly. In addition to this the same company has recognized that much used motor oil is disposed of by pouring down sewers where it ends up polluting water supplies. It thus developed a unique refining process to recycle used oil on a commercial scale.

Liquid washing products such as Palmolive use cleaning agents which are biodegradable. There is increasing use of bottles made from recyclable plastic. Few households and local authorities are sufficiently well-organized to recycle efficiently so one alternative is to create liquid refill packs. It uses 70 per cent less plastic than a conventional bottle and takes up 95 per cent less space in landfill sites. Much of the exterior packaging and measuring scoops are now made of recycled fibre.

The motor industry claims that in the last 20 years the average car has reduced its three major polluting gases (hydrocarbon, carbon monoxide and oxides of nitrogen) by 90 per cent. For lorries these emissions have been reduced by 75 per cent. This has come about by the introduction of catalytic converters, exhaust gas recirculation systems, electronic fuel injection and on-board computers.

Discarded batteries have a major impact on the environment so improvements in battery technology to lengthen life and the use of mercury-free batteries will help. More recent developments include units to replenish conventional batteries, even superseding the use of rechargeable batteries as a source of energy.

Proctor and Gamble is another major company to consider environmental issues seriously. It has established a group of senior executives to lead a campaign to reduce solid waste. Already many detergent cartons are made of 100 per cent recycled papers and some products are packaged in reusable containers and light-weight plastic refill pouches. Their disposable nappies have used new technology to make them equally effective, yet thinner, thus reducing the volume by 50 per cent. With 3–5 per cent of landfill being attributed to disposable nappies this should make a large difference to the environment.

These examples apply more to multinational policies and their impact on the environment. They all operate on the three Rs principle of *reduction, re-use and recycle.* Every company could embody this principle and become environmentally healthier as a consequence. The examples given above could be incorporated in a limited way with most companies. All companies use cleaning products and 'greener' options could be used. In offices a recycling strategy could be used for the mountain of paper created weekly by most administrators. Packaging could be examined for its volume and whether it is based on recycled products. Company cars could all be using lead-free petrol and driving techniques encouraged which reduce consumption. Every policy of the organization could be reviewed to ensure the most sustainable power options were chosen. Rather like Proctor and Gamble an advisory team could be established to audit the company's approach to environmental issues.

Hazardous Substances

Employers are required to assess the risks to health arising from hazardous substances in the workplace, so a regular audit on these is essential.

The Control of Substances Hazardous to Health Regulations 1988 or COSHH aims to protect the health of workers by adopting good practice. The main provisions require employers to:

- assess the risks to people's health caused by workplace exposure to hazardous substances, taking account of the specific circumstances of the workplace, and decide what precautions are needed. In all but the most straightforward situations an assessment should also be reviewed as appropriate
- prevent such exposures or, where this is not reasonably practicable, implement control measures
- ensure that control measures are used and that equipment is properly maintained and procedures observed
- where necessary, monitor environmental contaminants and keep records of the measurements obtained. Where records refer to individual exposures they should be kept for 30 years or in any other case for five years
- in certain cases, carry out and record health surveillance. These records should be compatible with those above
- inform, instruct and train employees about risk and the precautions to be taken

The provisions are intended to be sufficiently flexible to cover a range of workplaces. Even those apparently 'safe' such as offices may contain hazardous substances such as solvents used in photocopying and cleaning.

The substances hazardous to health include:

- toxic, harmful, corrosive or irritant substances
- those with an occupational exposure limit
- micro-organisms (e.g. legionella bacteria) which can create a health hazard
- high quantities of dust
- any other substance which can create comparable hazards to those listed above

Having assessed the risks to health, the employer should either prevent or control the risk by appropriate measures. The provision of protective clothing is not necessarily adequate as the hazardous substance could be eliminated, substituted or controlled in other ways. These may include total or partial enclosure of the process of the systems for handling, improved ventilation, or changing work practices to reduce exposure.

Monitoring, using for example atmospheric sampling devices, is normally carried out annually and will concentrate on airborne contaminants. Monitoring is defined as 'the use of valid and suitable occupational hygiene techniques to derive a quantitative estimate of the exposure of employees to substances hazardous to health'. The COSHH regulation requires monitoring to be performed whenever 'it is requisite for ensuring the maintenance of adequate control of exposure. . .'. Inhalation, although the most common route for exposure, is not the only one as ingestion or skin contact is also applicable. Most monitoring procedures are designed to establish exposure levels for individuals, but in certain cases it is acceptable to use group sampling when employees are likely to be similarly exposed. Certain substances such as vinyl chloride need to be monitored more regularly than once a year. Clear records should be kept which include information on the date, procedures adopted, the results, the location, the operation in progress and the names of individuals involved.

In situations where adverse health may occur it is necessary for health surveillance of individuals to be undertaken. Substances known to cause asthma or dermatitis, carcinogens and special situations such as man-made mineral fibres are all examples where health surveillance could be invaluable. A particular example would be skin cancer which, if detected sufficiently early, can be treated with significantly more success.

An excellent example of a company responding to the COSHH regulations for hazardous substances is Kelloggs who employ about 3000 people at five sites in the UK. The company instituted training days for the managers to ensure that the COSHH assessment procedures were fully understood. They then undertook five model assessments at specific sites. In parallel, a list of objectives and a timetable was established to implement the COSHH assessments at each Kellogg's location. This involved the production of a product inventory which revealed much duplication, products no longer in use and products being called by different names. From an original list of

500 chemicals, rationalization reduced the figure to 300. Suppliers were asked to produce safety data sheets on their products. This was not totally successful mainly because small suppliers were concerned about loss of trade if their products were deemed hazardous. The assessments were carried out by responsible persons at the worksite. Consistency was attempted by standard documentation being provided. All departments were required to ensure that all chemical substances had been assessed for their potential health risk. If necessary control measures were identified and implemented. Kelloggs produced a standard assessment form which included:

- the product
- the supplier
- the substances assessed
- the hazard rating
- routes of entry
- control measures
- use
- personal protection
- occupational hygiene
- risk assessment

Kelloggs concluded from this exercise that the company, on the whole, was already taking adequate measures to control chemical hazards. The exercise was successful because of the teamwork approach and it helped to focus the attention of employees on the risks of hazardous substances at work.

Although hazardous substances are rather exceptional because they are covered by government regulations, they represent the principle of audit. Most of the other examples that follow will be more discretionary but, in a company promoting health positively, may be considered equally important.

Smoking

A health audit on smoking can reveal the extent of the habit and also determine attitudes of employees. This could include the views of smokers to smoking cessation, the concerns of non-smokers to passive smoking and the general attitude to no-smoking policies if planned or implemented.

The recent Incomes Data Services survey shows that most workers are now banned from smoking at work or can smoke only in special areas. Of the 36 organizations surveyed only three did not have a formal policy on smoking. It is only relatively recently that this change in attitude has taken effect. As recently as 1991 there was evidence that smoking policies were being seriously considered but now the implementation rate is extremely high.

The government in its concern to reduce passive smoking targeted in 1992 the provision of smoke-free areas to include:

- at least 80 per cent of public places to have no-smoking policies by 1994
- workplace no-smoking policies to be available to a large majority of employees by 1995
- the NHS to implement a virtually smoke-free environment for staff, patients and visitors as rapidly as possible

In the workplace, the pressure has often come from the employees, although employers are recognizing the advantages in terms of reduction of sickness and absenteeism from introducing such non-smoking policies. Introduction of such policies can cause resentment if senior managers are exempt. Smoking cessation also needs to be managed well to avoid it seeming patronizing or interfering. There is also the danger that introducing a no-smoking policy can act as a catalyst for other grievances.

A common action is to confine smoking to certain areas (76 per cent of organizations), educating employees about the health hazards associated with smoking, and providing assistance to those wishing to give up the habit (40 per cent). Almost 80 per cent of employers in a recent survey had some form of smoking policy, although there is still a wide variation of practice. Some companies have no overall policy but leave it to individual departments to decide whether or not they should have no-smoking areas. There is a clear trend for companies to introduce some form of smoking policy, with some concentrating on designated smoke-free areas, some banning the sale of cigarettes on the premises and others restricting smokers to their private rooms.

The instigation of a smoking policy at work does not necessarily mean that it is properly implemented. It is possible, for example, to have a policy which only permits smoking in single-use offices. If, however, the office doors are left open regularly the corridors can become smoky. Departmental offices which may normally house a single secretary and therefore designated as a single use office, will be used regularly by other staff for photocopying, filing, etc.

Confinement of smoking to certain areas has been shown to be the most common type of smoking policy in industry. Often the reason is less one of health and more a matter of safety. Companies such as Kelloggs and Crown Berger where either food or inflammable products are being processed are examples of this approach. Some companies do not permit smoking in canteens and others have a no-smoking policy during all meetings. An unusual policy, which has been adopted by Sun Alliance, is to restrict smoking to certain hours. In this case it is before 9.00 am, after 4.00 pm and during lunch and coffee breaks.

The introduction of a smoking policy will usually involve consultation within the company, hopefully on the basis of consensus. A recent audit of smoking practices within the London and Manchester Group resulted in the following actions:

- the existing ban on smoking in open-plan offices was extended to corridors, meeting rooms and lifts
- the restaurant smoking area was reduced
- smoking was allowed to continue in certain private offices providing there was adequate ventilation and there was no impact on open-plan offices
- smoking was restricted to one toilet per floor

Thorn Lighting was another company that recently undertook a smoking audit designed specifically to establish in which departments the smokers were most heavily concentrated. Having obtained the results they are attempting to reduce the problem without infringing personal freedom. The company has insufficient space to provide no-smoking areas within its general office environment. However as offices are refurbished they are becoming no-smoking areas under a voluntary arrangement which will be policed by the employees themselves.

The consensus approach seems to work well. A number of companies such as National Nuclear Corporation, which restricts smoking 'by co-operation', and Wimpey's 'employee-regulated' no smoking areas demonstrate its success.

Part of a smoking audit can establish the extent to which employees consider themselves to be the victims of passive smoking. The damage caused by passive smoking is not conclusive. Recent legislation in the United States is based on suggestions that passive smoking or 'environmental tobacco smoke' is causing 3000 deaths per year. The equivalent number in the UK is about 300 deaths per year. The difficulty in the medico-scientific literature is that there are two types of lung cancer. Normal smokers tend to contract one type whereas passive smokers contract a different form. This difference has not been satisfactorily explained and until it is the jury must be considered 'still undecided'. However putting clinical uncertainties aside, there is mounting pressure from authoritative medical bodies and the public to recognize the possible dangers of environmental tobacco smoke. This has been emphasized in the recent case of Veronica Bland, the council worker who claimed her health was damaged by passive smoking at work. Her employer, Stockport Metropolitan Borough Council settled out-of-court with a damages claim of £15,000. As it was an out-of-court settlement it makes no legal precedent but the case certainly indicates the problem that other employers may face in the future.

Part of a smoking audit could also identify those smokers who wish to stop. Asda Stores introduced a blanket ban at its head office in Leeds in September 1993 but also recognized the needs of addicted smokers. The company offered free hypnotherapy to assist those wishing to stop smoking. Other companies have introduced smoking cessation programmes. These include Lubrizol who are working closely with a local hospital's cancer research trust and its team of health visitors. These run courses during work time on the company's premises. Shell UK Oil provide individual counselling and encouragement to those wishing to give up smoking.

It is less commonly known that the recently renegotiated GP contracts have emphasized the need to achieve the government's smoking reduction targets. This means that primary health care teams are being encouraged to record smoking status and to offer advice on smoking cessation. This resource should be available to companies needing advice and assistance as is the support of the anti-smoking charity QUIT.

Safety

Although this book concentrates on health issues, it is inevitable that safety is considered because of the close link between the two terms in the workplace. This is probably the area where most companies undertake audits as a matter of course and build in a 'safety check' as part of their regular working practice. The safety philosophy of a major company like BP can be summarized as:

- the requirement for active management, with plans and resources fully considered
- the quantification of safety performance with the level of compliance measured for each objective
- weakness in management control to be assessed as part of accident or incident investigation
- all superiors and managers should achieve minimum safety training standards
- regular audits should establish whether safety management processes are effective

Dow Chemical Company were one of the first companies to establish a line management system on safety from the supervisor right through to the board. They have instituted a number of programmes including fire and explosion risk, reactive chemicals, loss prevention and a review system for self-inspection audits to check that minimum requirements were being met. Shell uses advisers within its organization to develop safety standards, to conduct audits and technical reviews and to act as a specialist source of information and guidance. A safety management policy was issued in 1985 with the following elements:

- a commitment to safety by a visible management especially with respect to resourcing and personnel training
- a comprehensive and clear safety policy which has an equal status with other business practices
- the responsibility of the safety officer is mainly advisory with a clear line management in place
- safety advisers to have high levels of competency to provide managers with specialist support
- safety standards are practical, understandable and available in writing
- comprehensive measurement of safety performance
- measurable and achievable safety objectives, tasks and targets
- safety training, motivation and communication to be effective
- all injuries and incidents to be thoroughly investigated
- safety standards and practices to be regularly audited

Du Pont was a company with an excellent safety record up to 1986 – some 90 per cent lower than typical in the chemical industry. However as the company was restructured to cope with a leaner marketplace, safety standards seemed to deteriorate and management soon addressed the problem. It required an increased level of instruction and training to place more emphasis at an individual level. Du Pont have also ensured that managers at every level are re-committed to this component of their responsibilities. Much of this effort has been concentrated on modifying behaviour. It is attempting to enable a common approach of all personnel working cooperatively to improve safety performance.

The HSE's Accident Prevention Advisory Unit consider that 90 per cent of accidents are caused by human error and that 70 per cent are preventable. Three separate studies have suggested that about 70–75 per cent of accidents are as a result of reasonable precautions not being taken by management. Dow Chemicals estimate that about 80 per cent of accidents are caused by employees not following procedures or by inattention to detail. Based on this type of information an audit on safety not only provides information on procedures commonly in use but more importantly the compliance with such procedures.

It is possible to list the features of an audit for one sector of a company – that of the offices. A similar list should be developed for all sections of the company, but the following is indicative of areas to be considered:

- appropriate registration under the Offices, Shops and Railway Premises Act 1963
- requirements for a Fire Certificate
- information supplied or posted on relevant Acts
- cleanliness of furniture, fittings and furnishings
- space allocations
- temperature levels and safe heating methods
- adequate ventilation and lighting
- toilet and washing provision for males and females
- drinking water supply
- seating arrangements
- state of floors and staircases
- safety of machinery
- first aid support
- emergency evacuation procedures

- fire precaution and appliances

A general safety audit should be concerned with the reduction or elimination of any danger to the workforce. It should examine:

- premises
- environment
- plant and machinery
- materials
- processes
- working systems
- supervision and control
- training
- personal protective equipment
- specially vulnerable groups
- unsafe behaviour
- personal hygiene
- awareness of health and safety procedures

The audit can take a variety of forms; a combination or a selection or just one of the following depending on the exact requirement of the audit:

- surveys: an examination in detail of selected areas of the workplace usually based on employees' evaluation of procedures
- tours: unscheduled examinations of operational areas often used to assess compliance with safety requirements. Can be undertaken by an individual but more commonly on a group basis
- critical examination: questioning each area of the organization to ensure safe working systems, compliance with policies, etc
- inspections: a scheduled inspection, usually by specialists to establish legal compliance levels on company policies
- contact schemes: sharing information with colleagues to discuss topics on safety
- sampling: identifying omissions or defects by random sampling of working procedures. Observers can note use of protective equipment, correct handling techniques, etc. Items can either be noted and acted upon or a pro forma produced which scores items numerically to show changes in performance over time
- hazard analysis: a study of the potential for accident or injury. Often

undertaken by an independent observer who will not have been involved in the process design
- damage control: damage to property, products and plant may relate closely to injury, especially if the incident or 'near miss' level is high. Elimination of 'near misses' should reduce accidents

Manual Handling

Manual handling results in more than one third of the accidents reported annually. Although fatalities are rare, major injury such as fractures account for 6 per cent of all major injuries reported. Most accidents caused by manual handling result in employees being off work for over three days, usually as a result of sprains or strains, and most commonly with injuries to the back. On January 1st, 1993, the Manual Handling Operations Regulations 1992 came into force and this requires employers 'to make a suitable and sufficient assessment of the risks to the health and safety of their employees while at work'. In other words an audit is required of manual handling working practices. The Health and Safety Executive (HSE) publication (HMSO) on *Manual Handling* provides very full guidance to the regulations and should be consulted for those involved in this aspect of health at work. The remainder of this section will paraphrase the appendix on numerical guidelines for assessment.

In essence the Regulations suggest the following measures:

- any hazardous manual handling should ideally be avoided
- those tasks which cannot be avoided should be thoroughly assessed
- the risk of injury should be reduced whenever possible

It is recognized that large individual variability exists between workers of both sexes. Any numerical guidelines cannot be interpreted as limited at either end of the scale. Individuals vary so much in strength and fitness that a lower limit may be damaging, yet a higher limit may be acceptable in certain cases.

Generally speaking a task involving lifting and lowering a load is more manageable nearer the body. When the person is standing upright, the area from the elbow to the hand is the safest. The two areas from elbow to shoulder and buttock to mid-lower leg can support loads reasonably well and the head and foot areas are those capable of supporting least load. Any twisting action will produce a torque on the body which should be compensated by a lighter load. This especially applies for people with a history of low-back pain. The frequency of lifting and lowering is an important variable with much lower loads being recommended if the frequency goes above 30 operations an hour. The principles of lifting and lowering apply equally to carrying over a distance up to ten metres. Any longer distances and loads should be reduced proportionately. During pulling and pushing tasks, the guideline figure to start or stop a load is a force of 250 Newtons. It is assumed when keeping an object in motion (about 100 Newtons) that the force is being applied in the abdominal region of the body and that adequate rest periods are given. When seated the guideline load, because of the less stable base, is reduced to about 5 kg and should ideally be restricted to an area close to the body between hips and shoulder. This same region when standing has an advisable maximum of 20–25 kg, so the advantages of standing can be appreciated.

The HSE publication on *Manual Handling* provides an example of an assessment checklist. This has been modified by the University of Liverpool safety adviser and is reproduced in Appendix 2 to show how one organization is responding to the Regulations. The flow chart which is shown opposite was also produced by the University Safety Adviser. It gives a good example of how an audit which starts with a simple question can go through a series of stages, each with a suitable action to reduce the risk of injury.

Lighting

Poor lighting is one the of the contributors to 'sick building syndrome'. A recent Gallup survey of over 700 office workers revealed that over a quarter had complained about glare and reflection from VDUs. Over half of those who responded to the survey indicated that the office lighting had not changed since the introduction of the VDUs. A lighting audit can consider the personal levels of comfort or discomfort experienced by the employees. As lighting levels can be measured directly, a lighting audit can also examine how lighting compares with the recommended standards.

Lighting design has two dimensions:

- the quantity required for a given task
- the quality with respect to its distribution, colour, brightness and the avoidance of glare

Manual Handling Flow Chart

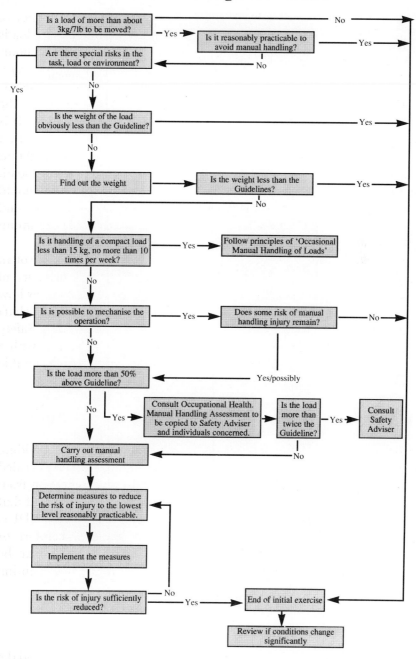

Table 4.3

Average illuminances and minimum measured illuminances

General Activity	Typical locations/types of work	Average illuminance (lx)	Minimum measured illuminance (lx)
Movement of people, machines and vehicles	Lorry parks, corridors, circulation routes	20	5
Movement of people, machines and vehicles in hazardous areas; rough work not requiring perception of detail	Construction site clearance, excavation and soil work, loading bays, bottling and canning plants	50	20
Work requiring limited perception of detail	Kitchens, factories assembling large components, potteries	100	50
Work requiring perception of detail	Offices, sheet metal work, bookbinding	200	100
Work requiring perception of fine detail	Drawing offices, factories assembling electronic components, textile production	500	200

(Source HSE Guidance Note HS(G) 38 'Lighting at work')

HSE Guidance Note HS(G) 38 entitled *Lighting at work* provides lighting standards and the reader is recommended to this for further details. It is necessary to distinguish between average illuminance levels for working activities and the minimum levels required. Table 4.3 provides this information. An audit can establish the discrepancy between the standards recommended by the HSE and actual levels.

It is also important to examine the relationship between the specific working locations and the surrounding area. Visual discomfort can occur if the ratio is too great especially if there is frequent movement between areas. Once again the HSE Guidance Note HS(G) 38 *Lighting at work* provides a table to indicate suitable ratios for illuminating adjacent areas as shown below:

Table 4.4
Maximum ratios of illuminance for adjacent areas

Situations to which recommendation applies	Typical location	Maximum ratio of illuminances	
		Working area	Adjacent area
Where each task is individually lit and the area around the task is lit to a lower illuminance	Local lighting in an office	5 :	1
Where two working areas are adjacent, but one is lit to a lower illuminance than the other	Localised lighting in a works store	5 ⋅ :	1
Where two working areas are lit to different illuminances and are separated by a barrier but there is frequent movement between them	A storage area inside a factory and a loading bay outside	10 :	1
(Source HSE Guidance Note HS(G) 38 'Lighting at work')			

Glare is a special case which can cause discomfort and impaired vision. It can occur by reflection off a surface or when there is an unusually bright part of the visual field. Glare can be reduced by keeping lighting as high as possible, parallel to the main direction of lighting, designing appropriate shades to screen the lamps. The way in which ceilings, walls and floors reflect light is an important consideration in visual comfort. The type of surface will be the major factor contributing to this with a carpeted floor clearly providing less reflection than a white tiled floor. The ideal ratio between the illumination level of the task is for ceilings 60 per cent, walls 30–80 per cent and floors 20–30 per cent.

Temperature and Humidity

An audit on temperature and humidity can, rather like lighting, be based on subjective comfort or direct measurement. Not only are high temperatures uncomfortable but they can influence personal hygiene adversely and add costs to the company for unnecessary use of fuel. Hot, stuffy conditions can cause lapses of concentration through drowsiness which is potentially serious when employees responsible for heavy machinery. Although it is necessary to take into account preferred styles of work clothing, culture and changes in styles of work during the day, the following table, Table 4.5 provides a recommended temperature range.

Table 4.5
Temperature ranges for different types of work

Temperature range	Type of work
19 - 30^0	Sedentary e.g. office work
15 - 20^0	Light work e.g. cleaning
12.5 - 16^0	Heavy work e.g. plastering

Relative humidity is ideally maintained between 30–70 per cent. A level below 30 per cent will cause the throat and nasal passages to dry out. Above 70 per cent may cause a feeling of stuffiness or clamminess.

Ventilation

Ventilation becomes especially important in working environments involving dust, gases, fumes, and other airborne pollutants. The requirement to maintain comfortable conditions means that all harmful fumes, dust and other impurities should be rendered harmless. For areas which do not involve pollutants, such as offices and shops, adequate ventilation must also be provided.

Mechanical ventilation systems are needed when natural ventilation is inadequate. These include:

- extract or exhaust ventilation which can duct air to a collector system. The charcoal filter above a cooker is typical of this type
- capture systems which transport the pollutant to a remote point
- high-volume low-velocity systems which prevent the contaminant reaching the operator in the first place

The alternative type of ventilation dilutes the contaminant until it is no longer dangerous. This is usually used for gas or vapours of low toxity.

A ventilation audit will ensure that the most appropriate ventilation system is operating, that it is working efficiently and that the employees find the ventilation adequate.

Noise and Hearing

A noise audit will reveal the level within the workplace and give the opportunity for action to be taken. Noise exposure levels should be reduced to 90 decibels wherever possible and, if not reasonably practical, some form of personal hearing protection should be provided. At the lower level of 85 decibels, hearing protection must be available to all employees who request it. There is also an obligation on the employer to provide 'noise awareness training' to employees whose daily exposure is 85 decibels or above. The shift from 'request' to 'provision' may seem a major difference for a small difference in sound levels. However the decibel scale is logarithmic so that a change of only 3 decibels is in fact a doubling of sound intensity. These logarithmic differences can be viewed in a different way when legislating for the maximum noise dosage over time. An increase in 3 decibels means a halving of the time permitted to tolerate the noise. Thus 90 decibels can be tolerated for eight hours, but 93 decibels can only be tolerated for four hours and 96 decibels for only two hours.

Theoretically, if employees refuse to wear hearing protectors, having been provided with them by supervisors and told to wear them, they could be prosecuted. A more likely scenario is for the employer to be served with an enforcement notice to ensure that they are worn by the workers.

A noise audit should be able to identify ear protection zones where exposure is likely to exceed 90 decibels. Having identified the area and the personnel likely to be affected, the employer should then:

- erect suitable warning signs
- clarify that protectors must be worn in the zones
- ensure that anyone entering the zone is properly protected

The protection from noise will depend on its source. In certain areas it can be questioned at source by designing quieter machines, by damping, by isolation, by insulation, by absorption, by the use of silencers, or at the very least by reducing the exposure time. In many cases the only practical protection is by using personal ear protectors. These need to be comfortable, efficient and compatible with other forms of protection.

Most ear protectors are either muffs covering the whole ear or plugs covering the ear canal. Their performance is not only influenced by quality of fit but also by the frequency level of the predominant sound. There is also a big difference between the laboratory performance of ear protectors and the 'real world' performance. Studies at the University of Salford indicated that the degradation (real versus theoretical) was greater in ear plugs than muffs. The ear plugs provided about half the claimed decibel performance, whereas the muffs were about two-thirds efficient. These results are not placing the blame on the products themselves, but often on the user. This is why appropriate training should be given by the employer and, in work circumstances when noise becomes an issue, an audit should reveal the training practice.

Noise is another example where legislation is effectively a form of audit. The regulation requires that if any employee is likely to be exposed to a level of 85 decibels then a competent person must make a noise assessment. The *a priori* assumption is recognizing the possibility of such exposures to noise in the workplace in the first place. This is when a more general health audit could reveal the possibility.

Ergonomics

Ergonomics is the science of fitting men and women to machines in a workplace environment. Inevitably compromises have to be made between the cost of installing the perfect machine for a given operation and the wide variation in size, shape and strength of the prospective worker. Even so reasonable planning and observation can make a big difference to the working conditions for many employees. Normally if operators are more comfortable they will be less subject to accidents, injuries and distractions. If they are working in an ergonomically healthy environment they are more likely to be productive.

The ergonomic audit may, simply on the basis of intelligent observation, reveal a number of features which would predispose discomfort. The following may be observed:

- work surfaces too low to allow adequate clearance for the upper surface of the thighs
- office furniture which cannot adjust to accommodate different physiques
- angle of sight inappropriate between eyes and screen causing tense neck and shoulders
- inability to reach certain key controls without excessive movement
- vision of display panels partially obscured
- tools not designed to optimal specifications for the user
- lack of clear identification on controls, switches, dials, etc.
- temporary modifications to equipment can reveal poor design
- regular changes of position to accommodate poor lighting patterns

It would, however, be naive to consider ergonomics as simply observing a 'poor fit' and making adjustments to improve the task-person interface. It may be necessary:

- to analyse the training needs of the situation
- to identify and avoid the risks involved
- to be prepared to pilot the changes and design prototypes
- to audit not only the original situation but also the changes

The Health and Safety Executive in its pamphlet on *Ergonomics at Work* has provided a list of ways to tell whether something is ergonomically satisfactory. The first stage is to consider all the ways in which the equipment is to be used and then ask:

- does it suit your body size?
- does it also suit all other users?

- can you see and hear all you need to readily?
- do you understand all the information that is presented?
- do errors occur frequently, and is it easy to recover from them?
- does the equipment or system cause discomfort if you use it for any length of time?
- is it convenient to use?
- is it easy to learn to use?
- is it compatible with other systems in use?
- could any of these aspects be improved?
- do other users have similar reactions?

Such questions will indicate the extent to which the equipment or operation performs its desired function.

In designing or redesigning a workstation (used in its broadest context) the first stage is to analyse the user and the task to establish the specifications for the design. The task may appear on the face of it straightforward – a secretary, for example, undertaking a range of wordprocessing skills. This indeed may be the perception of the task. However when analysed more critically, the secretary may spend more time answering the telephone, the door entry system, talking to clients at a 90 degree angle from the VDU and moving to use the photocopier. If so the task analysis may suggest a different workstation layout to optimize the activities to be undertaken.

With many tasks it is necessary to have the most current anthropometric data to ensure the least discomfort. One example is the height of work surface, especially when the operative is standing. There have been relatively few adjustments to sink heights over recent decades even though the average leg length has increased significantly.

The next stage is to attempt to design-out conditions which are potentially injurious. For such conditions as repetitive strain injury or work-related upper-limb disorders (RSI/WRULD see Chapter 5.7) it may be appropriate to examine the workstation from the aspects of:

- excess force
- repetition
- rest intervals
- activity changes
- posture
- excess individual stress
- excess organizational stress

A thorough understanding of the potential risks in workstation design and operator factors will not necessarily result in risks occurring. However the aspects of

- frequency
- intensity, and
- duration

will be three major determinants in likely outcome. The combination of these, with a high frequency and intensity combined with long duration, is likely to be the most damaging. Reduction of one of these aspects is likely to reduce risk but working practice may constrain the amount that they can individually be changed.

In addition to aspects of frequency, intensity and duration, the job design and the manner in which work is organized is critical to ergonomic evaluation. Manual handling, as seen earlier, is an example where redesign of a job can cause major benefits but it is also important to appreciate the consequences of any redesign strategy. Sometimes a change in work practice may have a temporary effect without solving the root of the problem. Job rotation, for example, has been often used as a means of reducing RSI/WRULD but this does not resolve the cause of the initial problem. It may mean that less efficient workers are undertaking the task and that resentment is built up because work practices are constantly changing.

There is a great danger in trying to resolve an ergonomic problem in a theoretical manner. Far better to try the solution with a prototype, pilot or temporary solution. It does not matter if the solution looks 'Heath Robinson', if it not only works, but satisfies the operative. Obtain feedback from the workers on proposed changes before implementing them permanently. This is especially the case if the improvement has a number of options. It is important for the employee to recognize the cost implications, especially if competing options differ widely in price. Time and money spent at this stage could save errors being made which when fully implemented could prove to be expensive and not resolve the problem satisfactorily.

It is also worth re-auditing the ergonomic situation further down the line when any changes have been in place for some time. On a purely psychological basis many changes will produce positive results initially because the employee recognizes that there is interest in his/her situation. However once a situation settles the change may have introduced other ergonomic aspects which were not previously recognized.

Any changes in workstation design are both costly and disruptive. It is far better to incorporate at the initial 'design and build' stage principles which will allow the operator to perform efficiently, in comfort and safety. The following design principles should assist this process and could additionally be used as an audit checklist:

- make the workstation adjustable so that the tall person will fit, and the small person can reach easily
- provide all materials and tools in front of the worker to reduce twisting motions. Provide sufficient work space for the whole body to turn
- avoid static loads and fixed work postures. Avoid job requirements where the operator must: lean to the front or the side, hold an extremity in a bent or extended position, tilt the head forward more than 15 degrees, bend the torso forward or backward more than 15 degrees, or support the body's weight with one leg
- set the work height at 5 cm below the elbow
- provide adjustable, properly designed chairs with the following features: adjustable seat height, adjustable back rest including a lumbar (lower-back) support, padding which will not compress more than an inch under the weight of a seated individual, and the chair should be stable on the floor at all times
- allow the workers, at their discretion, to alternate between sitting and standing. Provide floor mats or padded surfaces for prolonged standing
- support the limbs. Provide elbow, wrist, arm, foot and back rests where needed
- use gravity to move materials
- design the workstation so arm movements are continuous and curved. Avoid straight-line, jerking arm motions
- design so arm movements pivot about the elbow rather than the shoulder to avoid stress on shoulder, neck and upper-back
- keep arm movements in the normal work area to eliminate excessive reaches of 40 cm
- provide dials and displays that are simple, logical, and easy to read, reach and operate
- eliminate or minimize the effects of undesirable environmental

conditions such as excessive noise, heat, humidity, cold, and poor illumination

Source : Occupational Health Review, April/May 1991

Electromagnetic Fields

Electromagnetic fields or EMFs emanate from a variety of electrical sources as disparate as power lines to electric razors. It is relatively recently that concern has been expressed as to the possible health risk, largely because the quantity of EMFs has never been as high as at present. The actual health risks are as yet unknown with a number of studies reporting no increase in risk whereas others show up to double the average risk. As with many epidemiological studies the other contributing factors cannot always be standardized or eliminated. Thus what may seem to be an increased risk could be caused by another unknown aspect. Nevertheless until further research produces definitive results, scientists will probably argue for prudence over the issue and suggest reducing the exposure to EMFs until the issue is settled.

The reason for concern is that EMFs have been implicated as a cause of cancers, especially leukaemia. Other possible risks include birth defects, weakened immune systems, hypersensitivity/allergies, pregnancy problems, pacemaker problems, headaches, fatigue, suicide and even cot deaths.

The mechanism that has been suggested is that once a cell becomes cancerous it is more likely to produce a tumour and at a faster rate if EMF exposure is high. The mineral magnetite, found in very small amounts in the brain, may interact with the altered magnetic field caused by EMFs. Some studies have suggested that EMFs may suppress the production of melatonin. This hormone is involved with such health problems as depression, seasonally affected disorder, jet lag and cancer.

Over 50 studies have investigated whether employees who are exposed to high levels of EMFs at work are more likely to develop cancers. Three studies on a rare cancer affecting the male breast have found that there appears to be about double the average risk of the disease for workers exposed to high EMF levels. The range of all studies is from no increase in cancer to double the risk compared with the general public.

One of the major occupational studies on EMF and cause of death compared electrical workers with age and race matched controls. Overall it was shown that men employed in any electrical occupation had a mortality odds ratio of 1.4 for brain cancer but only 1.0 for leukaemia. However brain cancer odds ratios were higher for electrical engineers and technicians, telephone workers, electric power workers and electrical workers in manufacturing industries. It must not be forgotten that these same workers could be exposed to other hazards which influence brain cancer. This study implies an increased mortality among some groups of electrical workers but gives little support to an increased incidence of leukaemia.

The problem with these epidemiological studies is not only are confounding variables often present but the actual numbers of cases presented are very small. This makes statistical analysis extremely difficult. In the case of EMFs it is also very difficult to find a target population which is exposed to higher levels than normal. The current position of the World Health Organization is summarized as:

> human data from epidemiological studies, including reported effects on cancer promotion, congenital malformations, reproductive performance and general health, although somewhat suggestive of adverse health effects, are not conclusive.

Accepting this, it would still seem reasonably prudent for a caring employer to audit EMFs in the workplace and within reason take action to reduce exposure levels. Sweden, for example, already has legislation requiring the use of low radiation monitors for computers and wordprocessors. The cost of a low radiation monitor to meet the Swedish standard is about £50 more than the high radiation versions more common in Britain. Workplaces, if practicable, could be redesigned to reduce long-term exposure to high EMF sources such as high-voltage power lines, electric storage heaters, mains adaptors, halogen and fluorescent lamps and high-powered machinery. A building that is incorrectly earthed will produce high levels of EMF so this should be audited and corrected if faulty.

Research is still being conducted by companies such as the National Grid into exposure levels and until this is completed, it would be unwise to suggest that anything more than 'prudent avoidance' was necessary.

Shiftwork

Shiftwork is common in industries requiring 24-hour continuous operation such as heavy manufacturing when stoppages would dramatically reduce the efficiency of the process. For companies or organizations which require shiftwork it is important to recognize the health impact on the employees.

The basis for many health changes is a disturbance in the normal biological rhythm of daily life. Humans have certain circadian rhythms which if allowed to 'free wheel' would dictate a wake–sleep cycle of about 25 hours. However time cues such as clocks, light, work patterns and social contact overlay these biological rhythms and bring people regularly back to 24-hour cycles. Shiftwork can entrain the circadian rhythms but this will take time and assumes no other disturbances. Most shiftworkers have time cues conflicting with the body's constant attempt to adjust circadian rhythms and this can have an effect on health.

Rather like studies reported in the section on electromagnetic fields experimental designs may be flawed because of bias. Shiftworkers may have a different lifestyle such as greater use of convenience foods and alcohol which would make any comparison with non-shiftworkers tenuous. However, allowing for this possible error, the health of shiftworkers can be summarized as follows:

- prolonged sleep loss may increase mortality rates
- a 40 per cent increase in cardiovascular disease was shown in one study compared with dayworkers
- digestive disturbances are more common
- possible link with peptic ulcer development
- greater incidence of nervousness, anxiety and depression
- average sleep loss of two hours per day
- sleep patterns are affected
- variation in tolerance to shiftwork, possibly affected by natural inclinations
- in long shifts (e.g. 12 hours) greater likelihood of errors and performance decrease at end of shift
- greater fatigue on nightshift with tendency to fall asleep at work
- diabetics may be especially affected by changes in eating patterns
- epileptic seizures may be increased by sleep disturbances, especially when the individuals are tired

- asthmatics with an allergy basis may worsen at night if they respond to variations in histamine release
- medication compliance may be more difficult as normal instructions such as 'three times a day' may be difficult to interpret on a rotating shift
- morale may be lower as a result of isolation from family and friends and disruption of recreational activities

Although with most people there are no contraindications to working shifts, an audit of the characteristics listed above may highlight the people least suited. Employees who exhibit a combination of existing health problems most likely to be exacerbated by shifts should be counselled as to its advisability. Those suffering from gastro-intestinal disorders, diabetes, thyroid problems, epilepsy, emotional instability, heart, lung or kidney problems would be most susceptible to worsening health as a result of shift work.

The type of shifts to minimize ill health has not been established with certainty. The length of time will depend on the task. Work requiring concentration, heavy labour and monotony can be tolerated for short periods of time. A regular pattern of shifts gives greater opportunity for planning off-duty hours. Weekends should be free of work as often as possible to permit normal socializing. Recent experimentation in the United States suggests that it is preferable to design shifts consistent with the circadian rhythm. This means in practice that the shifts should rotate by successive phase delays (worked later in the day) with the interval between each phase delay being as long as is possible. This appears to reduce the upset to the circadian rhythm. When this approach was tried there was greater employee satisfaction, health was improved subjectively and productivity increased. These principles were applied in a coking plant in France when a more frequent rotation of shifts was applied. Each person worked either two or three days on one shift and then went on to the next later one, going through the cycle of the three shifts, three times per four week period. This replaced changing shifts only once per four week period. It also meant having two periods of 48 hours off work and one of 72 hours. They never worked more than three shifts without a continuous rest period of at least 24 hours.

The audit should ensure early and continuous consultation if shifts schedules are to be changed and a careful assessment of the consequences of the changes shortly and regularly after implementation.

Sick Building Syndrome

Sick building syndrome, like many syndromes, is a combination of a number of symptoms, in this case apparently related to the workplace. Some investigators have found a mild illness associated with a particular office. Occasionally the cause is identified, such as inadequate ventilation, but in others no reason is established. Some researchers suggest the cause is related to dissatisfaction with working conditions. Although office buildings contiguous with industrial premises are likely to suffer from poor air quality, it is the increasing incidence of mild ill health in independent offices that is giving rise to the so called 'sick building syndrome'.

Open-plan office design has changed heating and ventilation approaches, gives more opportunity for cross-infection and provides greater communication to take place to compare symptoms.

A US study on 203 sites showed that inadequate ventilation accounted for over half of the cases cited. The non-specific complaints of headaches, respiratory and eye irritation were so high in one building that staff were moved once contamination was eliminated as a cause. Having re-located the staff it was established that the air intake had been sealed to protect against fall out from the Mount St Helens volcano. The building was re-occupied with little difficulty once the outdoor intake was resited.

It is important to examine all possible causes of symptoms. A recent case of lethargy at work was originally attributed to car exhaust fumes but further investigation revealed that the culprit was excessively high air temperature. Although environmental causes are common, the possibility of psychogenic disease should not be overlooked. A large group of telephone operators sought medical treatment to a reported odour yet environmental analysis failed to find any toxicity. When the progress of the disease was mapped it back-tracked to one individual who had a history of psychological problems in the forces and had clearly initiated the outbreak of mass psychogenic illness.

Sometimes the cause is very specific such as a group of printers who suffered from microbial infection caused by the humidifiers used in the printing process. However in most reported cases the health complaints are diverse and non-specific. There is rarely a common cause.

One way to try to establish causes is to review symptoms from a variety of types of buildings and see if any pattern emerges. A study in 1985 by Robertson and others showed very clear differences between office buildings which were air-conditioned compared with those having natural ventilation. The air-conditioned buildings had a much higher incidence of employees reporting stuffy nose/dry throat; blocked, runny or itchy nose; watering or itching of eyes; lethargy and headache.

Another study, reported by Wilson and Hedge in 1987, analysed over 4000 questionnaires about work-related symptoms and environmental conditions at 46 sites. This survey was used to produce a score for the average number of symptoms per person (3.11) which was designated a *building sickness score*. Although there was considerable overlap of results between buildings and pre-conceptions in the mind of the respondents, the results reinforced the earlier study to show that on average the air-conditioned buildings had a higher building sickness score (3.47) compared with the natural or mechanically ventilated ones (2.36). One interesting outcome of this survey was that there appeared to be a relationship between the incidence of symptoms and the degree of control respondents had over their environment. People who could alter ventilation and lighting at will had fewer symptoms than those who could not. This may be a contributory factor in the poor outcome from uncontrollable air-conditioning systems. This gives some credence to the theory that 'organization sickness' is part of the sick building syndrome. There could, of course, be other non-behavioural explanations and a more detailed analysis of the differences between air-conditioned and conventionally ventilated buildings might help.

- air conditioned buildings tend to be deep plan having fewer outdoor views and greater dependence on artificial light
- there is little individual control over air movement, ventilation air or temperature
- there is often a greater use of business machines such as mainframe computers; the cooling required to offset heat generation by the machines is greater
- location is commonly in inner-city areas with air filtration limited to particulates
- air-conditioning systems need to be maintained to a high specification to avoid becoming pollutants
- most use filters, silencers, ducting, etc., made of man-made fibres which as they disintegrate release fibres into the air
- air conditioners can remove negatively charged atmospheric ions from the environment

One of the consequences of air-conditioned buildings which have winter humidification is that the humidity levels throughout the year could favour the multiplication of the house dust mite. The faeces of the house dust mite are a well-known allergen responsible for asthma. Other allergens have been implicated in sick building syndrome, although like many causes the case has yet to be fully proven.

Prevention of sick building syndrome involves identifying and controlling potential contaminants in offices. Maintenance needs to be a priority for air conditioning and mechanical ventilation. Consultation between the staff and those responsible for the building might increase perceptions of control. The needs of the users should be given a high priority over the budgetary factors. Should prevention be unsuccessful then expertise is now available to resolve minor health problems which have no obvious cause.

4.3   Occupational Health

Occupational health is a term which has a variety of meanings depending on the company and the attitude within the company. Many companies are too small to consider occupational health as a major issue but at the other end of the scale Shell UK have included health and safety within their primary business objectives.

The organization of occupational health will vary depending on the company but for many the occupational health nurse will be a key person. She will have a number of functions including:

- health supervision and assessment
- training and education
- occupational safety and environmental monitoring
- counselling
- treatment
- rehabilitation and resettlement
- administration and record keeping
- liaison with other organizations

This list could relate to either skills or tasks and the profession and the management tend to look at occupational health from these two approaches. The analysis of the function of occupational health is both, and the approach can be re-cast as a list of goals as in the HSE publication *Review your occupational health needs*. The four main occupational health goals are:

- *prevention of work-related disease* (including maintenance of conditions which are comfortable and conducive to effective work)
- *placement and fitness for work* (including safety-related standards, rehabilitation and job design to meet individual needs)
- *first aid treatment* (incorporating immediate treatment of injury and illness, disaster management and non-urgent treatment services such as physiotherapy and dentistry provided in the workplace)
- *general health promotion* (health education, screening for non-occupational illness, dietary and other intervention campaigns)

The rationale for these goals will differ. Sometimes it is to comply with regulations, often to reduce absenteeism and occasionally to promote health in general within the workforce.

Each of the goals listed above can be best achieved through a sequence of activities. Each activity, once completed logically follows to the next:

- assessment of the details of the problem
- planning what action to take
- evaluating the effectiveness of the action taken

The combination of the goals and the activity sequence produced a grid as follows in Table 4.6.

The occupational health practitioner imports appropriate skills to each of the activities exemplified in Table 4.6. These skills include following instructions, adapting information, observing and analysing a process or even an individual. Sometimes the task will be given to different people within the organization who may not be the occupational health specialist. It could include employers, employees, suppliers, trade unions, advisory and regulatory bodies.

For some companies that do not have occupational health specialists on site, it is possible to make use of external services. One such company is Safacare which originated as a Liverpool-based supplier of medical and first aid equipment to industry. Safacare can provide a service to companies by:

- designing a health and safety policy as required by the Health and Safety at Work Act
- assessing health hazards
- surveying workplace environments

Table 4.6
Outputs of Occupational Health Unit Tasks

Goal	Prevention of work-related diseases	Placement and rehabilitation	First aid and treatment	General health promotion
Task Assessment	Health risks of each agent present in workplace	Health-related performance criteria for jobs	Needs for emergency response and benefits of providing other treatment	Benefits from health promotion at workplace
Planning	Arrangements for control of risk-engineering, work practice etc.	Methods of applying criteria or modifying jobs	First aid and other treatment provisions	Arrangements for appropriate education, counselling
Implementation	Absence of adverse effects or over-exposure	Improved performance, equity, safety, productivity, retention	Reduced harm from emergencies, less time lost from routine treatment	Improved general health
Evaluation	Appraisal of health risk management	Appraisal of effectiveness of placement and rehabilitation	Appraisal of effectiveness and targeting treatment	Analysis of benefits of intervention to promote health

SOURCE: *Carter, J.T. Occupational Health Review August/September, 1989*

- advising and providing information on work-related health matters and their prevention
- evaluating first aid service
- monitoring statutory and voluntary healthcare
- advising on welfare provision
- interpreting and applying legislation concerning health at work

- liaising with statutory organizations
- assisting with major incident/disaster planning
- providing vaccination/mass screening programmes

Companies such as Safacare will provide their services either from their own premises or in the clients' own place of work. They will deal in direct maintenance of first aid boxes through to the provision of seminars on a range of topics. The expertise provided can be offered in conjunction with an existing in-house service or operate independently.

A third option in occupational healthcare is a relatively recent development in which projects are established in cities by people without medical expertise. Occupational health projects in Sheffield, Liverpool, Bradford and Camden (London) aim to establish links between occupation and ill health by interviewing patients when visiting their GPs.

The first of these projects started in Sheffield in 1978 although it was ten years later before it was officially constituted. A brochure produced in 1989 by the Sheffield team states that:

An occupational health worker:

- interviews people in the waiting room
- receives referrals from GPs
- liaises with other health workers
- maintains occupational histories in patients' notes
- carries out health surveillance, audiometry, spirometry, etc.

An occupational health worker advises on:

- support groups where people with similar problems can share information and experiences
- compensation for industrial injury and disease, including state benefits and common law settlements
- safe workplace systems, including ergonomic design
- health and safety at work, legal rights and duties
- handouts and books available on hazards, including chemicals, stress and noise

An Occupational Health Project:

- uses its occupational health database to relate diseases to specific industrial, workplaces or hazards
- reveals 'new' health problems caused by substances or a change in work processes
- publishes reports and literature surveys on hazards and disease profiles by industry

These statements have been the model for the three other projects. The Liverpool project which was funded primarily by the Family Health Services Authority (FHSA) is involved in surgery work, researching the link between work and ill health and in sharing skills to produce change. The following summarizes the activities of the Liverpool Occupational Health Project (OHP).

- pilot scheme started March 1990
- project fully running from 25 March 1991
- project was originally funded with £15,000 from the Inner City Partnership. FHSA funding is paid every three months and runs for three years
- 70 per cent of the funding comes from the FHSA, and the running costs come from the health promotion fees now available which can be claimed back by the doctors
- Four full-time workers
- backgrounds of the staff are varied: one trade union safety representative, one local authority/environmental and two scientific/ research. Two are women and two are men as this facilitates interviewing in the surgery
- steering committee (includes two GP representatives) which meets once a month
- most surgeries are contained within a five-mile radius of the city centre
- main industries include dock service, car production and machining
- major employers include Metal Box, Tate and Lyle and Plessey
- project workers spend 70 per cent of their time in surgeries
- project workers receive weekly training at a local university
- there is no administrative or other back-up
- resource library and up-to-date computerized databases to supply information to patients, doctors and affiliated organizations
- issued first *Liverpool Occupational Health News* in March 1991 which

contained details of the project, RSI, noise-induced hearing loss and a brief history of occupational health and medicine

The 1992–3 executive summary is reproduced in part as follows with permission from the authors:

SURGERY WORK

(i)   Interviews:

The project operates in the waiting rooms of fourteen geographically scattered GP surgeries in Liverpool. The four occupational health workers carry out two hour clinics where they approach patients in the waiting room and ask them a series of questions relating to their health at work and their working environment. A record of the information is retained in the patient's medical record for future reference by their GP. Taking work histories is a crucial first step towards identifying work-related health problems, both for individuals and more generally for the population. Patients often fail to recognize that their work may be affecting their health. Many hazards, such as excessive noise and upper limb disorder, can take many years to show health effects; therefore knowledge of previous jobs is important. Patients attending the surgery for a reason not connected with work are often grateful to be able to discuss their working environment in a neutral setting.

(ii)   Requests for health and safety information:

Patients are often given immediate advice at interview when it is clearly within the competency of the interviewer. Patients and GPs are supplied on request with further information and advice on workplace hazards and diseases, from the project's extensive range of health and safety literature. In 1992–3, 400 patients were provided with additional information on request. Spreading the word on good working conditions and providing people with detailed knowledge on work hazards helps to promote safer working conditions. The project has produced a number of leaflets on specific issues in response to local demand, including asbestos exposure, women and work, and war pensions. News bulletins highlighting a number of occupational hazards are regularly distributed to patients, GPs, trade unions, employers and other organizations and agencies.

(iii)   Audiometry screening:

Hearing tests are offered to patients who feel their hearing has been affected by noise at work. The service has proved highly successful – over 400 tests were carried out in 1992–3. Most patients are referred by their GP, but a proportion are 'picked up' through the interview. In many cases, workers have carried out a test on a patient who was attending their doctor for a matter unrelated to their hearing. The workers also provide patients with advice and information on the hazards of noise exposure at work. Almost half of the patients who had hearing tests conducted by the workers and were referred to the Hearing Aid Departments were issued with a hearing aid.

RESEARCHING THE LINK BETWEEN WORK AND ILL-HEALTH

Much is already known about the harmful effect of hazards at work and much of the work of the OHP involves using this knowledge in a way that is relevant to help solve immediate problems. Much however is not known and OHPs in different parts of the country have a good track record of identifying previous unknown problems.

The amount and range of information collected during patient interviews is vast, with approximately four thousand patients interviewed each year. During the first two years of the project, patient interviews were based on an individual approach. Retaining this in-depth interview method is seen as remaining important in the years ahead; however, the project will consider other less detailed interview techniques to produce more superficial data which is easier to analyse. A database system has been developed to act as an index for previous interviews to investigate suspicions of trends in work-related ill-health. One such suspicion led to a research study on the health of residential caretakers in high rise flats. The final report, produced in November 1991 and which validated the workers' suspicions of stress related to the residential aspect of the work, resulted in media coverage which facilitated the need for employers, both locally and nationally to reconsider the nature of these residential posts. In a similar way, the project has developed suspicions that cleaners suffer health problems due to the use of industrial buffer machines. A study is being planned to investigate this.

SKILL SHARING TO PRODUCE CHANGE

The project's unique position as part of the Primary Health Care Team, but also linking closely with major organizations, has allowed networking between different disciplines and outside organizations, facilitating group action by bringing together people from different professions who share a common goal. By using an Action Research approach (involving many people in the study and feeding back information regularly) people can learn immediately from the project's work and action to change gets linked with data gathering in an immediate way that is locally owned and locally sensitive. This is much more efficient and effective at causing change than conventional research methods.

The project has developed profitable links with the University of Liverpool, Liverpool John Moores University, the Health and Safety Executive, the City Environmental Health Department, trade unions, welfare groups and community groups, including a Somali linkworker.

During 1992–3 the project established two support groups – a Repetitive Strain Injury (RSI) or Upper Limb Disorder and an Asbestos Support Group. Both groups originated as a result of the workers interviewing an increasing number of patients suffering from RSI or an asbestos-related health problem. Both Support Groups have attracted the support of MPs, GPs, welfare groups, trade unions and employers. The main aim of these groups is to provide an information, advice and counselling service for sufferers and their families for whom there are no services available on Merseyside.

5

Examining the Individual's Health

5.1 Health Screening

A number of companies make use of private health screening. This tends, because of the cost, to be offered to senior management and may operate in association with private health insurance. There is an opinion that providing health screening for the most costly staff, and presumably those with the greatest influence in the company, is a wise investment. An alternative view is to provide health screening for the sector of the company at greatest risk, which is far more likely to be at the non-management end of the employee continuum. Another option is to provide health screening for all staff on the basis that a small shift by everyone towards better health is likely to produce a better outcome overall. Epidemiologists would argue for the latter option as most studies have shown that if the normal distribution can be altered towards better health, then this will have the most impact. The consequence of this option is that the quality of screening may not be as high as if fewer individuals were targeted, largely because of budgetary limitations.

The operational definition of health screening will be an investigation (normally medical) which does not relate to an employee seeking advice for a specific complaint. The justification for health screening is on the basis of:

- early identification of disease
- public health protection

- research, such as checking an intervention strategy before being implemented widely

Any health screening will have consequences beyond the immediate benefits to the person being screened. It often produces a greater interest in health amongst employees, a statistical base to provide employers with an action plan and is often seen as an employment benefit.

Health screening, whatever the type adopted should fulfil certain criteria. These may include:

- the condition to be examined should relate to an important health problem
- anyone found with a problem should be treatable
- diagnostic and treatment facilities should be available
- a suitable test or examination should be available
- any test should be acceptable to the group being examined
- policy on treatment should be agreed
- the economic implications of screening and treatment costs should be known
- screening should never be isolated by part of a regular process

The choice of a particular test during health screening should also be considered with care. The test should ideally be simple, acceptable to the subjects being tested, accurate, cost effective, reliable or repeatable, sensitive and specific to the disease under examination. The sensitivity is especially important as psychological damage could occur to people who are given inaccurate information.

Too often a health-screening programme is instituted without due consideration to the employees and the workplace. If the workplace has any special environmental conditions or hazards then these should be part of the screening process. For example a factory for car production is likely to be extremely noisy and generate significant hearing loss. Audiometry tests, on the other hand, are unlikely to be appropriate for most office-based workers.

Health screening could usefully include tests which indicate special features of a job. Concentration on a display panel requires good visual acuity, firefighters require a minimum level of fitness and kitchen workers need to be free of infections. It is important to evaluate the requirements of the job with care to avoid discrimination based on inaccurate information. In addition to the specific requirements of a job, there may be more general health issues surrounding a type of employment. If it were known, for example, that an adverse health issue such as alcoholism affected a sector of the workforce (e.g. publicans) then screening could concentrate on that feature. Often a more general health screen may have to be undertaken before the features become evident.

Having considered the background to health screening, let us now consider which tests may be appropriate. The following is typical of the options available:

- coronary risk factors
- lung function
- well-woman, e.g. breast screening and cervical smear test
- stress
- hearing and vision
- obesity
- thyroid function
- diabetes
- back problems
- skin diseases
- smoking levels
- alcohol and drug abuse
- dietary habits
- fitness levels
- Aids/HIV awareness
- risk analysis
- safety procedures
- knowledge of resuscitation

You can see it is potentially a mixed bag of options and the list above is by no means exhaustive. The difficult judgement is which ones are appropriate, relevant, affordable, sensitive and likely to be responsive to subsequent health promotion. Ultimately this has to be a management decision, most probably taken on the basis of professional advice. Subsequent sections of this chapter will consider a number of tests on specific aspects of health screening. Those not examined later will be considered below and include hearing tests, vision tests, faecal tests, urine tests, blood tests, tests for lung, breast and cervical cancer and lung-function tests.

Hearing Tests

These will be particularly valuable for individuals whose hearing is likely to be damaged by the environmental noise at work. Audiometry involves exposing the ears to pure tone sounds and detecting the threshold levels. Hearing sensitivity at different frequencies can be detected and often hearing loss can be established before it becomes a serious problem. Preventative or protective action can then be taken.

Vision Tests

This is becoming more common with the use and over-use of visual display units. Some basic testing will indicate major defects but full visual analysis by a trained optician will be necessary before prescribing corrective procedures such as spectacles, contact lenses or laser surgery.

Faecal Tests

Occult blood in the faeces is widely used to screen colorectal cancers but evidence is weak to support a reduction in mortality. However a 13 year follow up study on over 46,000 people in Minnesota showed that when annual screening is undertaken reduced mortality of about one third occurred compared with a control group. Reduced mortality was accompanied by improved survival in those with colorectal cancer and a shift to detection at an earlier stage of the cancer. The test, which is initially based on observing the colour change of special paper, does produce a large number of false positive readings with the accompanying concern and discomfort from subsequent investigations. As testing is refined it may become more popular, with the potential benefits of reducing a major cause of death obvious.

Urine Tests

These are used mainly to detect diabetes based on glucose levels but can also test for blood and protein as an early indication of kidney disease. As this is not intrusive and relatively cheap it is likely to be used more routinely in the future.

Blood Tests

In addition to blood tests for cholesterol and lipids which will be considered in a later section on coronary risk factors, blood tests can reveal diabetes, gout, liver damage, renal disease, jaundice and anaemia. They can also be used to examine for illegal drugs and HIV/ Aids, although clearly the implications of such knowledge are far reaching.

Lung, Breast and Cervical Cancer Tests

A chest X-ray is of limited value in preventing lung cancer because a detected tumour is likely to be too advanced for treatment to be very effective. Prevention is a far better option. Health surveillance linked to particular work conditions such as high asbestos levels may justify this approach more readily. Mammography on the other hand can reduce death rates by early detection although once again the incidence of false positives is high. It should be available to all female employees over 45 to 50 years of age. Cervical cancer screening was rated as the highest health priority after smoking by employers in a recent survey. Encouragement should be given to employees to attend regularly for screening.

Lung Function Tests

These are used commonly in health screenings, most usually by single-breath spirometry. As an indication of satisfactory lung function, their inclusion may be justified but their usefulness to detect respiratory disease prior to more specific symptoms is questionable. If there is the likelihood of respiratory disease as a direct consequence of occupational hazards or asthma control, then lung function tests may well be justified. The benefits of routine lung function screening in jobs which are environmentally healthy may need to be considered carefully, although the capital and recurrent costs are relatively small.

Lifestyle Assessments

As preventative approaches to medicine gather momentum it is important to be able to quantify the current status of employees before taking remedial action. It will also provide the basis for targeting employment groups in special need. Perception of health status is one example of what may be a mismatch between a worker's personal beliefs and the realistic situation. This was shown clearly in the Allied Dunbar National Fitness Study when many respondents were reasonably happy with their personal health status whilst more objective evidence suggested much room for improvement. Exercise, dietary, smoking, drinking and health habits can all be assessed by asking appropriate questions. Similarly life and job satisfactions, mental and physical stress, and personality behaviours can provide useful information for subsequent health promotion. There have been clear differences shown between white and blue collar workers to many of these lifestyle measures, differences between shift and non-shift workers, between staff of different ages and between the sexes. Health promotion activities will be more effective if the working conditions and lifestyle background of each worker are taken into consideration.

Although it is not always possible to divide health screening into convenient approaches or styles, this section will examine:

- private screening – off site (e.g. BUPA)
- private screening – on site
- specialist screening – off-site (e.g. breast screening)
- in-house screening

The approach to be taken will be very dependent on the management policy. In most cases a number of factors will be considered including the size of the company, the facilities for health screening, the type of work and the availability of support resources. A large company with a strong occupational health department may operate a health-screening programme for all employees whereas a small company may be prepared to allow staff time off work for off-site specialist screening such as mammography.

Private Screening – Off-Site

There are now well over 150 clinics nationwide offering body check-ups. A *Which?* survey in 1989 found that a third of its members had check-ups in the last five years and most of these had been funded by their companies. Since that time there has been a massive expansion in the number of general practitioners offering a basic screening under such names as MOT, well-woman, etc., so numbers of private clinics have probably remained static. A BUPA Health Screen, for example, will include a full physical examination and consultation with a doctor, plus tests on blood pressure, urine, lungs, blood, hearing, sight, a chest X-ray and an electrocardiogram. Some companies will offer special combinations tailored for specific workers and women could have cervical smear and breast examinations. Within two weeks, clients should receive a personal health action plan setting out recommendations based on the findings of the screening.

A common feature of such off-site private health screening was that companies offered it only as a perk to senior staff. An alternative is to select specific tests to suit the type of employee.

Private Screening – On-Site

An increasing number of fitness consultants are prepared to bring their expertise to the premises and set up a range of services on-site. These will include health and fitness screening, lectures and workshops on health matters, installation of fitness equipment, organization of rehabilitation classes, nutritional courses and re-assessments. Increasingly use is being made of computerized systems to evaluate the results from health screening. The advantages of this approach include a rapid result, a hard copy for the patient to take away, back-up files for comparison and a quality-looking report. The disadvantage is that the values produced are only as good as the normative data. These are likely to be based on material collected elsewhere – often from another country. Although most companies offer some consultation time, feedback based on a standardized report gives no opportunity for interaction. Some fitness companies provide a very comprehensive report including a complete exercise prescription programme. Appendix 3 illustrates the type of detail provided by Wellsource, an American company specializing in employee health appraisal.

The advantages of on-site private screening are that employees take minimum time off work to attend, it can be fitted into company work schedules and there is no need to provide a permanent specialist venue as the equipment will be removed after use. The disadvantages are that certain tests using specialist equipment (e.g. mammography) will not be offered, the clinical environment will not be as safe compared with testing in a hospital and consultants are less likely to have the financial resources of a major medical insurance organization. One major advantage of consultants who visit the company is that they should be in a better position to assess all aspects of health and tailor their screening to the specific needs of the employees.

Specialist Screening – Off-Site

This type of screening will often be associated with the NHS and will include such screening options as cervical smear testing, breast screening, chest radiography for tuberculosis. In such cases appointments may be made during working hours and employers will need to be sympathetic to staff's wishes to be screened.

In-House Screening

This type differs from on-site private screening in that it is a permanent feature of the company's health policy. For companies with well-established departments of occupational health this may already be in evidence. However some occupational health staff may not have the specialist skills to undertake comprehensive health screening and will need to be trained. Others may not consider this to be a priority for their work, although recent evidence suggests that this aspect of primary healthcare is of great interest. Some companies will invest in the equipment for health screening and employ specialist full- or part-time staff to undertake the testing, often linked to health-promotion activities.

5.2 Coronary Risk Factors

Seventy million working days are lost to industry and commerce each year as a result of coronary heart disease (CHD). This is well over ten times more than those lost through strikes and industrial disputes. Apart from accounting for 30 per cent of all UK deaths, it also affects the lives of many people associated with the deceased person.

Coronary heart disease is statistically linked with over 200 risk factors, but the more significant ones are:

- age
- blood cholesterol level
- blood pressure
- cigarette smoking
- diabetes

- family history
- lack of exercise
- obesity
- high-fat diet unrelated to obesity
- sex (male)
- stress, tension and anxiety

A number of these can be modified and emphasis will be given to those in this section. It must not be forgotten that these risk factors should never be considered in isolation. Even a multiplicity of risk factors does not guarantee heart disease, although in epidemiological terms the chances are bound to increase. There is plenty of anecdotal evidence of people who have a number of risk factors and never develop heart disease. Similarly there are individuals who have no risk factors yet die of heart attacks. It is possible that some people have a protective gene which overrides other risk factors. However, until further evidence accumulates the current view is to consider risk factors seriously and for those that can be reduced to make every effort to make the appropriate changes.

Total Cholesterol

Cholesterol is a white fatty substance which is produced in the liver. It is an essential component of human cells but a high-fat diet will produce more cholesterol than is required. This will result in fatty deposits in the artery walls which constrict blood flow and can eventually lead to a heart attack. Cholesterol can be measured using a drop of blood taken from a finger prick. This is commonly analysed by a desk-top machine using a dry chemistry process. The blood is placed on a special slide, inserted into a machine such as the Reflotron, and after two minutes a cholesterol value is produced. Any value below 5.2 millimoles of cholesterol per litre of blood is acceptable. People with values of 5.2–6.5 mmol/litre will probably benefit from dietary advice. The Flora Project for Heart Disease Prevention which is sponsored by Van den Berghs and Jurgens provides an educational resource for health professionals. Their free literature can be obtained from 24–28 Bloomsbury Way, London, WC1A 2PX. Values above 6.5 mmol/litre may require further action and the person's general practitioner should be consulted.

Triglycerides and Cholesterol Fractions

Triglycerides are more blood fats that contribute to the risk of CHD. Cholesterol can be divided into two transporting proteins, the high density lipoproteins (HDL) and low density lipoproteins (LDL). HDL cholesterol appears to have a protective effect so high values of this fraction is ideal. The same type of machine can be used to test for triglycerides and HDL cholesterol, although it may be beneficial to do this after a 14-hour fast to obtain more accurate results. The best strategy may be only to consider testing for triglycerides and cholesterol fractions if the total cholesterol value is high and not responding to dietary treatment.

The Glaxo company tested 1009 employees and found 20 with a plasma cholesterol of over 7.8 mmol/litre. When the test was repeated after fasting, eight were found to have levels below 7.8, eleven had confirmed high plasma cholesterol levels and one had normal cholesterol but high triglycerides. Those that had not already seen their GPs were advised to do so.

Benefits of Lowering Cholesterol Levels

Although the link between raised cholesterol and CHD, particularly in middle-aged men, is undeniable, the benefits of lowering cholesterol levels is still disputed. One study even showed that as cholesterol levels fall, the risk of death increases. Reducing cholesterol levels from drugs seems to be particularly associated with increased cancers, especially of the colon. The trouble with these sorts of statistics is that even if it were true that high cholesterol is associated with low colon cancer, the overall benefits may be greater by reducing cholesterol! A recent article in *The Times* by Jeremy Laurance states that:

> Reducing the amount of fat in the British diet by one sixth would cut blood cholesterol by 10 per cent, enough to prevent half of all heart attacks among men and women aged 40 and a fifth of attacks among those aged 70.

He goes on to say;

> Fears that reducing cholesterol might increase the risk of cancer, accidents and suicide are dismissed. The researchers say that the link

with suicide arose because people who are depressed lose their appetite and eat less, so lowering their cholesterol.

It is almost impossible to assess the specific contribution of lowering blood cholesterol because as stated earlier no risk factor should be taken in isolation. Even so there is more acceptance of the benefits of cholesterol reduction, with recent studies suggesting that a one per cent reduction leads to a 2 per cent decrease in CHD risk.

It is important to recognize that there is an ongoing debate but Dr David Roberts who is Medical Officer for UML Ltd, Port Sunlight is one who is prepared to accept the philosophy of the Coronary Prevention Group. This is to measure cholesterol in those at high-risk and others on request only. One of the special high risk categories are people who suffer from familial hypercholesterolaemia or FH. This is a common inherited condition which is estimated to affect as many as one in 500 of the UK population. FH sufferers have a reduced number of the low-density lipoprotein receptors. Recognition of this disease can be based on such aspects as a close relative having a heart attack at a young age, xanthomas (fatty lumps) on the tendons at the back of the hands or on the Achilles tendon in the heel, or a corneal arcus (a ring around the cornea). Clearly a group like this are likely to benefit most from intervention such as low-fat diet or drugs.

Blood Pressure

Blood pressure is now commonly recorded whenever anyone goes to a GP surgery. This is part of the preventative medicine policy being adopted by doctors. A high blood pressure is an important risk factor. This is because the increase in blood pressure (hypertension) can result in the arteries becoming thicker and more rigid. Once the arteries become rigid (arteriosclerosis) the heart then has to work harder to maintain the circulation at adequate levels. The maintenance pressure of the blood or diastolic BP were considered as elevated by the Glaxo company if over 95mm of mercury. Blood pressure recordings do need to be interpreted with caution as they can be increased simply because of the anxiety involved in taking the reading. If a blood pressure value is consistently high, medical advice should be sought to find ways to control it by exercise, diet or drugs. It must also be remembered that blood pressure varies not only on levels of anxiety, activity and time of day but also on age. Thus a typical reading for a young person of 120 systolic and 80 diastolic (recorded as 120/80) may be atypical for a person aged 70. An elderly person may have an acceptable systolic blood pressure of 145 which would be considered abnormal for an undergraduate student

The main causes of high blood pressure are high salt intake, low potassium intake, obesity and a high alcohol intake. There should be no need to add salt to food once it is cooked. Low potassium intake can be prevented by increasing the amount of fruit and vegetables in the diet. Obesity will be considered as a separate section later as will alcohol. High blood pressure not only affects CHD but is a very important risk factor in strokes – damage to part of the brain causing varying levels of disability and even death.

Cigarette Smoking

This has been considered at some length in Chapter 4 but at an individual level this is now recognized as one of the most significant risk factors. The major risk from smoking is lung cancer. It has a direct effect as a coronary risk factor by raising blood pressure and pulse rate, releasing adrenalin, raising low-density lipoproteins and carbon monoxide levels. The carbon monoxide increase means that the blood can no longer carry oxygen so efficiently, putting extra strain on the cardiovascular system. It also damages the lining of the arteries which in turn will result in more cholesterol being deposited.

For those addicted to nicotine it may appear difficult to change smoking habits. However individually or in combination such strategies as nicotine patches, chewing gum or lozenges, smoking cessation classes and even hypnosis may result in eliminating a habit which is increasingly recognized as anti-social and produces greater fatalities from CHD even than lung cancer. The key to smoking cessation which is successfully achieved by 1000 people a day is to use the following strategies all starting with the letter 'D':

- Delay – when tempted try to delay lighting another cigarette
- Drink plenty of water
- Deep breathing – holding the breath and letting it out slowly
- Distraction – go for a walk or find some alternative activity
- Diary – keep a record of your smoking habits
- Discuss with others – by telling others, you get support and encouragement

- Departure – going 'cold turkey' or total withdrawal is considered to be the best option compared with gradual reduction

Lack of Exercise

A number of studies have suggested that wholly sedentary people are at greater risk of CHD than regular exercisers. The reason for this may be associated with increased levels of obesity and the limited opportunity for the coronary arteries to be 'flushed through' as a result of increased blood flow during exercise. Also the heart, like any muscle, will benefit by being more efficient to operate as a result of regular overload training. Exercise could also act as a stress reduction opportunity providing it is undertaken in a favourable psychological climate. Exercise which is associated with extreme levels of competition, especially if taken infrequently, could be far more damaging than beneficial. Indeed *sudden violent* exercise is a potential risk factor in causing heart attacks. The middle-aged man who without any regular exercise accepts a challenge to play a squash match by a junior colleague is asking for trouble. This would be even more the case if some work grudge were being settled on court. Normally sedentary individuals who engage in sudden violent exercise increase their risk of CHD markedly. Even those who exercise regularly carry some increased risk of a heart attack if they exercise strenuously and suddenly. However the news is not all bad. On balance the person who exercises regularly and sensibly, at an intensity which allows a person to hold a continuous conversation, will significantly decrease his or her chances of coronary heart disease. Many people exercise at very specific times of year such as on holiday, often in climates both cold (e.g. skiing) and hot (e.g. playing beach volleyball). They should prepare for unaccustomed exercise by a gradual increase in their daily exercise several weeks before the planned holiday. For the person who normally does no more exercise than walk around an office, even a fell-walking holiday needs exercise training. A brisk 30 minute, flat walk daily for a few weeks before the event will make a great difference to both the enjoyment and safety of the holiday.

Obesity

Obesity becomes a risk factor for CHD primarily through its effect on hypertension and diabetes. It is reasonable to assume that if a person appears obese externally then fat is being deposited not just under the skin but in and around major blood vessels. This is particularly so in men who show the so-called 'apple' shape when the ratio of the waist to the hips circumference is high (i.e. exceeds 1.0). Although there is increasing interest in waist to hips ratio as a predictor of CHD a more common method is to divide body mass (what most people still call weight) by height. This is called the body mass index or BMI. The correct formula and units for BMI is body mass in kilograms ÷ height in metres squared. Thus a 75 kg person of 187 cm in height would have a BMI of $75 \div (1.87)^2$ which gives a value of 21.4. An acceptable range for BMI is 20–24.9. A value of 25–29.9 is considered to be rather plump for most people and a value of 30 and above is obese and should be taken seriously. Those of a BMI of 30 and above account for about eight per cent of the UK population. Note that in a previous sentence I used the term 'for most people'. This was deliberately included because people who are highly muscular will have a high BMI which is unrelated to obesity. These exceptions will be obvious, but it does illustrate the dangers of using a measure without due regard to the reasons for the result.

High Fat Diet Unrelated to Obesity

In many ways the above heading is misleading because the majority of people on high-fat diets do eventually become obese. However this need not be the case and many people do not come within the obese category of a BMI of over 30, yet increase their risk of CHD by eating an unsuitable diet. Current figures suggest that the average person consumes about 42 per cent of his or her calories as fat and more than half of this is from saturated fat. The Committee on Medical Aspects of Food Policy recommend that no more than 35 per cent of our energy should come from fat and less than half of it should be in the saturated form. This will be achieved by eating less convenience food, especially 'junk' food, and eating more natural foods such as fruit, vegetables and foods higher in fibre such as cereals. To give an example of convenience foods, a recent *Which?* survey indicated that chilled lasagnes, served at well-known supermarkets contained less than 10 per cent meat. Fat accounted for more than a third of the calories of the lasagnes and this is a dish which many people would consider to be at the healthier end of the food continuum. There will also need to be much better public education about the content of foods, especially the fat content. Most people recognize that butter, margarine and lard are predominantly fat, but even lean meat can have up to nine per cent fat and fat is half the composition of nuts. These so called 'hidden fats' are found in confectionery such as chocolate, in meat and meat products, in milk, cheese and cream, in biscuits, cakes and pastries and also in eggs.

For many people the conversion to a lower-fat diet is difficult, largely because fat imparts a taste which most enjoy. It is not necessary to have a highly restrictive diet eating nothing but fruit and salads. The progressive conversion to lower-fat alternatives without increasing the amount of food to compensate will often suffice. This especially applies when trying to eat foods lower in saturated fat. This will mean eating *more* foods such as:

- margarines which are high in polyunsaturates
- low-fat spreads
- vegetable and plant oils (except coconut and palm)
- fish
- white meats
- cottage cheese, fromage frais, Edam and Brie
- skimmed and semi-skimmed milk

and *less* foods like:

- butter, lard and hard margarines
- cooking oil
- beef, pork and lamb
- hard cheeses like cheddar, full-fat cheeses
- whole milk, cream

In addition to considering carefully the total fat and the proportion of saturated fats in the diet, people planning a healthier eating plan should concentrate on:

- eating more fruit, vegetables, rice, pasta, bread and wholegrain cereals
- eating less full-fat diary products, red meat and meat products
- preparing food by grilling, steaming or microwaving in place of frying
- choosing dishes which combine meat with vegetables, pulses or pasta so the meat is not missed
- avoiding dishes with creamy or rich sauces

- limiting baked foods, cakes, biscuits and pies
- limiting whole eggs to three per week

It is quite instructive to observe how others eat and compare it with your own diet. A recent survey on children's eating habits show that many consume two packets of crisps a day in addition to a wrapped chocolate biscuit and many highly-sugared drinks. The non-nutritious calorie load of these 'snacks' alone, coupled with the high-fat content does not bode well for the future generation.

Risk factor screening

Cholesterol screening has already been considered and many of the statements that applied to cholesterol apply equally to other risk factors. An integrated approach is needed, preferably undertaken by a professional such as a GP who is familiar with the health history of the person being screened. This may not be possible in the workplace so employees identified at high risk should be advised to consult their doctor.

The Family Heart Association, as part of its Cholesterol Countdown Week, produced the questionnaire shown as Table 5.1.

It not only produces a personal risk score but also gives the respondent an action appropriate to the risk.

A more developed system, but working on similar principles has been developed by a company called Health Options. A master score card is completed as in Table 5.2. Tables at the beginning of the appropriate sections of an accompanying manual convert the measured value into a cardiovascular risk score. Respondents get feedback as to whether their risk is low, medium or high and advice on risk modification is provided.

Dr Baxendine, who is Director of Medical Services for United Biscuits (UK) Ltd is convinced that lifestyle screening and risk modification 'will assist in achieving targets and create a healthier workforce, in a rational and cost-effective way for large populations, and give focus to health education and additional screening activities'.

5.3   Fitness Assessment

Fitness assessment, especially that of aerobic capacity, could have been considered in the previous section under coronary risk factors.

Table 5.1
Is Your Heart At Risk

1. Has anyone in your family had a heart attack before the age of 60?	**How to assess your personal risk**
Tick as appropriate	**Yes** *Score*
Yes ☐	
No ☐	for one 'yes' tick, score 2 .....
Don't know. ☐	for two 'yes' ticks, score 5 .....
	for three or more 'yes' ticks score 9.....
2. Do you smoke cigarettes?	
Yes ☐	**Don't know**
No ☐	
	for each 'don't know' tick, score 1 .....
3. Is your cholesterol level above the 'acceptable' level of 5.2 mmol/l?	**No**
Yes ☐	for each 'no' tick, score 0 .....
No ☐	
Don't know ☐	
	Now add up your total score: .....
4. Do you have high blood pressure?	
Yes ☐	0 You have a relatively low risk of coronary heart disease. Ensure that you maintain your healthy lifestyle.
No ☐	
Don't know ☐	
5. Do you eat any fried or fatty foods such as chips, cakes etc more than twice a week?	1-4 You may be at risk of coronary heart disease. To assess your risk, consider consulting your GP for a blood pressure or cholesterol test.
Yes ☐	
No ☐	
Don't know ☐	
	5+ Your risk of coronary heart disease is increased. If you smoke, eat an unhealthy diet or you are overweight, try to correct these risks. You should consult your GP for further help in dealing with your risk factors.
6. Are you more than slightly overweight?	
Yes ☐	
No ☐	
Don't know ☐	

However as fitness assessment includes health assessment measures which are distinct from coronary risk profiling, it is being considered separately.

Table 5.2
Risk Factors Master Score Card

NAME: COMPANY:	John Doe Anyco	
RISK FACTOR	See Manual Section	Your Score
CARDIOVASCULAR SCORE	Heart Disease	17
ALCOHOL (Units)	Alcohol	11 - 12/week
STRESS	Stress	4
SMOKING	Smoking	0
BODY MASS INDEX	Obesity	27.8
BODY FAT %	Obesity	-
NUTRITION	Nutrition	3 - 5
EXERCISE FREQUENCY	Exercise	1 - 2 weeks
CHOLESTEROL LEVEL	Heart Disease	4.1 - 5.1
BLOOD PRESSURE	Heart Disease	121 - 140 < 100

To illustrate different approaches to fitness assessment three individual approaches will be examined.

Private Fitness Test

This inadequate description refers to the type of fitness assessment offered by private hospitals or companies, usually at a cost which gives it the label 'executive test'. The following tests are typical of the fitness profile:

- height and weight
- percentage body fat
- lung function
- strength

- muscular endurance
- cycle ergometry

Most of these 'private' assessments will include a full medical examination, blood pressure, blood and urine sampling for cholesterol, triglycerides and sugar.

The percentage fat is most commonly taken with a skinfold caliper. These days electronic alternatives are available such as the Futrex device which predicts body fat by using infra red optics.

Lung function is measured using a spirometer and can indicate the prevalence of a viral chest infection in addition to lung power, efficiency and volume.

Muscular strength can be measured isometrically with a specially-designed chair. The subject's leg is attached to an ankle strap, with the knee at 90 degrees. The other end of the ankle strap is attached to a sensitive tensiometer and as the subject attempts to straighten the leg, the electronic display shows the strength of the main leg muscles. It is also possible to show muscular endurance by either measuring the time a muscular contraction can be maintained or showing the decrement in force over repeated contractions. A simpler method of measuring strength is to use a grip dynamometer which examines wrist strength.

Cycle ergometry is a common way of measuring aerobic capacity. This important component of fitness assesses the cardiovascular system, especially in terms of its oxygen-carrying capacity. It works on the basis that as one exercises progressively more intensively a point will be reached when the cardiovascular system can no longer cope with the demand placed upon it by the working muscles. As you sit reading this book your aerobic or oxygen carrying system is easily able to cope with the low muscular demand of limited movement. In theory the progressive increase in work will be reflected by an increase in oxygen consumption until a plateau is reached. This plateau reflects the inability of the cardiovascular system to process any more oxygen even if the work continues to increase in intensity. The level at which this happens is the best predictor scientists have for aerobic capacity, endurance or stamina. If the heart and lungs are working efficiently it will be of great benefit to many aspects of an individual's health. The measurement of oxygen consumption requires special equipment called a metabolic analyser. This collects all expired gas and measures the volume of gas and the fraction of oxygen and carbon dioxide in the gas.

The cycle ergometer is not the only work machine to be used. Slightly better estimates of aerobic capacity can be achieved using a motor-driven treadmill, but these can be quite costly. It is even possible to use a simple step test when the subject steps up and down off a bench at a given height for a specified length of time. Heart rate can be used as an alternative to the metabolic analyser and some of the simpler tests employ heart rate to make the estimation of aerobic capacity. Experience has shown that in most people a good relationship holds between work intensity, heart rate and oxygen uptake. This means that not only can heart rate be used to predict aerobic capacity, but in certain cases the work intensity alone will give a fairly good approximation. One test that uses this principle is the 20 metre progressive shuttle run. Each subject runs between two markers 20 metres apart. The speed is set by a tape recording of a buzzer indicating that the subject should have reached the end of the 20 metres. It starts fairly slowly, but the speed (and hence the intensity) increases every few minutes. Eventually the subject cannot keep up with the speed and this point estimates the aerobic capacity. This method has been used with the highly successful England rugby team of the early 90s for both training and testing. A test like this would be totally unsuitable for very unfit people such as cardiac patients. Much slower starting speeds are required with smaller increments. People such as these would start with slow walking on a treadmill and increase over several minutes to a brisk walk.

An essential component of these fitness assessments is the counselling session that should follow the test. This gives the opportunity for the subject to have the results discussed and to agree a training plan.

For many years the American College of Sports Medicine have recommended 20–30 minutes of exercise, two to three times per week as the best basis of training the aerobic system. The intensity of the training would depend on the current state of fitness and/or other factors such as age or maximum heart rate. As it may be dangerous to measure maximum heart rate in many people, it is better to estimate it from age by using the simple formula 220 − age. Thus a 48 year old person could be assumed to have a maximum heart rate of 220 − 48 = 172 beats per minute. Knowing this it is then possible to set a 'training threshold' based on maximum heart rate. A common approach is to use a heart rate threshold of 70–85 per cent of maximum. Thus for the person with a maximum of 172 the training threshold would be 120 to 146 beats per minute. For someone starting to exercise after a long lay-off it would be prudent to exercise initially at an intensity which keeps the heart rate near the bottom end of the threshold and then progressively increases the intensity over several months until able to work at the higher heart rate threshold. The same principle of progression applies to the duration, starting at 10 minutes per session and working up over many weeks to the full 30 minutes. The form of exercise is not critical providing it is rhythmical, uses the large muscles of the body and allows a full range of movement. Thus swimming, brisk walking, stair climbing, aerobics to music, dancing, jogging and skipping are ideal activities.

More recently it has been suggested that the 20–30 minute duration requirement does not need to be continuous. Providing a *daily* cumulative total of 30 minutes is achieved, a training effect may be possible with shorter bursts of activity of say five minutes each. It will depend, for many people, what fits into their lifestyle best. Shorter sessions may be theoretically sound but may not prove to be very practical. To show how one company plans its fitness profile the following information is taken from a catalogue produced by an American company called Wellsource.

====================

Description

This programme provides a system for conducting fitness assessments. For comparison sake, personal test results are shown in graph form along with standard population norms. An exercise prescription is produced based on test results.

Data Input

The profile is derived from the following fitness tests:

- Per cent body fat determination
- Tests for musculoskeletal fitness including:
    - Grip strength
    - Muscle endurance, timed situps
    - Flexibility, spine flexion
    - Posture and back/lifting test
    - Bench press
    - Leg press

- Cardiovascular fitness
    - Resting pulse
    - Blood pressure
    - Graded exercise test monitoring heart rate and blood pressure response, using one of the following protocols:
    - Treadmill
    - Cycle ergometry
    - CHFT step test, utilizing multiple stages and work loads.
    - YMCA (KASCH) step test
    - STPR step test, pulse recovery
    - 1 mile fitness walking test
    - Cooper 1.5 mile run
    - Maximum oxygen uptake is calculated on all cardiovascular fitness tests.

Features

- An individualized exercise prescription is generated based on test results
- The overall results are reflected in a total fitness score. Easily understood, this score provides an excellent means for setting goals and monitoring progress
- Additional explanatory and educational fitness material to accompany the report are available through Wellsource
- Guidelines for testing are provided, and on-site training can be arranged

Scientific Basis

Test procedures follow the guidelines of the American College of Sports Medicine. Norms are derived from a study of some 10,000 people in occupational settings in the United States and Canada, and are age and sex specific.

=================

Occupational Fitness Test

A number of jobs require special levels of fitness to ensure that the work is carried out effectively and with minimum risk to the employee.

Examples would be firefighters, the police, ambulance crew and even football league referees. Some, such as the referees, cannot be licensed without passing a suitable test. Others have minimum standards at entry which are rarely confirmed later in their careers and yet others take physical fitness seriously. An example of the latter are firefighters who require fitness checks every three years and medicals every six as a minimum. At entry to the service, they are required to have a grip strength of 35kg, a leg and back strength of 117kg and an aerobic capacity of 45ml per min per kg. Dr Kevin Sykes at Chester College of Higher Education has been working for several years with the Cheshire Fire Brigade, testing and advising on fitness. The monthly fitness test is shown in Table 5.3.

Table 5.3
Cheshire Fire Brigade Monthly Fitness Test

Test	Target
Fitech step test	Good
Press ups in 1 minute (*to 90⁰ elbow*)	25
Squats in 1 minute (*from standing, sit to 90⁰ thighs*)	25
Sit ups in 1 minute (*feet held, knees bent at 90⁰, hands behind head, touch knees with elbows*)	25
Star jumps in 30 seconds (*standing feet together, jump in air to star position, return to ground with feet together*)	10
10 metre shuttle run for 35 seconds	10
Squat thrusts in 45 seconds	20
1 minute recovery is allowed between each test	

This test is conducted in a confidential manner at firestations and demonstrates the fitness of each watch. A summary of the results is sent to the brigade training officer. Training in association with testing has resulted in the number of firefighters achieving the pre-set standard to increase from 30 per cent in 1987 to 80 per cent 18 months later.

Cardiac Rehabilitation Test

The benefits of exercise as part of a rehabilitation programme for cardiac patients are now widely recognized. However the type, frequency and duration of exercise is much more difficult to determine. This is mainly because the range of conditions presented could vary from heart replacement, to recent myocardial infarction. The key to assessing the optimal exercise prescription is a graded exercise test. This will provide information as to the heart's response to progressively increasing workload. It requires a 12-lead ECG to be recorded throughout the tests. This will give essential information on the heart's response to exercise and provide the criteria for stopping the graded exercise test. This is an essential pre-requisite for setting a precise exercise programme. Without it the programme would either be too risky or too gentle to give the optimal benefit. These statements, however, apply only to very high risk individuals or people who have known heart disease. This is because the use of an ECG as a screening tool for normal populations can produce invalid results. These can be divided into false positive and false negative results. False positives mean the results suggest that there are problems when there are none. Research published in 1989 by Campbell suggests that a 40-year-old male with no obvious risk factors would have only a 23 per cent likelihood of heart disease if he had a positive result from an exercise test. This means that 77 per cent of such men with a positive result could be subject to further, more intrusive testing and a considerable amount of anxiety during this time. Considering a male aged 50 with one risk factor, a positive result in that case would be correct 88 per cent of the time, making it a much more sensitive measure. False negatives means the results suggest that there are no problems when there really are. An example of a false negative might be a 60-year-old man with many risk factors. A negative result in such a case could be very misleading as there will still be a 92 per cent probability of heart disease. It can be seen that the wisest application of the graded exercise test is for those at greatest risk. Staff from the University of Liverpool, working in conjunction with the Wirral Cardiac Rehabilitation Centre at St Catherine's Hospital, Birkenhead, are trying a new approach to cardiac exercise prescription. The normal practice is to rely solely on the level reached on the progressive exercise test to set intensities for training. The University staff are measuring metabolic responses to exercise and using this information to set the exercise prescription. This will eliminate some of the assumptions and generalizations made by most workers in cardiac rehabilitation. It will also be much more sensitive to different types of cardiac disease.

5.4 Alcohol and Drug Abuse

Alcohol

Alcohol is regularly used by 90 per cent of the workforce yet its harmful consequences have only been recognized relatively recently. The excess mortality rate from alcohol misuse is around 28,000 per year. As alcohol is implicated in many diseases from CHD to cancer it is difficulty to quantify the total impact on health. However drink is considered to be a contributory factor in 5–10 per cent of deaths and a major cause in 40 per cent of hypertension cases. Lost productivity, accidents and days off work account for over £2 billion annual cost. Fifty per cent of assaults, 75 per cent of public order offences and 60 per cent of criminal damage are drinks related. It is also a factor in 50 per cent of drownings. There seems little likelihood of a natural reduction in consumption with the Institute for Fiscal Studies predicting a major increase in alcohol consumed as the UK harmonizes duty with the EC. Government initiatives have been very modest and largely ineffectual with most doctors believing that increased cost is probably the only measure to make a major change. A recent study in the Lothian region has demonstrated that heavy drinkers as well as moderate drinkers cut their consumption when prices increased.

There is clear evidence of concern for problem drinkers in the workplace with the Health Education Authority (HEA) launching its *Alcohol Awareness at Work* campaign in 1990. Research for Alcohol Concern shows that nearly three out of four firms discipline drinkers if they refuse counselling. Over 42 per cent of firms dismissed people on the grounds of misconduct due to drinking. Increasingly companies are testing employees for alcohol and drug abuse. This evidence alone indicates the importance attached to the problem in certain companies. With it being a general population problem it seems logical that the majority of companies will give it a high priority.

The main findings on awareness of alcohol at work are summarized as:

- alcohol is not considered an important issue, especially in small companies
- it is viewed as a matter of health and safety more than efficiency
- it is perceived as having a limited effect on performance, although those with an alcohol policy consider it to be more detrimental

- most believe that alcohol policies would be welcomed
- drinking at lunchtime was not perceived as a problem by most companies
- alcohol was not seen as an issue at an individual level
- alcohol policies were only needed for problem drinkers
- it was not seen as a greater problem for any particular sector of the workplace
- an alcohol policy was generally considered worthwhile
- at least one in three companies saw no problems in implementing a policy

This list indicates that there is a variety of attitudes to alcohol at work and some inconsistencies with respect to action. The major action is to institute some form of formal alcohol policy. The Industrial Society's survey showed that public sector respondents (58 per cent) are more likely to have an alcohol policy than the private sector (41 per cent). UK organizations (44 per cent) were more likely to have policies than Japanese companies based in the UK (32 per cent).

As part of the HEAs Alcohol Awareness at Work Campaign, work-based alcohol policies were reviewed. It was found that:

- 48 per cent had a formal alcohol policy
- 22 per cent had some form of 'informal understanding'
- larger organizations are more likely to have a policy
- policies are more likely in manufacturing and engineering companies
- a policy has never been considered in one out of every six companies. This is usually because the problem is not considered to exist
- a ban on on-site drinking is most often included
- problem drinkers are specifically targeted

A more recent survey by the Occupational Health Review (published August 1992) confirmed most of the above but added other information in its executive summary. These are:

- an alcohol policy was to be introduced within 18 months in 46 per cent of those companies without one at present
- half of those with policies have introduced them within the last six years

- 21 per cent of companies with policies have revised or updated them since they were originally introduced
- the primary instigators of alcohol policies are senior management
- policy preparation involves the trade unions in 50 per cent of the cases
- most organizations involve alcohol policies as part of a wider health strategy
- external agencies are often involved including the HEA and Alcohol Concern

Alcohol policies range from basic advice to company legislation. Appendix 4 gives an example of one organization's policy which is specific to that sector of work (a University). The mix of staff in a University is not typical of all companies so policies may need to reflect the activities of the business.

The contents of alcohol policies vary. The Occupational Health Review survey provided the following information on content:

- 81 per cent offer confidential counselling or help with problem drinking – usually provided by the occupational health staff
- 33 per cent had a complete on-site ban
- 30 per cent stated how to help or treat employees
- 28 per cent stated how to deal with problem drinkers
- 22 per cent gave advice on sensible drinking
- 21 per cent included disciplinary procedures
- 17 per cent stated how to deal with drunkenness at work
- 8 per cent had a complete ban during working hours
- most policies set out an individual's rights to return to the same job after counselling or treatment. Sometimes this right has limitations

For most companies with an alcohol policy, the social events are held at times when people are not expected to return to work. Disciplinary action is used by the majority of companies only as a last resort after counselling and treatment has failed to improve work performance.

Having established an alcohol policy, it is necessary to consider its implementation. Once again it is possible to itemize the results of surveys undertaken:

- provisions on training for management to implement a policy is only included in 38 per cent

- primary responsibility for implementation is given to line managers and personnel departments
- trade unions are often involved in communicating a policy but have a more moderate responsibility for implementation
- responsibility is often given to all employees to voice concerns about the alcoholic problems of colleagues
- communicating an alcohol policy is prevalent when first introduced, not subsequently
- special attention is given to inform new members of staff
- less than a third of the companies monitor or evaluate the effectiveness of their policies
- most evaluation is a combination of general personnel data and specific information on alcoholism treatment
- a small number of companies monitor the policy by surveying employees attitudes to drinking
- nearly half of the companies believe that the effectiveness of their policy could be improved by better training and commitment from managers

It is relatively rare for companies to have provisions within their alcohol policies for the screening or testing of employees. In more safety-conscious organizations such as the chemical or oil sector over a quarter do have such a provision. Most commonly this is in the form of pre-employment screening. Testing is sometimes introduced when there is good grounds for belief that alcohol or drugs are impairing work. This is achieved by the provision of a urine sample with it being considered positive if the levels exceed the limits set for a drink-driving offence.

Alcohol Concern's Workplace Advisory Service suggests the following principles when establishing and implementing an alcohol policy:

- establish the reasons for adopting a policy
- keep the well-being of all employees to the fore
- educate employees about the risks of drinking, especially at work
- assist employees who have a drink problem
- provide treatment for those in need
- have a company procedure for employees with a drink problem
- separate this procedure from disciplinary action

- provide special training for staff who will be expected to identify the problem
- guarantee confidentiality
- ensure the policy is equitable across the company
- review and monitor the policy regularly

The experience of the many companies who have become fully committed to an alcohol policy is that it is of benefit to the workforce. None have considered it anything but a valuable exercise and one which is likely to spread to more companies as a matter of course.

Drugs

Although alcohol is a drug, because its use is legal and it is consumed by most people, it has been considered as a special case compared with other drugs. The Industrial Society survey on British and Japanese companies shows that 30 per cent of all UK companies have a drugs/substance abuse policy which is about the same in the Japanese companies. Like alcohol, the public sector lead the way with 41 per cent having a policy compared with only 28 per cent of the private sector.

In the work context, drug abuse is of concern because of the impairment in performance. This is because many common drugs act on the sensory or motor systems and disrupt normal function. The range of psychoactive drugs are probably of most concern in the workplace and those include those prescribed as antidepressants, sedatives and to induce sleep. Some drugs have a secondary psycho-active effect and these include analgesics and antihistamines. It is quite possible that staff operating machinery, handling chemicals or driving would unwittingly have their performance or behaviour modified by use of drugs prescribed to them in good faith. There is little doubt that employees using tranquillizers are significantly more likely to have accidents than non-users. This especially applies with older people. A two year study showed that those using minor tranquillizers were five times more likely to be involved in a serious driving accident. A number of studies show a relationship between those at fault in accidents and drug usage.

Alcohol combined with psychoactive drugs is often additive with the sedative effect of anti-depressant drugs being exacerbated by even small quantities of alcohol. The relationship is not simple because personality, mental state, the work situation and the type of drug is a complex interaction. However a greater awareness of the risk of accident with psychotrophic drugs is essential.

A variety of tests can be used to evaluate the effects of these drugs and they include choice reaction time tests, tracking tasks, short-term memory tasks, continuous attention tasks and even getting the subjects themselves to rate levels of alertness, tiredness, drowsiness, etc.

Some older anti-depressants impair performance and have sedative effects on such tests. Common tranquillizers such as diazepam have the same effect the next day. Part of the problem is that many people do not read labels or instructions provided with the drugs.

Psychoactive drugs can be detected by non-skilled personnel from urine tests. These rapid tests have a varying degree of accuracy so positive responses should be confirmed with standard laboratory procedures.

Many of the issues raised under the previous section on alcohol policies at work equally apply to drug abuse policies. An example of such a policy used by the University of Liverpool, the third largest employer in Merseyside, is shown as Appendix 5.

5.5   HIV/Aids

By far the majority of people at work have no cause for concern about HIV and Aids. Only in specific employments such as those in contact with infected materials does it become an issue. However as the disease is a major social issue it is something which should at least be considered by a caring employer. The reason it is not in the same category of health hazards as more common infectious diseases is that it can only be transmitted by transferring body fluids from one person to another. Thus infected blood can be transmitted by intravenous drug users and infected semen can also transmit the disease. A carrier of the virus should not pose any risk to others in most working environments. The exception would be the health services where use of needles and blood products is common. Until a carrier of the virus develops one of the related diseases, the capacity for work should be unimpaired.

There are occasional work situations such as the administration of first aid when an increased risk of infection is possible. Although transmission of the disease via saliva is unproven, mouth to mouth resuscitation may be a concern for a known HIV carrier. Similarly, an accident at work which could cause blood mixing may potentially be a source of infection. This is why in a sporting context it is now required to have bleeding wounds covered before the player can continue. Sensible precautions such as the provision of equipment such as 'airways' for ambulance crews is probably the best policy.

The issue of testing for Aids is of interest to employers and questions are now being asked as to whether it should be included in health screening. Testing is undoubtedly possible, usually based on a blood test for the antibodies to the Aids virus, HIV. The test has certain limitations, one being that it is some time after infection that the antibodies can be detected. This could be as long as six months, during which time further infection could have occurred. Another problem is that no therapeutic action can be taken at present as there is no drug or vaccine currently available. A further problem is that the test only detects one strain of the virus (HIV 1). An important issue associated with the test is the extent of confidentiality. As most tests are undertaken in an STD clinic, case notes will be recorded and assurance must be given that they will remain there. However if disease develops and other specialists become involved, a positive result is likely to be known more widely. This would occur if the person's GP were informed. Individual consent is required before the test is undertaken and most health workers recognize the value of providing counselling *before* the test to discuss the procedure and the consequences of a positive result. Counselling after a positive finding is even more crucial. In most employment situations an HIV-positive individual does not present a risk to other employees. It is probably, therefore, of little benefit to undertake Aids testing for all workers. A far more positive approach to health would be education as the disease is largely preventable.

Health care workers may present a special case for HIV/Aids awareness because of the greater possibility of infection. Public confidence in the healthcare profession is also an issue. A recent survey indicated that over half of the respondents would no longer seek medical attention from a health care worker if they knew that the provider had Aids or HIV infections. This is largely irrational because the chance of actual transmission from healthcare worker to client is minimal. Concern for the healthcare worker is more justified. Although to place it in perspective by 1991 there were only 28 documented cases worldwide of healthcare workers who have become infected after contact with infected blood. There are however a high proportion of sharps injuries in hospitals and reducing this statistic may be a valuable preventative measure. This would not only be for Aids protection but other blood-borne diseases such as hepatitis B.

The Department of Health and the BMA have issued guidelines for the protection of healthcare workers against HIV. They include:

- sound basic hygiene practices
- the use of gloves, waterproof gown, masks and eye protection during procedures which might cause splatterings
- covering all wounds with waterproof dressings when splattering may occur
- clearing up blood spillage promptly
- disinfecting surfaces promptly
- sharps injuries should be reported
- disposal of sharps should be a personal responsibility
- re-sheathing of sharps should be avoided and sharps containers should be close to the place of use

Fewer companies have an Aids/HIV policy than have policies on smoking or alcohol. The Industrial Society survey indicates that 26 per cent of UK organizations have a policy compared with 14 per cent of Japanese companies based in Britain. The public sector, once again, leads the way with 53 per cent and the private sector just 20 per cent. The larger the company the greater the likelihood of an HIV/Aids policy. A more recent survey produced for the Health Education Authority indicated that nine per cent of all workplaces had in the past year arranged some activity related to HIV/Aids. It appeared that government guidelines on HIV/Aids at the workplace had minimal impact with most being unaware of government action. Very few required employees (present or potential) to disclose their HIV status.

The policies tended to be more concerned with health and safety than discrimination and recruitment. British Rail is one company to have produced guidelines and this is mainly because staff may have to deal with the consequences of violent death (accidents, suicides) or clean up railway sites used by intravenous drug abusers. Appendix 6 shows extracts from a leaflet produced by the University of Liverpool entitled *AIDS in Perspective*. It has sections on prevention of infection in everyday life, occupational prevention of infection and the rights of individuals. Appendix 6 is only part of the University's leaflet on Aids but it is interesting to compare its content with a list of concerns found in formal policies produced by other organizations. Table 5.4 shows what policies are included most commonly.

Table 5.4
Content of formal HIV/AIDS policies

Policy Issues	%
Health and safety measures relating to non-infected members of the workforce.	83
Health and safety procedures relating to an infected person.	75
Employment protection and benefits of HIV employees.	54
Discrimination against HIV employees.	38
Recruitment policy in relation to HIV positive people.	23
Source : Health Promotion in the Workplace: Health Education Authority, 1993.	

There is some concern about discrimination against workers with HIV and Aids. *Companies Act* is a national charter for dealing with Aids and HIV infection in the workplace. Although by early 1993 only 25 companies had joined, interest is growing and the standards required are being met by an increasing number of organizations. Signatories must have a clear policy and achieve one of several goals in the first year. They can educate staff, publicize senior management commitment, raise the issue in the business community, support the charter financially or provide practical help to any HIV or Aids agency. Large employers like Marks and Spencer, National Westminster Bank, the Body Shop and IBM have been attracted to the charter. With widespread discrimination against HIV-positive staff, it is important to produce a policy which advocates equal treatment of employees. *Companies Act* will assist employers in the production of such policies.

For smaller companies who may not have occupational health staff, it would be useful to have at least one person who is sufficiently well-informed to provide an unbiased view. Dr J. T. Carter, director of medical services of the Health and Safety Executive considers that HIV control depends on 'decisions made in bedrooms rather than boardrooms'. To avoid the possibility of industrial relations problems and as a social duty to employees, companies should seriously consider becoming involved in a positive education programme to reduce the spread of Aids.

5.6   Work-related Upper Limb Disorders

Increasingly companies are becoming aware of work-related upper limb disorders (WRULD) as a condition which in some cases merits compensation and in others reflects poor quality of work, high sickness and absence, problems with high staff turnover and even recruitment. WRULDs, commonly called by the misnomer repetitive strain injuries (RSIs), are not restricted to the workplace. It has been recognized in musicians and in oarsmen. However as this book is concerned with health at work, it will concentrate on employment issues alone.

WRULDs include a range of conditions which include diffuse pain in the back, arms, neck or shoulders to clear clinical symptoms such as swellings and inflammation. There is quite probably a psychological component to many WRULDs, both in terms of the cause and the consequence. There is no doubt that a genuine sufferer has pain, often intense, and an inability to continue to work. Certain types of WRULD such as tenosynovitis and writer's cramp are accepted industrial injuries and consequently entitled to compensation. There is no blanket treatment and most can be avoided by removing the risk factors with improved working conditions.

In 1990 the Health and Safety Executive produced a guidance document (HS(G)60) which classified WRULDs as follows:

- inflammation or trauma of the tendon, muscle-tendon junction or surrounding tissue, particularly the tendon sheath. Such inflammatory conditions in and around the tendon are, for the most part, of a temporary nature but in some individuals may become chronic
- inflammation of the tissue of the hand caused by constant bruising or friction of the palm (a similar condition may occur in the elbow or knee). Collectively these are known as the 'beat conditions'
- compression of the peripheral nerves serving the upper limb, particularly the hand. Many of these conditions, such as carpal tunnel syndrome, may arise spontaneously in the general population and may be aggravated by work conditions
- temporary fatigue, stiffness or soreness of the muscles comparable to that following unaccustomed exertion but where no permanent pathological conditions results. Full recovery occurs after appropriate rest

There is some question over the inclusion of the latter as it is temporary and hardly injurious.

A more medical approach is to state known pathologies such as the following. Unfortunately not all WRULDs exactly fit the clinical definitions:

- tendonitis
- epicondyliis
- peritendonitis crepitans
- De Quervain's disorder
- carpal tunnel syndrome
- radial tunnel syndrome
- diffuse conditions

There is some overlap even in the above list both in terms of strict medical definition and symptomology. Scientists are working on a physiological explanation for these, especially the diffuse pain which is less clearly defined.

Another approach is to classify the WRULDs on the basis of pain. A number of scales have been suggested and that of Fry published in 1986 is illustrated as follows:

- **Grade 1**: pain in one site on causal activity
- **Grade 2**: pain in multiple sites on causal activity
- **Grade 3**: pain with some other uses of the hand; may show pain at rest or loss of muscle function
- **Grade 4**: pain with all uses of the hand, post-activity pain with minor uses, pain at rest and at night, marked physical signs of tenderness, loss of motor function (loss of response control), and weakness
- **Grade 5**: loss of capacity for use because of pain which is continuous; loss of muscle function, weakness, and gross physical signs

In the presence of pain, but in the absence of a clear pathological condition (normally the diffuse type), the employee and employer are faced with a dilemma. The employee may sometimes find it difficult to report the disorder for fear of repercussions. The employer may resist recognition of the condition because it is ill-defined and the doctor may be reluctant to diagnose WRULD because of uncertainty or the concern about becoming involved in litigation. It is also extremely difficult when presented with a case of this nature to be certain if it is work-related. Many people undertake activities in their recreational time which could be the cause of the condition.

Treatment for WRULDs may involve a variety of approaches. Surgery is rare, but drug therapy, rest, physiotherapy, counselling and re-designing the task are all options. An individual analysis to attempt to establish the cause, such as the pain sequence, psychological factors, and the non-work elements, is essential. Of all the treatment options physiotherapy is possibly the most likely to succeed but specialist postgraduate training within the profession may be necessary to understand more fully the ergonomic implications.

It is generally accepted that WRULD onset is rarely based on a single factor. However there is evidence for a series of linked factors such as:

- static posture
- repetitive tasks
- insufficient rest periods
- working at extremes of posture
- excessive manual force
- awkward posture, especially of the hands, wrists or shoulders
- unsuitable rates of work
- anxiety and psychological concerns
- unaccustomed exertion

The occupational groups at most risk seem to be supermarket checkout operators and stackers, poultry pluckers, sheep shearers, hairdressers, musicians, keyboard operators, cleaners and machine operators. Most of these occupations are not new so unless reporting has previously been inadequate there must be some changes in work practice which have contributed to the phenomenon. An example of this was a national newspaper which replaced traditional production techniques with a computer-based publishing system. This required all writers and sub-editors to use a display screen. Before the change, no cases of WRULD were reported but in under three years over 100 staff reported the disorder. Most pain and discomfort occurred within two hours of a newspaper deadline where staff had limited opportunity to alter their working posture and keyboard activity was at its most intense. Psychological factors were also identified. Worries about computer breakdown, skills being lost and the new technology causing redundancies were issues raised. A study in Australia found that the places of work reporting high numbers of WRULDs were those with many complaints of boredom, stress, poor job satisfaction, lack of variety and individuality. Psychological factors are not necessarily a major cause but could exacerbate a physical condition for a number of reasons. People who are anxious for whatever reason are less able to allow their muscles to relax during work breaks and recreational times. Dr Howard Bird stated in New Scientist in 1990 that

> careful interviews with patients usually reveal the classical history of mechanical strain. It is hardly surprising that people who suffer from the disorders are upset when their livelihoods are in jeopardy, and so anxiety is probably a secondary phenomenon.

Like coronary heart disease, WRULD can be considered from the perspective of risk factors. The main ones are (a) posture, (b) movement and force and (c) the nature of the work and psychological factors. These may provide the basis for considering preventative measures. Prevention can be tackled by considering (a) the environment at work, (b) the task itself and (c) the individual.

The environment is not always easy to control. Factors such as the assembly process, the space available and the cost of top-quality equipment must be considered. However the work environment in many companies, especially the older manufacturing industries, is far from adequate. A recent judgment against BT indicated that 'strain has been substantially added to by the strains that arose from the working systems in place and poor posture due to poor ergonomics of the workstations'. Fully adjustable seating, keyboard positions, lighting levels and leg room should permit a comfortable working environment which minimizes unnecessary effort, twisting or stretching.

The task should be adapted to the needs of the worker. Sometimes a task is assessed with a higher grade, remuneration or other reward given to high rates of repetition. This can apply to lifting by poultry workers or car plant workers, to key depressions in data processing or letter production in banks. A higher speed can reduce safety and suitable breaks can decrease the potential for repetitive strain. Job rotation, redesigning work to avoid intense periods and realistic target levels are all issues to be considered in avoiding WRULD.

The individual will vary in terms of size, strength, skill, concentration, personality, attitude and other factors. Although not every aspect can be considered, the individual is a part of the risk assessment in designing the work process. Individuals respond differently to the demands of work and early opportunities to comment on the task will be beneficial as will a regular routine of stretching exercises to reduce muscle tension.

Management action can be successful in reducing WRULD. Modifications to a car assembly plant of the type mentioned earlier were highly successful. Reaching problems were reduced by the introduction of narrower work surfaces. Automation reduced vibration. Padded arm supports reduced static work loads. These types of changes reduced WRULDs significantly. In the case of the national newspaper, the changes included reduction of intense activity periods by better copy flow, forming user groups, improved training and information on WRULDs, implementing user trials and improved collaboration between doctors and the company.

Access to computer screens is now commonplace. The consequence of this is that many users have no formal training in their use. Until recently a typist would go through a rigorous full-time course, but today many workers will use computer screens, often with minimal typing skills. The consequence of this is potentially hazardous and as it is unlikely that keyboard skills will be trained, the other option is to reduce the potential for injury by applying sound ergonomics.

An operator's arm needs to be supported and most commonly this is provided by the work surface on which the keyboard rests. An alternative is a device to give full support of the arm, while leaving the hands and wrists free. The following recommendations summarize the main issues for a visual display unit (VDU) worker:

- seat height adjusted so the forearms are horizontal
- Elbow, wrist and fingers are positioned in a straight line with the fingertips touching the middle row of the keyboard
- a foot rest should be used if the seat is too high for contact with the floor
- the desk or keyboard should be raised if the working surface is too low
- the backrest should be adjusted to support the lower back
- full lumbar support should be maintained by sitting back into the chair
- screen height and angle should be adjusted so that the head remains upright with the top of the screen at eye level

- neck flexion should be less than 15 degrees and with a visual angle of 0–21 degrees
- A copyholder should be used to raise the text to eye level
- screen and keyboard glare should be avoided by either re-positioning the machine or lights
- screen size should be a minimum of 35cm diagonal
- contrast and brightness of the screen should be adjustable
- operators should be able to move while working. Alternate foot positions and rock the chair if possible
- use software which is friendly and intuitive to avoid frustration and stress. Microsoft Windows reduces the reliance on memorizing program sequences

One of the conditions listed at the beginning of this section was carpal tunnel syndrome (CTS). Patients often complain of pain at night with intermittent numbness which sometimes wakes the patient early. It can also be experienced when driving, reading or working with a flexed wrist. It often occurs from forceful and repetitive arm, wrist and hand movements. If associated with hand-tool vibration the condition hand-arm vibration syndrome (HAVS) is often presented. Although diagnostic standards and precise clinical definitions have yet to be established for both conditions, there seems to be a better chance of reversibility from CTS once the cause is eliminated. HAVS sufferers are less likely to recover although in younger persons, removed from the source of vibration, the prospect of permanent vascular damage is slight. Conservative treatment such as rest, splinting, and anti-inflammatory drugs should be tried with surgery as a last resort. Like other WRULDs the best management is preventative strategies in the workplace.

Work-related upper limb disorders cannot be discussed without a brief comment on the current medico-legal situation. Recently Judge Prosser in a high court damages claim ruled that RSI was meaningless as a medical concept. The fact remains that courts have awarded damages in the past and a number of out-of-court settlements have been made. Part of the problem is the use of the term RSI because the condition is not always related to repetition. The judge also intimated that the condition was associated with psychologically weak per-sonalities. It has been stated earlier that a psychological component may be involved but that knowledge does not remove what is for most people a very real and often chronic pain. At the end of the so called

'RSI epidemic' in Australia the *British Medical Journal* noted that it had arisen from the mutual misunderstandings of the medical profession, management, trade unions, judiciary and the media. Little seems to have changed since this was published in 1987, but at least it is now considered seriously as a health issue.

5.7   Back Problems

In a recent survey, 60 per cent of people had back pain at some time and 15 per cent had back pain at least once a week. In certain occupations as many as nine out of ten workers experience low back pain once in their lifetime. Anyone who has suffered from acute or chronic backache appreciates the effect it has on work, irrespective of the type of employment. The overall national incidence is difficult to determine but figures in 1988 suggest that 46.5 million days were lost annually from back pain. More recent figures on nurses suggest a figure of 1.5 million for that profession alone.

Over 50 per cent of large organizations have some form of written policy, standards or guidelines relating to back protection or injury. However the absence of a policy does not necessarily mean inactivity with many companies taking the issue seriously, offering advice and treatment. Policies varied greatly from a simple reference to safe manual handling to ergonomic assessments, back screening and training courses.

The cause of back pain was predominantly manual handling, although verification was not always possible. Posture was quoted as another cause as was vehicle accidents although some of these would have been away from work. Other activities away from work causing back pain were gardening and do-it-yourself and some estimates put the non-work cause of back pain as high as 80 per cent.

The human resources used usually involve health and safety managers, the occupational health department and physiotherapists. A few used external agencies such as the HSE and the National Back Pain Association. The consultation process was varied with a quarter of all respondents failing to consult their employees at all. The most common form of consultations was with trade unions or safety committees. Pre-employment screening for back problems occurred in half the respondents, mainly as part of an overall medical. When back problems occurred it was most common to refer the employees to their own GP or to an occupational health physician. Other strategies were redeployment, new equipment, training and treatment by a physio-therapist.

To alleviate the problems of back pain and injury, changes were made to equipment and procedures. Seating was the most common alteration, followed by work equipment. An example was the provision of electrically powered trolleys for porters and delivery staff. Up to one third of companies surveyed had changed the work patterns to reduce the amount of manual handling. Posture was considered by a number of companies and equipment altered to produce an improvement. The shape and size of chairs was one area under consideration as was staff uniform to assist in lifting when tight clothing would be restrictive.

An excellent, straightforward booklet on *The Back at Work* is available, free of charge, from the Health Promotion Research Trust, 49–53 Regent Street, Cambridge, CB2 1AB. It states that there are many ways to help individuals with back pain:

- treat a person's first experience of back pain with greater vigour, with the aim of preventing its recurrence so that the sufferer does not accept back pain as inevitable
- pay greater attention to the design of work, to achieve a better match between what workers are asked to do and their capacity for doing it safely and efficiently. This ergonomic approach is already being taught to many therapists and clinicians
- while it may not be possible to avoid getting the occasional twinge, people need not let it get the upper hand

The last bullet point above is hinting at the aspect of psychology in low back pain which is increasingly becoming an important issue. Recent research suggests that the nervous system may undergo changes following injury which result in pain transmission being more common. Also chronic pain, combined with decreased mobility and other life stresses, may eventually have a psychological impact.

Personality has been implicated in low back pain at an anecdotal level. There was some evidence in broad descriptive studies that subjects with back pain were associated with aspects of neuroticism. However the sensitivity of the tests could not operate at an individual level and general personality factors and pain have yet to be clearly established.

Psychological distress and chronic backache are commonly related, although it is important to recognize that this is not always so.

Depressive symptoms are very variable and dependent on the population and the methods of assessment. About a quarter of chronic back
pain patients have depressive symptoms often associated with the
amount of failed treatment and fearing the worst outcome.

The behaviour associated with back pain illness is starting to be
investigated. The plan is to replace inappropriate behaviour with
better responses. Physical examination, video analysis and simple
check lists are often used.

People's beliefs about pain, influence of their personal behaviour and
the extent that external forces govern life can all affect symptomology.
Attitude to pain in the context of overall control over life is undoubtedly
important. The workplace environment could well be a major factor
here with people who are in greater control of their employment better
able to cope with back pain. Coping strategies vary from *behavioural*
ones such as changes in activity and posture to *cognitive* ones such as
mental distraction, reassurance and imagining pain reduction.
People's ability to use different coping strategies may be the basis of
more productive treatment.

The link between psychological and physiological aspects must be
appreciated. Stressful events can cause muscle tension which can have
a direct bearing on an anatomical feature such as an intervertebral disc.
This in turn causes more pain and the circle is complete with more
strain being the outcome. It has been shown experimentally that a
given stressor can cause a higher level of muscle tension in back pain
sufferers and that they take longer to recover. An holistic approach is
necessary to reduce the chronic pain initially and then find an
intervention which removes the cause.

Industrial back pain has been studied by Bigot and others who
published in 1990 in a book entitled *The lumbar spine*, edited by
Weinstein and Weesel. Bigot lists the influences on industrial claims as:

- severity of symptoms
- perceptions of safety
- perceptions of impact.

He also considers the risks of chronic back pain to be influenced by:

- history of low back pain
- distress, and
- low job satisfaction.

Bigot and his co-workers stress that normally-occurring back symptoms were often unreasonably being attributed to industrial injuries. Psychological influences were clearly important and they conclude that

> once an individual is off work, perceptions about symptoms, about the safety of returning to work, and about the impact of returning to work on one's personal life can affect recovery even in the most well-meaning worker.

It would appear inappropriate to under-estimate the importance of psychological issues in back pain. This applies with treatment, rehabilitation or at work. A better understanding of low back pain should extend to the psychological risk which includes an individual's belief about pain, personal distress which includes job stress, personal views on safety and the effects of work.

The employer's response to back pain varies from provision of back clinics for employees which includes a psychological dimension to minimal compliance with manual handling directives.

In the healthcare sector, some 80 per cent of those who lifted patients did so alone and without lifting aids. A large Flemish study showed that there is a big departmental variation in the frequency of back pain with some sections reporting 36 per cent higher values than others. Eighteen per cent suffered back pain at any one time, with the average sick leave being 15 days and 63 per cent of staff suffering over the last year, the majority with repeated episodes of pain. Nurses and physiotherapists are especially at risk. Professor David Stubbs from the Robens Institute has shown that 16 per cent of days lost in nursing is attributed to back pain with almost half at risk of developing problems. Moving and lifting patients was the major factor with one study revealing that two nurses in a geriatric ward lifted the patient-equivalent of 2.5 tonnes in an hour. One study by Gilly Gladman has shown that nursing recruitment tends to be from older recruits. This means that more time has passed to allow back pain to develop prior to nurse training. This would especially apply to those who were nursing auxiliaries before training.

The following were all identified as reasons for back problems in nursing:

- lack of available help

- badly designed environment
- shortage of lifting aids
- inappropriate clothing
- lack of suitable skills
- inadequate specific education

Although most episodes of back pain were preceded by a specific handling incident, there was evidence that the problem was cumulative. This reinforces the argument that early intervention is essential.

Back pain is found in many areas of the healthcare sector. Nottingham Ambulance Services Trust assessed the operational tasks of its personnel using a lumbar-monitoring device strapped to the back. It identified the levels of bending and twisting, the next stage being to reduce those manoeuvres likely to cause pain.

A problem identified by Margaret Hollis, who has acted as an expert witness in over 400 cases of back injury in healthcare environments, is the inconsistency of naming lifts and grasps. This meant that different descriptions and rules were being applied to so called 'proper lifts' making training and consolidation very difficult. The lack of availability (and if available the use) of hoists was also poor, an example being that only five per cent of health authorities provided a mobile hoist when it was deemed necessary.

The construction industry, based on HSE figures, is the worst for back injuries. Unfortunately the *ad hoc* nature of the industry, the macho image and the use of subcontractors makes it difficult to evaluate or educate. Injuries could be reduced by reducing the mass of cement bags, using smaller blocks and redesigning building practices to take more account of handling needs.

The retail industry has most of its back problems from the transport of roll-pallets loaded with stock in the warehouse and resited at the retail outlet. Attempts are being made by Tesco to assess the risk of this process using a 12 factor checklist (e.g. stability of load). Once new procedures are implemented it is anticipated that a fall in accidental injury will follow which should also reduce insurance premiums.

The brewing industry has changed little in a 100 years. Manual handling training is encouraged but the problems of confined spaces and a range of lifting requirements makes back injuries common. The industry is likely to become more mechanized in the future which should reduce the current incidence.

There is evidence that a back injury prevention programme can cause a modest decline in the prevalence of back pain. An intervention group was given a combination of education, training, physical fitness activities and ergonomic improvement. The most significant change was in satisfaction and reduction in risky behaviours. At the same time a cost-benefit analysis was undertaken with the return in the investment of the programme being 179 per cent.

Prevention of back injury is based on education, ergonomics, supervision and exercise. Key points for each of these will be examined in turn.

Education

- basic anatomy and physiology
- biomechanics of movement and posture
- common back problems – description and causes
- work methods
- personal responsibility

Ergonomics

- work stations; height, distance and angles
- frequent handling
- loads; size, weight and awkwardness
- prolonged standing and sitting
- working in confined spaces
- working in static positions
- lifting
- video analysis of person/task mismatch to establish causes
- cost effective solutions

Supervision

- workplace environment
- encouraging good body mechanics and manual handling
- communication with employees
- early positive action

Exercise

- posture correction

- spine mobility assessment and training
- strength assessment and training
- relaxation

Although prevention is by far the best policy, the fact remains that back pain will occur and then sound management is essential. Views differ on back pain management but four stages can be identified:

- initial treatment
- industrial assessment and treatment plan
- returning to work
- ergonomic changes

Initial treatment involves identifying the symptoms and causes, relieving pain and muscle spasms, increasing mobility, spinal muscle strengthening, patient education, restoration of confidence and establishing personal responsibility for lifestyle changes. Note that this is proactive and not the more common option of rest and painkillers. The next stage involves a more detailed clinical assessment and the development of a treatment plan. Returning to work involves a work plan which may involve consultation with a supervisor and some modification of duties. Finally ergonomic changes at work should be based on a thorough evaluation of the task and the environment. Once problem areas are identified then immediate, mid- and long-term changes can be agreed with all concerned.

5.8   Driving and Fatigue

Pharmaceutical representatives typify an occupational group that spend a large amount of their work time in driving. The average representative spends two to five hours per day in a car, driving between 60–120 miles daily, often in busy traffic. Some occupational groups such as coach, truck and train drivers will spend considerably more time at the wheel. The following aspects are of concern for those involved in healthy driving:

- vehicle safety
- design of the cab
- ergonomics of loading and unloading
- driving position and seat design

- skill of driving
- stress of driving
- accident and injury reporting
- alcohol consumption
- stereo volume
- fitness to drive
- driver fatigue

A number of these issues will be the responsibility of the employer to ensure that within budget the safest vehicles are provided. Safety does not only refer to ABS braking and the design of the outer shell of the car. It also means a seat design in which the level is adjustable and lumbar support is available, a head rest which can be positioned so the top is at eye level, and an adjustable steering column. Driving skills vary dramatically but special courses on 'defensive' driving techniques are available, as are advanced driving skills.

Driving stress is mainly associated with the aggressive behaviour of other drivers, bad weather conditions, road and traffic conditions and keeping to strict timetables.

An excellent pamphlet has been produced by the Health Promotion Research Trust (Tel: 0223 69636) on the basis of a study undertaken at Aston University. Driver stress appears to be based on:

- driving aggression
- dislike of driving
- frustration in overtaking
- irritation when being overtaken
- heightened alertness and concentration

The pamphlet recommends actions to be taken by an employer to reduce driving stress. It includes:

- auditing your driving resources – suitability and necessity
- including driving in training programmes
- educating about driver stress
- teaching relaxation techniques
- targeting young employees
- planning journeys to avoid problems
- checking that maps and guides are available
- carrying out regular health checks

- advising drivers on issues that could cause stress

The car is the most dangerous weapon that most people have control over. To be responsible for that weapon under conditions of stress increases the risk of severe consequences dramatically. Employers need to recognize the dangers and act accordingly.

Alcohol consumption on the day of work would for most responsible drivers be zero or minimal. What often goes unrecognized is the effect of a high alcohol intake the evening prior to a day of driving. A heavy consumption of alcohol up to midnight will result in a person still being above the legal driving limit of 80mg/100 ml at 8.00am the next day. For those who depend on their driving licence for work it is a sobering thought!

A health issue for drivers which is rarely considered is the volume of car radios and cassettes. Studies have examined the frequency and volume of car stereo systems at the driver's normal levels and durations. For the majority there was no evidence of hearing damage but at the extreme of the range there was clearly a risk.

A number of medical conditions will question the individual's fitness to drive. For PSV, HGV and vocational licences appropriate regulations apply and employers have a responsibility to ensure their compliance. For many occupational groups who undertake extensive driving the situation is less clear. The booklet *Medical aspects of fitness to drive* published by the Medical Commission on Accident Prevention makes a number of recommendations which are invaluable.

The conditions of most concern are:

- cardiovascular conditions
- diabetes
- epilepsy
- other nervous-system disorders
- psychiatric disorders
- vision
- deafness

In the case of cardiovascular conditions the recommendations or regulations depend on the licence required and the type of heart disease. The publication by Gold and Oliver called *Fitness to drive: updated guidance on cardiac conditions in holders of ordinary driving licences*, in Health Trends, 1990, 22, pp. 32–3 gives specific advice. In summary:

- uncomplicated myocardial infarction: discontinue driving for at least one month
- angina: do not drive if it occurs during driving
- coronary artery surgery or angioplasty: discontinue driving for one month
- peripheral vascular disease or well-controlled high blood pressure: acceptable to drive unless side effects of drugs cause problems in which case do not drive while symptoms persist
- arrhythmia: cease driving until symptoms are controlled
- conduction abnormalities (e.g. heart block): advised not to drive
- symptom-free congenital heart block: three year licence after specialist evaluation
- surgery for vascular disease: cease driving for one month after surgery

It must be recognized that these are only guidelines which will be subject to individual differences. All patients should be more specifically guided by their GP. A number of these conditions warrant the DVLA to be informed.

Common conditions which can impair driving such as diabetes, epilepsy and other disorders of the nervous system may also require the DVLA to be informed, once again in conjunction with advice from a GP. Even the use of contact lenses for vocational drivers who are driving for long periods may be hazardous.

Probably the greatest health hazard in driving is fatigue. It is estimated that 50 per cent of motorway fatalities are caused by drivers falling asleep, however *briefly*. A third of all motorists have nodded off for short periods of time at the wheel of a car, a substantial minority of whom are now dead. One study in the county of Leicestershire established that up to 25 per cent of all accidents were due to drivers falling asleep at the wheel. The same study found that time of day was an important factor with 6.00am being the time when most accidents occurred. This is two hours after the point when the body's diurnal rhythms are at a low ebb with temperature and thought processes especially affected. A small proportion (about 4 per cent) of middle-aged men, particularly the obese, suffer from sleep apnoea. This condition, featuring heavy snoring, causes daytime drowsiness and may be a major cause of accidents in sufferers. Overwork, shifts, extensive duration of work, stress, alcohol, the side effects of drugs and many other factors can be responsible for drowsiness. The strategies that employers use to avoid it or counteract it when present will vary. Adequate in-car ventilation, eating, and suitable rest intervals are all logical responses. The fact remains that as a result of work deadlines, etc., there will still be a number of drivers who are unfit to drive through fatigue yet persist in doing do. This situation should never be condoned and drivers in that situation should stop. For those that refuse to do so, the old lorry drivers trick of holding a pop bottle between their knees so it crashes to the floor as the muscles relax is one rather unsatisfactory alternative.

5.9   Weight Control

Aspects of nutrition have already been considered in Chapter 4. In addition to being an issue for the company's health it needs to be examined at an individual level. In many ways the term weight control is a misnomer because the major problem is fat levels. In most cases the two are closely related but as someone reduces fat and replaces it with muscle the body mass for the same volume will increase. Alternatively if doing the same thing causes no change in mass, then the volume will decrease. It is therefore in most cases preferable to look in the mirror than look at the bathroom scales. The United Kingdom has been in the forefront of obesity research. It has explained the causes and consequences but the area of least success is in obesity therapy. Strong evidence for successful, permanent weight reduction methods is notably lacking.

Evidence is increasing to show that obesity *per se* is clearly a risk factor in cardiac disease but in combination with other risk factors the morbidity and mortality increases significantly. There is a differential sensitivity of individuals to the effects of weight gain. If an adult is susceptible then moving into the BMI range of 25–30 is likely to be especially hazardous. Forward projections indicate that by the year 2005 the *average* BMI of adults in the UK will increase from the current level of 25.6 to a new level of 27.5. The consequence of this will be a doubling of the number of people in the obese category. The most effective strategy at a population level may not be to focus on the obese to ensure that they all slim successfully or to focus on the overweight to prevent them becoming obese. The best strategy may be to focus on the predicted secular trend by establishing preventative methods to avoid any further upward trend in weight distribution. If the expected doubling of obesity can be prevented this may have far greater impact than attempts to reduce the weight of the currently obese. This strategy, although developed for society at large, will equally apply to a smaller community such as a factory, business or institution.

Whatever the arguments proposed for differential metabolic rates by the obese, the fact remains that obesity develops because energy expenditure is less than intake. The progressive decline in physical activity in society has contributed to this. The reasons for decline include personal transportation, working practices, and the home becoming more mechanized and warmer. Recreational physical activity has not compensated for this decline. School-organized sport has declined as has walking to school and 'natural' exercise largely because the outside environment is deemed less safe for children. As most active adults were active as children, the inactivity spiral is likely to continue downwards.

Eating habits have changed so that light meals precede a heavier evening meal. Decreased energy input is unconsciously compensated later and in most cases overcompensated. The reverse does not seem to be true so that people who eat more energy than required compensate very slowly, over a matter of weeks. This means that skipped meals, inadequate breakfasts and low energy diets are likely to fail as methods of weight reduction. The relationship between the percentage of fat in the diet and the level of activity is crucial. Inactive people need an especially low fat diet to expect any degree of compensation. The solution which individuals must accept in the process of weight control is to change their lifetime habits with respect to exercise and fat percentage in food.

Businesses can make a great contribution by the provision of shower and changing facilities. This will encourage staff to walk, cycle or run to work. Companies can also be more proactive in organizing activity breaks and permit workers who become active to have additional time off work for changing to make the activity viable. The use of local sports facilities could be explored more fully by employers or even better the provision of on-site facilities.

Employers need to ensure that all employees are aware of the need to reduce the fat level in the diet and educate them as to the appropriate methods. Works canteens could display the fat targets and fat-content of meals. Occupational health staff need to be fully informed about preventative health strategies of weight control and be prepared to counsel staff and their families. The food industry needs to become active in promoting low fat options and labelling foods clearly. Not only should canteens provide information but they should also extend choices. The option of fresh fruit, high fibre foods, low energy foods and other healthier choices should become commonplace. This can extend to vending machines in businesses, to office deliveries and especially opportunist sales such as at supermarket checkouts.

It has been established that healthy eating initiatives in the workplace are very closely related to the number of employees. The larger the organization the more likelihood there was of a healthy eating activity. The same occurred with healthy catering, with almost half of the large employers (500+ staff) offering healthy catering compared with only four per cent of the smallest companies. This in part reflects the use by large organizations of external organizations who follow nutritional guidelines more closely.

The source of the healthy eating initiative is quite variable. Irrespective of company size about a quarter originate with management. It is only in the large (100–499 employees) and very large companies that occupational health seems to have any impact. Staff demand influences the smaller companies (up to 99 employees) only.

In summary weight control is predominantly a personal issue and all the evidence points to the benefits of prevention rather than restoration. Natural inclination and education are key factors but these can be supported significantly by efforts of key personnel in the workplace.

6

Work Stress – A Special Case

Whole books have been written on the topic of stress, even on coping with stress at work. This chapter is a resumé of literature from sources such as the Health Education Authority, Look After Your Heart, occupational health journals and other pamphlets and booklets. Work stress has been given special consideration because it is on the increase, it is a serious health issue and susceptible to modification by appropriate action.

6.1 What is Stress?

Stress results from a perceived imbalance between the demands made on an individual, including self-imposed ones, and the personal and environmental resources available to meet those demands. Stress can therefore result from an undemanding environment in addition to an over-demanding one. A physicist would prefer the term strain to be the consequences of stress. Thus the causes would be the stress or stressors. In the definition above the important term is the imbalance because it is that which elicits the problem.

It is essential not to confuse stress with arousal and demand. Some situations make very heavy demands on people but only become stressful if the person cannot cope with them. High and low levels of arousal can be demanding but only become stressful when not managed effectively. In the workplace the pressures of employment can often be greater than the person's ability to cope and this results in overload. This can take the form of things being too difficult or too much or more often a combination of both. However certain jobs are monotonous and boring, providing insufficient challenge and stimulation. In this case the outcome is underload and can be equally stressful.

Stress should not always be viewed as harmful. Controlled utilization of a stressful environment can be very invigorating and satisfying. Certain mental stresses can improve managerial performance, provided it is kept within the bounds of coping. People have a wide variation in their capacity to absorb stress. It may be a feature of management training to predict stress and learn a variety of coping skills.

One of the earlier workers to suggest the body's general response to stress was Hans Selye, a Canadian endocrinologist. Selye considered that there were three major stages:

- the alarm reaction
- the resistance stage
- the exhaustion stage

The alarm reaction is not dissimilar to the body's response to danger and preparation for 'flight or fight'. To do so a complex series of chemical reactions come into play, in the main to make energy available for expected action. One of these is muscular tension, essential to provide the rigidity to do battle with a perceived foe. The consequence of this is that the after effect is residual muscle ache, often in the back, shoulders and neck, and commonly a 'tension headache'.

The second stage, the resistance stage, is when the original alarm reaction seems to dissipate but high levels of corticosteroids remain in the bloodstream. This can make substantial demands on the energy reserves of the body, reducing nutrients, vitamins and sex hormones which generally reduce the ability to cope with physical damage.

The final stage is that of exhaustion when the body's reserves are exhausted and all resistance collapses.

Stress cannot be implicated in every disease, but in some it is causal and others contributory.

6.2   The Causes of Stress

The causes of stress are varied and extensive but as stated above will only result in damage if the person is unable to cope adequately. One of the often-cited studies was by Holmes and Rahe who gave a whole series of life events a stress rating based on experimental evidence. The *highest* stress rating was given to events such as:

- death of a partner
- personal injury or illness
- loss of a job
- marital separation

A *high* stress rating went to such things as:

- business readjustment
- change of financial state
- retirement
- pregnancy

A *moderate* stress rating applied to, amongst others:

- foreclosure of mortgage or loan
- change in responsibilities at work
- trouble with management
- partner begins or stops work

The *lowest* stress rating is given to changes in:

- work hours or conditions
- eating habits
- change of residence
- social activities, etc.

The list is considerably longer than given above but it represent aspects which may especially apply in a working context. When these events are unpredictable, unfamiliar, of great magnitude or intensity, compulsory or especially impelling then the outcome is particularly stressful.

In addition to major life events, the causes of stress could be a consequence of too many demands, insufficient stimulation or relationships with others.

The demands on us will include:

- insufficient holidays or weekend breaks
- inability to organize breaks in the day
- responding to tough deadlines
- insufficient support, training or experience
- an environment which is too competitive or difficult
- too much to do in the allocated time

The lack of stimulation may involve:

- having insufficient to do
- not meeting enough people
- undertaking routine and boring tasks
- requiring more responsibility

Relationships with others will be influenced by:

- getting upset or angry
- being treated badly
- insufficient personal time or space
- conflicting demands

As with many things, self-analysis may reveal potential causes of stress. Some people care too much about others' opinions, bottle up emotions, set personal standards too high and are not assertive. Others worry about health, insecurity, money, their job or partners. Many people find that their inability to express themselves well is a cause of stress, new technology concerns them and they do not see their role in the organization clearly.

It must not be forgotten that small stresses which accumulate over time can be very damaging. People can have stresses at home which when brought to work can be exacerbated. It may not even be possible to identify with clarity the causes of stress at work. Minor changes of management, technology, resources or attitude may not be recognized by all personnel but only influence the people directly affected.

6.3   The Symptoms of Stress

It is crucially important to recognize the symptoms of stress at work as early as possible so that appropriate action can be taken. Unfortunately few things in isolation are predictive of stress. It is usually a combination of a number of stressors, persistent stressors or changes which do not have a logical explanation.

It may be useful to break the symptoms down into early signs and longer term effects. The early signs can be further sub-divided into emotional, physical and behavioural.

Emotional or mental early signs include:

- reduced concentration
- sudden changes in work style
- more mistakes at work
- becoming forgetful
- judgement impaired
- depression
- becoming irritable and anxious
- loss of self-esteem

Early physical signs of stress could include:

- cardiovascular changes (pulse, palpitations)
- appetite loss
- sleeplessness and tiredness
- aches and pains
- sweating and trembling
- digestive problems

Early behavioural changes are not uncommon, such as:

- becoming less interested in work
- decision-making less easy
- loss of temper
- judgement impaired
- changes in personal and work habits
- increases in smoking, alcohol and coffee intake
- aggression

The longer-term effects can also be broken down into emotional, physical and behavioural effects. It might also be appropriate to add hormonal effects.

Long-term emotional effects may have some influence upon:

- nervous or mental breakdown
- a less rational approach

The long term physical signs of stress may in part involve:

- gastric and intestinal ulcers
- rheumatism
- arthritis
- allergies and skin rashes
- diabetes
- high blood pressure
- heart disease
- cancer

The behavioural long-term effects could include such things as:

- frequent absence from work
- alcohol and drug addiction
- breakdown of personal and family relationships
- accident proneness and clumsiness
- overall work inefficiency

6.4   Likely Candidates for Stress

A commonly used division into candidates more or less likely to become stressed is the so-called type A and type B behavioural patterns. Type A personality traits are far more likely to result in the characteristics of stress described earlier in this chapter according to the original work of Rosenman and Friedman.

In broad terms the Type A characteristics are:

- a strong commitment to work with great personal involvement in the job (workaholic)
- a highly-developed concern for urgency usually manifest in time pressures and working to tight deadlines
- marked competitiveness often associated with aggression

Such an individual is always trying to overcome events which are seemingly slightly out of control. In trying to gain control more effort and time is expended and success is rarely seen to be achieved. The consequences can literally be fatal with the risk of coronary heart disease being twice as high for type A as non-type A.

It is dangerous to be too stereotypical about individuals because not all research confirms the type A behaviour and there will be exceptions. However a more extensive list of characteristics of a type A personality would include:

☐ high competitiveness
☐ irritated easily
☐ constant striving for achievement
☐ when relaxing feels guilty
☐ aggressive and hostile tendencies
☐ impatient with people
☐ undertakes excessive responsibilities
☐ acceleration of common activities
☐ attempts to master uncontrollable situations
☐ restlessness
☐ becomes upset if things go wrong
☐ hyper alert
☐ cannot confide in people
☐ explosiveness of speech
☐ difficulty solving domestic problems
☐ tenseness of musculature, especially facial
☐ constantly struggling against time urgency
☐ prefers work to personal life
☐ insensitivity to the environment
☐ works on two or more projects simultaneously
☐ leisure time reduced or omitted
☐ rapid eating, moving and working

Clearly the number and extent of these characteristics will vary between individuals who eventually become stressed, or suffer 'burn-out'. People who consider themselves indispensable to their organization, work closely with the public, are over-committed to their jobs and most importantly have unrealizable goals are far more likely to suffer burnout. However the issue is a complex interplay of personality, situation, physical make-up and susceptibility and it is dangerous to be too rigorous in predicting a stressful outcome. Probably of greater importance is the awareness and to be alert to such characteristics in individuals. This will provide the basis for subsequent action.

There are many tests to establish the extent of an individual's type A behaviour. The Thurstone Temperamental Schedule is one and it is now possible to obtain a software package which will analyze and produce a report on occupational stress (OSI Screentest, ASE, FREEPOST, Windsor, Berks., SL4 1BU). The book by Jacqueline Atkinson on *Coping with stress at work* gives checklists for both behavioural signs of stress and type A behaviour with a simple scoring procedure. Alternatively you could simply tick the boxes in the list given above to get an indication of the characteristics that apply to you.

The work environment, as considered in Chapter 4, can often impinge on established personal characteristics to cause a cumulative effect. Noise, lighting, air pollution, repetitive jobs, shift work, travel and driving could all be the extra stressors which cause a type A prone person to reach the point of exhaustion. It must also be recognized that some organizations may actually encourage the competitive characteristics of the type A individual. The more aggressive sectors of marketing and management, for example, may view certain aspects from the list above as being very positive for the work ethos. The very culture of certain organizations is type A and those working in such companies would not thrive unless they showed these attitudes.

6.5   Stress and Lifestyle

Having considered the type A personality in the previous section, there appears to be a missing ingredient in the stress story. The notion of the 'stressed executive' who is constantly under pressure does not seem to relate to the incidence of stress-related diseases such as coronary heart disease. Studies on large number of civil servants have shown that lower grade workers consistently suffer from a greater prevalence of heart disease. Personal autonomy at work may be the missing factor or indeed overall control of life. With higher levels of unemployment it is not easy to describe work autonomy as a major feature as many people are not even at work. Unemployment itself lacks autonomy because such people are often dependent on external influences such as benefits for their basic needs. If overall lifestyle lacks independence, control, options, motivation and overall meaning it is far more likely to be stressful. There are a number of people who have such overwhelming responsibilities (e.g. captains of industry, government ministers, senior officers in the forces) that it is sometimes difficult to comprehend how they cope. They are, of course, well briefed but even so to avoid stress-induced exhaustion their lifestyle must compensate well. A number of world leaders historically had high blood pressure. Presidents Taft, Wilson, Roosevelt and Eisenhower had hypertension as did Lenin, Stalin, Khrushchev and Brezhnev. Churchill suffered from strokes in old age and George Bush collapsed as a younger man as a direct result of the pressures he was under. However Bush adapted his lifestyle as a result of his experience and started to exercise regularly and enjoy active recreation such as fishing and golf. John Major suffered from exhaustion after the Gulf War in 1991 probably as a result of insufficient sleep. Margaret Thatcher was known for the small amount of sleep she needed. This is also a characteristic of Giulo Andreolti the former Italian prime minister who takes a 15 minutes siesta. This is a strategy adopted by Lech Walesa, another world leader who only needs five hours sleep a night in the form of regular 10 minute 'power naps'. Many world leaders have strategies for unwinding. John Major enjoys watching cricket, Francois Mitterrand of France plays golf twice a week and Felipe Gonzalez the Spanish prime minister unwinds by walking in his garden of bonsai trees. These people who might be assumed to be under stress are all fundamentally in charge of their lives.

For the rest of us who are not presidents, premiers or prime ministers, we still have to examine our lifestyles to gain as much control as possible within our particular circumstances. The major life events described originally by Holmes and Rahe are unlikely to happen often but the daily nuisances and bonuses may become important. Many daily events cannot be clearly divided into either a nuisance or a bonus. The sudden change of plans required by a demanding manager may initially be construed as a nuisance but if the purpose turns out to discuss an exciting new venture it becomes a bonus. On the domestic front the heavy cold that keeps you indoors may allow you to watch a video that you have been longing to see. A common nuisance for many people is the planning and preparation required for a holiday. The eventual bonus is the benefit that the holiday provides. It is not surprising that many people report that it takes a few days of the holiday to unwind sufficiently to begin to enjoy it. Even though holidays are recognized by most people as an essential lifestyle benefit, it is surprising how many Europeans do not take their full holiday entitlement. This appears to be particularly so with the professional workers, who have a high commitment to their jobs. Similarly those high-income earners who have the money but not the inclination show this characteristic. Within EC countries only 46 per cent of those on high salaries took a long holiday of more than 14 nights. Thirty per cent of British workers do not use their holiday entitlement each year compared with 41 per cent in Italy, 43 per cent in France and 60 per cent in Holland. Although holiday entitlement in the USA appears less generous than Europe, much greater recreational use is made of weekends and this compensates significantly.

Probably the greatest lifestyle factor is dealing with personal relationships whether at work or at home. Stress and conflicts will arise as a result of failures with personal relationships. The basis of good relationships involves a number of factors, but there are three of special importance. The first is to establish clear ground rules for the relationship whether it be with a partner at home or a colleague at work. If there is uncertainty over key issues to do with relationships it can produce a stressful outcome. It is said that it is better for a child to be brought up in a harsh, but fair and clear, relationship with a parent than one in which no consistency occurs and the child has no constant frame of reference. This equally applies at work. Uncertainty breeds insecurity and possible resentment. Secondly it is important to be objective about individuals, their problems and their personalities. It is unrealistic to expect every worker to be a clone of management, sharing the same views and motivations. Finally it is essential for problems to be discussed not kept bottled up. Employers may simply be unaware of employees' problems which, if known, they could take suitable action to alleviate. Some people do not see the value of establishing good relationships with others, especially in a work context. As people are the most important resource in any company, the benefits of positive relationships are paramount.

As the nuclear family becomes increasingly rare people may have to turn elsewhere for their social support. The sympathetic view, the praise, the advice or the comfort of a partner is bound to be less readily available as the number of single people increases, especially single parent families who may have job concerns to add to their domestic life. The traditional support structures are being eroded and increasingly the place of work may become the only alternative. All sectors of the workforce need to be aware of this and be prepared to provide mutual support if applicable.

One of the most noticeable individual differences is the way in which people can perceive the same situation so differently. Some people are eternal optimists, others pessimists. Some people have irrational beliefs which will eventually govern their attitudes. A friend of mine has a very senior job in local government in which it is always necessary to be totally realistic. This person is always positive about every aspect of life. The effect is refreshing and engenders respect and loyalty amongst colleagues. People can crudely be categorized into what I call 'radiators' and 'drainers'. Faced with an identical situation, the extremes of what is probably a continuum will react totally differently. There is a view that beliefs or assumptions that are irrational can affect our opinions and expectations. This may in turn bring about the prevailing attitude of the drainer or radiator. There are three types of irrational beliefs:

- internal focus
- assumptions of others
- life expectations

The first type takes the line that everything I do must be correct, acceptable, outstanding, pleasing, respected and loved. If I do not meet these criteria then it is unacceptable, I am a failure and consequently worthless. The second type implies that everyone else should follow my example, do things my way, give me what I expect. If they do not, then once again life is intolerable and other people are worthless because they fail to please me. The third irrational belief is that life itself should be relatively easy, be painless, consistent and provide all my wants. Once again if life does not fulfil these criteria it is unacceptable and intolerable for causing me unnecessary upset. Written down in this way, a normally balanced person may find these irrational beliefs surprising and perhaps outside their experience. It is surprising, however, how many people share them in part or whole, to a limited degree or completely. Identifying people who think irrationally, such that their attitudes become hardened in a negative direction, may not, on reflection, be too difficult. Consider the family member who acts in this way (sometimes transitionally, such as when adolescent) or the work colleague with a 'chip on his/her shoulder'.

Once the belief is recognized as irrational then remedial action can be taken. Taking the first type as an example, it would be almost impossible to be liked, respected, revered by everyone. This especially applies in industry where harsh decisions, taken for the good of the company, will inevitably cause resentment by some people. A belief in wanting to be liked by everyone means that a person cannot enjoy being approved of by those that do. Exactly the same logic can be applied to the other two irrational beliefs, the assumptions of others and life expectations. How many times have you heard a critical comment made of a colleague: 'She/he believes the world owes her/him a living!'? The negative consequences of these irrational beliefs can be very stressful and it may be worth re-assessing this aspect of lifestyle on the basis of the following questions:

- what is my view of this issue?
- is it based on a particular belief?
- am I making any assumptions?
- are these sensible, rational assumptions?
- if this belief is unfilled or I do not get what I want, what will really happen?

One of the consequences of re-evaluating long-held beliefs is that it is very difficult to change. Especially so when a belief has appeared to be successful. An ambitious person who has worked hard, putting extreme industry and effort into his company is likely to be rewarded by promotion. The consequence of this may be more responsibility, more projects to manage and more overall work. A point may be reached when the previous exemplary attitude, perhaps perfectionism, just is not possible. This person can either change and subscribe to 'the acceptance of incompleteness' or become overwhelmed by the situation with the prospect of a stressful reaction. Writing this book is a typical example. The contract specifies a given delivery date. Although the manuscript will be delivered on time, I would prefer another year to revise, improve and re-organize it. The publishers, however, have advertised its imminent publication and the contract becomes void if it is not delivered as agreed. I have to accept that it is not as 'complete' as I may wish but to avoid unnecessary stress I learn to live with that disappointment. I must accept that some people will not like the book (and therefore transfer their dislike to me). I cannot assume that everyone thinks like me over contractual issues and that I have to be prepared to accept the knocks in life as a consequence of writing the book. Hopefully the confidence that comes from knowing that the manuscript has been written is better on balance than the disappointment which could accrue if the book was deemed a failure. As was once said by Ray Bradbury, the science fiction writer,

If we listened to our intellect, we'd never have a love affair. We'd never have a friendship. We'd never go into business, because we'd by cynical. You've got to jump off cliffs all the time and build your wings on the way down.

Perhaps this is the problem with those who stick to irrational beliefs. They cannot risk the change which allows them to jump off the cliff!

Another feature of lifestyle is the meaning of life itself. Although answering this in its entirety may never be fully resolved, stress control may depend on an overall life plan and clearer meaning. Indeed the exhaustion state is often verbalized as 'Life has no meaning for me any more'. It is not possible to give an answer to the meaning of life because it is very personal, but everyone should aim to have a sort of 'mission statement' for their life which may have a number of short-, medium- and long-terms goals. These goals could be philosophical, moral or spiritual. Although few will have a personal 'meaning of life mission statement', making sense of everyday activities from a broader horizon may put some of the stressful trivia into perspective.

6.6   Stress and Organizations

Stress is monitored within the workplace in a number of ways. The most common method is absenteeism rates with almost half the companies surveyed reporting that they use this method. Lateness is also a common method with a third of the companies monitoring it this way. A third of the companies surveyed used no method of monitoring stress and less than 10 per cent used some physical method such as blood pressure.

The effect of stress on work is little different from other adverse health aspects. Typically employers might expect:

- absenteeism and poor time-keeping
- decision-making impaired
- productivity or service reduced
- negative social climate and morale
- cooperation reduced
- strained industrial relations
- accident rate increased
- increased vandalism and sabotage
- high turnover of staff including early retirements

All these features are unlikely to be evident simultaneously and may appear over a long time. Employers should at least be aware that the underlying cause of such features may be organizational stress.

The causes of stress in the workplace are a combination of aspects discussed earlier in this book but probably worth repeating. This list is taken from a pamphlet called the *Stress Action Plan* produced by the HEA in 1990. Copies of the full pamphlet and a more extensive booklet called *Action or Stress at Work* can be obtained from the Health Education Authority's Distribution Department, Hamilton House, Mabledon Place, London, WC1H 9TX.

Environmental causes:

- occupational hazards
- background
- equipment
- facilities for staff

Job causes:

- too demanding
- lacking a challenge
- lacking control
- insufficient workload
- inadequate training
- poor feedback

Organizational causes:

- style of management
- structure of work
- communication
- changes

Individual causes:

- job ambiguity
- conflicting interests

Relationship causes:

- personnel policies
- between colleagues

Recognition:

- company values
- training
- career prospects

Security:

- redundancy fears

The organization of the company in terms of its overall structure, its approach to management, the standard and attitudes it expects of its employees and to corporation culture are critical to company stress levels. The corporate culture may be in conflict with the individual's attitude. The quality of the product, the type of marketing, the cost cutting and other work practices may be unacceptable to an employee's personal preference. This would especially apply if the company's expectations and reward system is based on work intensity. Workaholics may suit the company but never the family. Management styles which are either too autocratic or too lax can be a source of stress. Most studies in the UK have revealed the lack of training in management training compared with counterparts in Europe and the USA. This especially applies to stress management. If employees have some degree of 'ownership' over decisions, stress levels can be reduced because staff feel they are involved and participating in management policy. The control people have over their jobs at every level is important. Efforts should especially be made to ensure that employees never loose total control because this is the basis of so much stress. People become bitter if communication between different levels of an organization is lacking. The success of many Japanese companies is based on having communication units when numerous work issues are debated. This leads into the important issue of recognition and appreciation. This is especially so if it is personal, either face to face or by personal letter.

The problems in many companies is that staff are so committed to the present, the immediate, that time is rarely available for a longer perspective. This understandable approach is potentially very dangerous because stress at an organizational level can be very insidious. Planning, training and better appreciation of the company's approach to stress is likely to be beneficial and more likely to prevent serious problems in the future.

6.7   Coping With Stress

The starting point in this section on coping with stress is to examine what stress reduction activities are common in the workplace. Most approaches to stress control have concentrated directly on individuals and paid little heed to the organizational issues covered in the previous section. Stress management courses and breaks head the list of activities. Forty-four per cent of participating companies are involved in one or both of these activities. Professional counselling is undertaken by 39 per cent of concerned companies, with background music (17 per cent), relaxation classes (15 per cent) and yoga (6 per cent) being the other cited activities. This pattern tends to persist irrespective of the size of the company.

Before considering coping strategies in general it is worth giving some specific activities in response to the type A personality type:

- find a time during the day or night to relax body and mind entirely
- protect personal time by learning to say no
- during an intensive working day take a number of stress-free breathing spaces
- avoid unnecessary appointments and impossible deadlines
- enjoy recreational opportunities such as the performing arts and exercise
- reduce time-oriented behaviour
- accept that everything does not require immediate attention
- reflective periods are essential
- re-assess the causes of your apparent need to hurry everything
- avoid being the centre of attention
- only talk when essential
- become aware of the obsession with time and re-establish a different behaviour pattern

The list above illustrates some specific, direct actions applicable to someone who may become stressed as a result of their dominant personality or behavioural type. The rest of the section will examine broader aspects of stress management including:

- sleep
- relaxation
- recreation
- spiritual beliefs
- time management
- communication
- working relationships
- team building
- establishing control
- crisis management
- counselling
- exercise

Sleep

Stress can have a potent effect on sleep and when sleep loss occurs people become more stressful by worrying about it. There is no evidence that people need eight hours sleep, the quality being more important. Sleeping tablets should only be prescribed when alterative behavioural methods have been tried first. These include:

- taking more exercise
- avoiding heavy meals prior to bedtime
- going to bed only when tired
- avoiding stimulants such as coffee and alcohol prior to bedtime
- having a warm bath before going to bed
- getting up earlier
- following a relaxation programme just before going to bed

Relaxation

Relaxation for many people is not natural. They even feel guilty if not constantly achieving things. If this occurs at work it is even more essential to relax during non-work time. Often the problem is made worse by very busy people who bring work home in the evenings having to cram in their domestic chores at weekends, leaving them little time to truly relax.

Relaxation means different things to different people. A recent survey indicated that reading was considered to be the most popular form of relaxation followed by watching TV, sport, taking a bath and hobbies.

The next most popular method is listening to relaxation tapes. Many of these are based on the neuromuscular techniques of Jacobsen and aim to help people become aware of physical signs of tension. The process should reduce the tension and subsequently prevent it occurring. The procedure involves tensing and relaxing all the major muscle groups. Attention has to be given to the sensations which occur at each level. Over time people become more aware of the feeling of relaxation and the experience of tension before it becomes necessary to undertake the relaxation programme. The benefits will not be immediate as it takes regular practice to develop the skill fully. Relaxation tapes rarely teach relaxation but provide the opportunity for an individual to learn to relax. A conducive environment, comfortable, warm and noise free is of great benefit while undergoing a relaxation programme. The attitude to relaxation is also important. It cannot be expected to succeed if the person is taking a negative approach or is constantly worrying about a specific issue. Once learned the muscle relaxation technique can be transferred to many situations and practised at other times such as when travelling, shopping, at work or when trying to get to sleep. The strategy applied to most relaxation programmes involves the features of:

- recognizing tension
- breath control
- adopting a basic relaxation position
- following the relaxation instructions
- recognizing the relaxed state

A variant on relaxation training which involves tensing and relaxing muscle groups is autogenic training. This can involve a deeper, almost trance-like state of relaxation and should best be taught by an experienced trainer. In autogenic training the arms, legs, neck and shoulders are made to feel heavy. A feeling of warmth should occur in parts of the body, particularly the thoracic cavity. Respiratory control is important as is the use of phrases such as 'my right arm is heavy' to invoke the required response. The physical exercises are followed by visualization exercises and a form of meditation. Further details on autogenic training are available from the Centre for Autogenic Training, 101 Harley Street, London, W1N 1DT.

Other relaxation techniques include:

- meditation
- yoga
- massage
- aromatherapy
- the Alexander technique
- biofeedback
- electronic 'mind machines'

All of these need special training, equipment or experience and further details can be found in libraries or from complementary therapists. The Alexander technique is a method of establishing correct body habits including posture but to be learnt correctly needs a qualified teacher. The electronic 'mind machine' uses intermittent sound and light pulses to stimulate brain waves and induce relaxation. Although many claims are made for its efficacy, more rigorous scientific research will be necessary before it can be recommended as a mainstream relaxation technique.

Recreation

Recreation is often synonymous with leisure which can be defined broadly as all non-work activities. For the purposes of this section recreation involves play, hobbies, dining out, enjoying television and theatre, going to the pub and above all laughter. Laughing with others and at oneself is a great stress reducer. Children mature and develop through play, yet adults often find it difficult to engage in relaxed informal play. It is also unnecessary for recreation always to be creative. Playing musical instruments and do-it- yourself could pro- duce other stresses because of the need to practise regularly or avoid mistakes. Non-serious recreation can be of real benefit to alleviate stress which is why laughter has been included in the list above. A company in the Yorkshire Dales is offering courses on dry stone walling to provide a recreational opportunity for those not used to manual skills. The course which involves hard work and the satisfaction of achieving something tangible in a few days is well-subscribed by company directors, management consultants and others keen to utilize this basic activity as a method of reducing stress.

Spiritual Beliefs

No one would suggest that spiritual belief is the antidote to stress and certainly it is not something that can be produced on demand. There is evidence, however, that having clear beliefs is beneficial for psychological health. These will not always be religious, but having a sense of the order of the world and one's place in it could be of real benefit.

Time Management

Whole books have been written on this topic, staff development courses include it regularly and those under stress constantly appeal for more time. In most cases more time is not the answer but more effective use of the actual time available. A brief examination of time management tactics may indicate methods for stress reduction. The tactics include:

- time diary
  - keep records of a typical day and examine honestly when time is ineffective
- job description
  - if you have a job description, does what you actually do match it. If you have no job description, produce one and reveal any discrepancies between what you do and what you ought to be doing. Then add what you want to do and see if you have given yourself the right priorities
- priorities
  - distinguish between important and urgent. Dealing constantly with trivial tasks because it is achieving volume will result in important tasks eventually becoming urgent. Then the time cannot be given
- procrastination
  - do so with purpose. Leaving the post until it can be dealt with properly is effective procrastination as is phoning at a later time because it is cheaper. Putting off most tasks is highly inefficient because the task has to be reviewed again when you come back to it
- task completion
  - plan; reduce to manageable parts; concentrate exclusively on the part; take breaks
- establish long-term goals first
  - this provides an overall mission within which everything else must fit
- examine goals in behavioural terms
  - do work practices, personal responsibilities and lifestyle permit the goals to be achieved

- set objectives in the context of your time scale
    – some objectives are long term, others immediate. It may be an annual report or the objectives of a single meeting or phone call
- list everything first
    – within a given day, project or assembly, state every aspect before starting. Give each item a priority rating, A, B or C. All A ranked items are completed first. Cs may never be achieved or may in time become Bs or As
- check the consequences of every task
    – are they really necessary or are they being done because they are interesting not essential?
- never substitute
    – it is too easy to fill work time with little jobs to be completed prior to the important one. The phrase 'I'll just do this first' must be eliminated
- action list
    – an action or 'to do' list is especially valuable at the end of the day. It signals the intention to start afresh next day, not worry all night
- avoid interruptions
    – plan times not to be interrupted by using appointments, by screening, by saying no, or by using the telephone
- value time
    – recognize the worth of your time. When more than one person is involved in wasted time the costs escalate. Calculating the cost of 11 people waiting 15 minutes for the twelfth to arrive for a committee meeting puts it into perspective
- maintain reflective time
    – reflective or thinking time is the first to be lost but may be the most creative and active work you do
- delegate
    – the most difficult thing to achieve for many people with time stress, yet highly productive in releasing time
- attending meetings
    – is your attendance essential? Could someone else attend and brief you later?
- proper breaks
    – ensure that quality time is spent with family and friends. Holidays and weekends must not be eroded and activities should be planned which keep work out of mind

Communication

Ineffective communication is one of the major causes of stress whether at work or home. It means that people are having to guess the intention and wrong guesses could be calamitous. Some jobs require highly developed communication skills to be successful. For many people presenting an open and direct message which is understood clearly by both parties will reduce the stress associated with uncertainty.

Assertive communication does not mean heavy-handed or domineering. It involves the qualities of self-respect, confidence, fairness, honesty, being positive and clear. Some people have personalities which make confident communication difficult. Some can communicate well in social situations but have problems in open meetings or with staff more senior than themselves. As communication is important to stress management at every level of work it is worth noting a few principles:

- clarify thoughts first
- ensure the statement is clear and specific
- remain calm
- explore alternatives
- express feelings (e.g. concern)
- choose the venue and the time
- accept if agreement is impossible
- reasons are better than excuses
- be responsible for the issue
- consider responses before reacting
- request more details if unclear
- appreciate the feelings of all parties
- always apologise sincerely if appropriate, but do not over apologise
- phrase questions to ensure a response
- give total attention
- accept praise graciously
- give praise generously
- ensure your body language, voice and environment is consistent with the form of communication

Although the above have been written with verbal communication in mind, most of them apply equally to written communications. In many ways written communications are more important to get right because the recipient can mull over them at length and spend time on the nuances of interpretation. In the written communication the content is paramount but in verbal communication the manner is often of equal importance.

Working Relationships

Good working relationships with colleagues are essential for any job requiring teamwork, even of a fairly loose type. Not everyone is expected to like all their colleagues but a working relationship based on trust, appreciation of skills, limitations and attitude is highly desirable. Of course it does not always work out. A system where staff perceive an unfair division of labour, wages, friendship or attention will soon build resentment. What needs to be recognized in trying to reduce stress by improving working relationships is a) the effects of change, b) the acceptance of different responsibilities within the workplace, and c) the value of social support from colleagues.

The workplace is dynamic and even in the most staid organization, staff will change, small work practices will alter, attitudes will shift. Almost every change will impact on someone within the organization but it is not always apparent. Those who introduce change should give more attention to the effect on others so that it does not increase stress but ideally reduces it.

No workplace can operate without people having different responsibilities. Sometimes one listens to casual talk about individuals, especially public figures, and from the viewpoint of the speaker it is difficult to appreciate their virtues or qualities. With very few exceptions, people only rise to senior positions by being approved of by numerous others along the way. MPs have to be selected, interviewed, and gain experience at grass roots. They become promoted by small increments based on doing a job in an approved manner long before they reach cabinet rank. It is facile to say that anyone in authority is no good. We may not agree with their policies and they will certainly have weaknesses and limitations, but they must have positive qualities at least in the eyes of the person or persons who appointed them. This knowledge will not necessarily dissipate the frustration of the employer who is not appreciated. However if the employee at any level, whether management, subordinate or equal member of a team, can recognize the stresses or potential stresses of colleagues then working relationships could be improved.

Team Building

Stress can be reduced by effective team building. There are few work places in which a team approach either does not exist, or would not benefit from its existence. Team building is concerned with:

- increasing mutual trust amongst members
- increasing awareness of personal and colleagues' behaviours
- developing interpersonal skills

The strategies for team building espoused by Making, Cooper and Cox in their book *Managing people at work* and published in 1989 include:

- sensitivity training
- role negotiation
- structured approach
- packages
- interaction process analysis
- team roles

These strategies in the main use role play, games, competitive tasks and open discussion to explain the structure of teams and improve team function. Hilary Lomas of the School of Health Sciences at the University of Liverpool has explained these approaches and remains unconvinced that such activities help reduce stress at work. Indeed activities which might identify a 'weak link' in a team could increase the levels of stress. She argues that stress reduction is better served by less structured and formalized team-building strategies. Similar time spent in more social pursuits could foster the more informal supportive networks. Other bonuses for those who have tried this include staff and management getting to know each other better and an increased confidence in relationships at work.

A team where people care for each other, are open and truthful, make decisions by consensus, have a strong commitment to each other and deal with conflicts fairly are likely to experience less stress. Team building in a relaxed, enjoyable and fun context is likely to have the best chance of success.

Establishing Control

Earlier in this chapter the issue of attitude was discussed. One of the most potent ways of reducing stress is raising levels of personal confidence and self-belief. An athlete who enters a race in the knowledge that (s)he has trained harder than anyone else should have the self-confidence to expect a good performance. Positive thinking, enhancing ego and being in better control are likely to reduce stress significantly. The following approaches may assist in this process:

- aim for something tangible
- place negative thoughts into a total life context
- concentrate on the pluses not the minuses
- establish the cause of the concern
- be specific not too general
- accept achievements
- confront the real probability of fears
- having done your best, accept the consequences
- publicize and celebrate success
- enjoy rewards and treats
- list accomplishments
- record achievements, however small
- balance bad points with good
- adopt constructive criticism
- examine the behaviour not the person
- share failures as well as successes
- become aware of areas to improve
- learn from mistakes
- consider a situation as if it were *slightly* better
- ask others if anything can be done
- when under stress, reduce your expectations
- rehearse the difficult situation
- the way you view it is stressful not the situation itself
- count your blessings

For a further explanation and examples of some of these suggestions Peter Making and Pat Lindley's book *Positive stress management* and Jacqueline Atkinson's book *Coping with stress at work* are both recommended.

Crisis Management

Having found ways to reduce stress, to be more positive and ideally to prevent stress in the first place, a crisis can still occur. This is the time when people under severe stress often capitulate. This need not be so.

Preventing every crisis is impossible but a strategy which reduces the impact could pay handsome dividends in terms of stress reduction. Some jobs build crisis management into their training. This is because they are likely to be in the front line of a serious, often life-threatening situation. Examples would be the fire, police, ambulance and hospital services. Not all crises will be as severe, but the impact on the individual concerned may be fairly disastrous. Three effective ways to reduce the impact on a crisis are:

- have alternative solutions to hand
- appoint different people to take responsibility for different types of crises
- learn how to prepare alternative plans

To take a simple example, a University professor is invited to give a prestigious lecture in another town. S(he) plans to give a slide presentation and has all the slides prepared. En route her/his car is broken into and her/his slides are stolen. Disaster. Possible solutions could include giving the lecture without slides, cancelling the lecture, producing overhead transparencies (OHTs) at the venue and recovering the slides in time. The last solution is unlikely, the first and second solutions would be unprofessional, leaving the production of OHTs the only immediate response. Preparing for this unlikely crisis would have added little to the preparation time. When the slides were drafted, a paper copy should have been retained and carried separately from the slides. The production of the OHTs would then be straightforward and the situation retrieved.

When the crisis does occur the following may help:

- if time permits, have a few minutes alone to plan
- review the action including revised deadlines
- change jobs to suit new deadlines and inform staff involved
- spread the extra work now required to avoid sudden overload
- explore alternatives
- delegate
- optimize concentration to resolve the crisis
- reconsider priorities and objectives
- request and accept help
- debrief afterwards to use the experience positively

But above all a crisis is only one if it is viewed that way. Every crisis is relative.

Counselling

Counselling has a number of levels from crisis counselling to providing straightforward advice on diet and exercise. In traditionally 'high risk' occupations crisis intervention teams have been established. Members of such a team should:

- have well-developed counselling skills
- have empathy
- have peer-group support
- appreciate their own limitations
- obtain regular counselling supervision
- not have related personal problems or recent similar trauma

For less major incidents an in-house team can be involved in first line counselling providing the members have the necessary skills. They will need professional supervision, peer group support and regular training.

Sometimes employees may benefit from counselling, even though they were not directly involved in an event. This crisis intervention counselling would be offered to anyone who had to cope with trauma, accident, abusive or violent incident.

The management of a company or organization need to be fully briefed about the counselling service on offer, stress its confidentiality, encourage participation and reassure staff of its non-discriminatory nature. One of the best ways to ensure commitment is for managers as part of their training to learn basic counselling skills.

Exercise

Exercise has for a long time been associated with stress reduction but only recently has more medical evidence been forthcoming. In one study patients who suffered from moderate depression were either allowed to exercise or given traditional psychotherapy. The exercisers improved impressively better than the others. Another study compared exercisers with controls and found that the exercise group felt a much greater sense of personal achievement, experienced definite reductions in anxiety, felt more energetic and less depressed. Exercise appears to have a tranquillizing effect which lasts for considerably longer than the period of activity. It can be used in the management of anxiety and depression and has been shown to improve mood, possibly through its effect on endorphins. Particular exercises which combine physical activity with relaxation and stretching such as yoga and tai chi are especially beneficial for stress reduction.

The biggest mistake made in using exercise for stress reduction is the context. Some people simply transfer their stress into the physical activity and maintain their aggression, competitiveness and time dominance. They add their exercise to an already crowded day and add extra pressures which may be disadvantageous. Exercise, like everything else in life, needs a clear perspective. Use it as an opportunity to become healthier of course, but also make it a social occasion, a fun occasion, a relaxing occasion. Exercise within the limits of the current fitness of your body. For most people who are new to exercise that means starting at a low level and progressing slowly. Exercise at a level that enables you to hold a conversation – and converse. Give time for the pleasant experience of the warm down, the shower and the sensation of physical tiredness. Vary the type of exercise so it does not become another monotonous routine in the day. Use exercise to try new experiences like hiking abroad, fun runs, mountain biking or using flumes in swimming pools. Share exercise with family and friends. Start to use exercise as a substitute for more stressful activities such as sitting at a workbench or desk trying to resolve a difficult problem. Plans can be made, problems reviewed and crises resolved almost as easily when walking briskly or swimming lengths. If nothing else, exercise provides that brief window in a hectic schedule when you are forced to concentrate on an activity more in tune with the original 'fight or flight' reaction which characterized the early stress response. It reduces stress by providing the correct physiological reaction and gives the added bonus of a healthier body.

6.8   Case Studies

An effective way to show how stress is being managed at work is to report cases which illustrate individual approaches. The following case studies exemplify the attitude which is becoming more common in industry – that of recognizing and taking action on stress issues.

Stress Counselling in the Post Office

The Post Office implemented a specialist counselling service in 1986. It had been recognized that psychiatric and psychosocial problems ranked second only to musculo-skeletal disorders for retirement on medical grounds. Counselling and control groups were established from the full range of staff. The counselling group were after three years less anxious, less depressed, suffered fewer stress symptoms and had a higher level of self-esteem. Absence was also reduced in the counselling group although job satisfaction and organizational commitment changed very little.

Occupational Stress in Nursing

A study on hospital staff nurses listed role ambiguity, overload, badly designed work schedules and client concerns as occupational stress hazards. As fewer nurses are required, these psychosocial hazards could become increasingly important. Another study on nurses indicated that behaviours were strictly controlled leaving limited room for autonomy and individual abilities to flourish. There was evidence of maintaining the *status quo* to the detriment of natural professional growth.

Tinnitus in a Sound Engineer

A sound technician having been promoted to supervisor complained of tinnitus which on specialist examination was normal. He was very concerned that loss of hearing could become permanent and affect his job. A definite imbalance was established concerning his life away from the sound studio – he was a workaholic. He was counselled to cultivate more outside activities and relaxation therapy. The tinnitus is now reducing.

Anxiety in a Studio Floor Manager

Floor managers have responsibility for organizing people in the studio as required by the director. Immediately after the company relocated the floor manager was certified sick with an anxiety state. After a premature return to work, counselling identified the source of his stress to be the problems of driving in London associated with the relocation.

He also recognized an over-protective mother causing him difficulty in living up to expectations. His identification of the basis of his stress started his rehabilitation. He relaxes with music and has a supportive wife. When under stress he hyperventilates but finds that writing helps. He is now coping much better and is optimistic of a full recovery.

Prison Riots and Absentee Counselling

In 1987, Barlinnie prison in Glasgow suffered serious riots which resulted in a very high absentee rate amongst prison officers. Those that remained were resentful of their absent colleagues and their inability to give prisoners normal privileges because of understaffing. Middle management recognized that many officers needed special encouragement to return to work. Schemes were established to reintroduce the absentee officers to prison duties in a progressive manner. Those visited at home were reassured that no punitive action would be taken. The high visibility of the governor was appreciated by staff. The opportunity was given to staff to seek consultation with professionals in confidence. Absenteeism reduced dramatically and those who were absent preferred to be visited by a colleague than a health professional.

Stress Factors in Industrial Workers

In Canada the highest incidence of stress-related illness was found in manual and industrial workers. They were less likely to acknowledge the harm and therefore less likely to recognize and seek early help. Many perceived health-threatening conditions as a consequence of particular jobs. The major factors for psychogenic illness was a high-pressured, noisy, alienating and insecure work environment. Poor communication and repetitive monotonous jobs caused most dissatisfaction.

Clerical Workers and Heart Disease

The Framington study of heart health in the USA shows the incidence of heart disease among female clerical workers to be twice that of managers, professionals, service and blue collar workers.

Telephone Operators and Management

The health problems of telephone operators were described as being related to poor worker–management relations. Role and status uncertainty, with a lack of social interaction were also identified as producing health problems. The main causes seem to be an interaction of psychological and social factors.

Stress Reduction in Sweet Manufacturing

A production process was reorganized to comply with a number of aims linked to stress reduction. The action involved:

- reorganization into small groups with a common machine and work area
- a production process which involved more local sequential operations
- greater decision-making and autonomy given to all workers
- greater variety and range of skills offered as well as increased interaction between working groups
- all employers given single status for key issues such as working hours and sick pay

Retirement Planning at Exxon

Employees who were to leave over the next year were given retirement planning and financial counselling. Those that were seeking another job were given coaching and assistance. Stress management was offered either in the form of group seminars or individual counselling.

Further Reading

Two short pamphlets on stress provide additional reading:

Wilkinson, G., 1987, *Coping with stress*, London, British Medical Association

Scriptographic Booklets, 1993, *What everyone should know about stress at work*, Alton, Scriptographic Publications Limited.

7

Becoming a Healthy Company

7.1 The Evidence

The starting point for deciding whether or not to become committed to a health company policy is to consider the merits of doing so. Chapter 2 has indicated the benefits of a healthy workforce and this section reinforces this but also gives evidence at a more specific level.

One course of evidence is to show that others are adopting a health policy. This follows the principle that if the majority consider it valuable, it should have some inherent value. Eighty-two per cent of all organizations surveyed offer healthy meals, 72 per cent offer stress counselling, 68 per cent offer all three.

Some form of voluntary health checks were offered to nearly all of the 50 organizations surveyed. Most provide a full and/or regular medical examination. Others tested simply for blood pressure. Kellogg's is an example of a company which offers a full annual assessment including height and weight checks, urinalysis, blood pressure, cholesterol and respiratory function tests. Kelloggs also offers a lifestyle assessment, together with periodic cytological screening. Blood pressure and cholesterol levels are tests which are commonly undertaken. Wimpy and Warner Lambert offer cervical and breast screening as part of their 'well woman' initiative. Some organizations offer urine, heart and sound/vision screening. Testicular and skin cancer screening is offered by Marks and Spencer. Biochemical and haemological screening as part of a voluntary health check is offered by Shell UK Oil. Full medical checks are offered annually by Kellogg's, whereas TBA Industrial Products offer theirs two-yearly and Shell UK Oil every five years. Companies such as the London and Manchester Group use mobile screening units from the health education authority for their checks. Some companies such as Granada Motorway Services and Acorn Computers use a private medical company such as BUPA for health screening checks. Acorn Computers limit this to employees over 40, whereas Atlas Copco (Manufacturing) only offers its medicals to senior managers and spouses. Some companies such as Cammell Laird restricted health screening to occupational-linked diseases. Health checks at Occidental Petroleum are only offered to employees operating in hazardous areas and to executive staff. Other companies operate a selective policy providing health checks mainly to executives, shop managers and supervisors.

Seventy-eight per cent of companies surveyed have a smoking policy with almost all of these restricting smoking in some manner. The figure drops to about 62 per cent for policies on alcohol/drugs/solvent abuse and there is a great deal of variation in the way substance abuse is managed by employers. The figure may not be truly representative because a number of companies offer help in the absence of a formal policy. Atlas Copco (Manufacturing), for example, arrange counselling for individuals where it is considered necessary. Kelloggs and Merseyside Police Authority operate in the same way. Policies on substance abuse tend to be more 'sympathetic' than smoking policies. Individual counselling is a popular approach either given by the in-house occupational health staff and/or by external organizations. The occupational health department is used by Macclesfield Health Authority, together with external units and a staff counsellor. Links with a local hospital and a drug dependency unit are used by Phillips Components. Some employers take things a stage further by referring those in need to treatment centres. British Telecom (NI) and Cammell Laird were examples of companies adopting this approach. The jobs of staff undergoing treatment are protected at Boots and Sheffield City Council and Marks and Spencer treat employees with substance-related problems exactly the same as those with any other medical condition.

In addition to individual companies who have adopted health promotion policies with enthusiasm, evidence can be culled from the support given by national industrial organizations. The Confederation of British Industries (CBI) provides information to employers on their legal duties under the Health and Safety at Work Act. It also encourages employers to undertake workplace health promotion. It will proactively give guidance on workplace policies for alcohol, smoking, drugs and Aids/HIV. The CBI recognized that voluntary lifestyle health promotion at work may take time to be introduced especially as employers and occupational health staff are committed to implementing the European directives on manual handling and VDUs.

The Institute of Personnel Management (IPM) has produced publications on substance misuse and smoking policies at work for all its 50,000 members. It feels best able to contribute by distilling the experience of larger companies in workplace health promotion and disseminating this information to smaller organizations. The IPM plan to produce guides for smaller companies on health at work with such topics as alcohol, smoking, healthy eating, exercise and defensive driving being considered.

The Trades Union Congress (TUC) are promoting better health in the workplace by lobbying government and being represented on national organizations such as the National Forum for Coronary Heart Disease Prevention. It is involved in many efforts to reduce accidents and work-related health damage by using legislation and training. Like the IPM, the TUC have produced guidelines for its members on problem drinking, HIV/Aids and women's health issues. The TUC recognized health promotion in the workplace as extremely important and welcomes a joint initiative involving themselves, government, employers, the NHS and the HEA. It suggests a practical pilot project to establish the levels of stress in department stores.

The Health and Safety Executive (HSE) exists to assist and encourage those responsible for providing and maintaining health and safety at work. The process of protecting people at work has direct application for promoting health at work. The experience of the HSE in promoting behavioural changes in industry should reduce risks. The HSE particularly emphasize the need to ensure the commitment of both employer and employee in health promotion enterprises.

Another approach in collating the evidence for becoming a healthy company is to see how the employees benefit. Most report statements such as feeling 'better', 'fitter' or 'happier' as a result of workplace health promotion. Mobil North Seal and Kelloggs have detected lower absence levels with the latter also showing an improved safety performance. Lower absence levels have also been reported by Gallagher (NI), Sheffield City Council, ICL (Kidsgrove) and Exxon Chemicals. Some companies have not been able to differentiate the health promotion activities from secular change as a cause of lower absence levels. A company like Inmos started with an absence level well below the national average and therefore would not expect to see any major changes. Cammell Laird, the former shipbuilders in Birkenhead, attempted to reduce their insurance premiums by quantifying the improved working conditions as a result of workplace health promotion.

The response of the employees to health promotion activities is a good index of success. Most organizations that have been surveyed have reported a very positive response from their employees. Unipart (Cowley), Michelin Tyres (Stoke), National Nuclear Corporation and Findus (UK) are all companies who reported a 'good' response from staff. Health initiatives were described as 'massively popular' by Mobil North Sea and as 'excellent' at ICL (Kidsgrove). Novelty value was the attraction of health promotion at the London and Manchester Group, whereas the opportunity to attend smoking-cessation classes appealed to Lubrizol employees.

7.2   Planning Principles

To conduct health promotion in the workplace in a constructive manner requires careful planning. The major phases are as follows:

- identifying the need
- gathering supportive evidence
- commitment and consultation
- establishing the structure
- planning the programme
- promotion, training and maintenance
- evaluation and feedback

Each of these phases will now be considered in more detail.

Identifying the Need

The starting point will be a view that health matters at work. The evidence of the previous section, combined with a knowledge of the benefits to the workforce and the cost of ill health, will lead those that influence decisions in a company to agree to take action. Note the phrase 'those that influence decisions' because it does not always have to be management. Influence may originate from occupational health, trade unions or the only employee concerned about aspects of health. Ideally health initiatives should be both top-down and bottom-up enabling joint ownership by the whole organization. It is important for maximum benefit not to adopt indiscriminate approaches. The tactics must be sensitive to the organization and the people employed there. It is desirable to create a mission statement concerned with health promotion which would be a blue print for the rest of the strategy.

Gathering Supportive Evidence

This will involve obtaining records of absenteeism, sickness, accidents, personnel information and medical records prior to the programme being established. It may involve gathering material from different sections of the company or reviewing the literature for information to mount a convincing argument.

Commitment and Consultation

It is vital to gain a commitment from the management to any proposed health programme. As most employers in industry are motivated by profit this may be the approach to take by linking absenteeism with financial cost. The cost in a non-industrial organization such as a hospital would be measured not in terms of profit but replacement of staff. It is also essential to gain the commitment from personnel, from those involved in training and line managers. This will require consultation with many staff, especially trade unions. A very important aspect of commitment and indeed consultation is the workforce.

Many of the activities will be voluntary in nature and it is essential to have a workforce who wish to support the proposed programme. Without it a biased sample of the workforce may become involved and the wrong people may benefit.

A very important aspect of commitment is funding. A business plan needs to be established to show the true costs, the possible revenue and what is expected of management to establish the programme.

Establishing the Structure

This involves the policies to be adopted, the way the programme will fit in with the overall company objectives and key personnel such as the coordinator. Revisions have to be made as to whether the programme will be run in-house or whether external consultants be appointed.

Planning the Programme

The starting point for this could be a needs assessment of the workforce based on a survey analysis. There is little point in planning smoking cessation classes if no one considers this useful and will therefore not attend. For each section of the programme the specific goals and objectives need to be established. The programme will then be planned in detail including the times and places to be used, the resources, the staff and paperwork. The latter will include the production of informed consent forms, pro forma for recording any test results and promotional literature. It may be necessary to obtain resources from the local community, the health education authority or local and regional health authorities.

Staff may need to be employed, trained or motivated to work in a different way than they had previously. A steering group or management committee may be necessary to oversee the operation and maintain continuity. A facility may need to be developed using existing rooms, as a result of conversion or by building new accommodation.

The content of the health promotion programme will depend on the needs of the company or organization. The following is a list of popular activities to be considered. It does not include all options, many of which could be unique to the needs of the workplace.

- films and videos
- displays of exercise clothing
- poster displays
- fitness testing
- health screening
- hazard appraisal
- individual counselling
- seminars and workshops
- special features such as 'nutrition month'
- health education literature
- newsletters
- bulletins
- exercise breaks
- educational campaigns on specific topics, e.g. HIV/Aids awareness

- exercise classes, e.g. aerobics
- special events, e.g. family fun runs
- relaxation classes
- smoking cessation classes
- back clinic
- nutrition and diet counselling
- cardio-pulmonary resuscitation classes
- yoga classes
- home exercise instruction
- weight loss challenge
- sporting weekend
- circuit or weight training
- stress reduction advice
- health promotion resource centre
- injury rehabilitation clinic
- guest speakers
- breast self-examination classes
- water safety week
- smoking and other policies
- healthy eating promotion in canteens
- provision of changing facilities
- cycle storage area
- low-alcohol option in bars

Promotion, Training and Maintenance

Promotional strategies are needed before the programme starts and should continue throughout. This can be divided into the three areas of awareness, education and motivation with the following aspects and suggestions as applicable:

Awareness

- presentations to supervisors and workers
- needs inventories and assessments
- creation of an advisory group
- recruitment of volunteer leaders
- poster and bulletin distribution
- articles in the company newsletter

Education

- distribution of literature
- special programme-related newsletters
- monthly lifestyle and fitness themes
- videos and speakers

Motivation

- contests (e.g. designing a logo)
- special events (e.g. facility opening)
- challenges (e.g. weight loss)
- appraisals and counselling

Training will be ongoing as various aspects of the programme develop. It may involve training in special skills to do with health promotion such as blood cholesterol measurement, in data handling or in areas such as counselling. The compliance rate in many health promotion programmes is poor so special attention needs to be given to maintenance of employee interest. This is often concerned with the relationships established between staff and clients, between groups who come together for a specific part of the programme and the degree of support given by line managers. Maintenance also applies to the facility and the equipment within it. Machines need to be kept working and stocks of supplies have to be optimal.

Evaluation and Feedback

It is essential to evaluate all aspects of the programme. This is often omitted which means that no evidence is available to measure the impact, assess the cost and therefore determine its worth. Evaluation can operate at a number of levels. A one-off event such as a family fun run can be evaluated on the basis of entries, enjoyment and other forms of immediate feedback. A cholesterol screening and advice programme may involve assessing the change in levels after a period of time. Absenteeism and sickness rates will need to ensure that no confounding variables such as time of year are introduced.

Feedback also operates at a number of levels. The employee for whom the programme is targeted is probably the most important recipient of feedback. This may be obvious if the health-promoting action was direct, such as the provision of an anti-glare VDU screen. However the outcome in relation to the original objectives may be less obvious but should be explained to all involved. Feedback on specific physiological measures is essential not only for peace of mind but so remedial advice can be provided. The management and trade unions will expect feedback and it should be provided regularly and appropriately. Positive messages need to be highlighted but honest conclusions reached with a full appraisal of limitations and errors.

7.3   The Well-Being Company

Wellness or well-being is a relatively recent term outside the USA. Some of the principles of becoming a wellness or well-being company overlap with those described earlier but the overall approach is sufficiently distinct to merit further explanation. Ten stages will be considered which provide an insight into the approach of certain North American companies and may transfer elsewhere.

A well-being company (WBC) is an organization that is 'consciously structured to support the maximum health and development of its employees and backs that commitment in every possible way. It supports personal health initiatives with on-the-job training in lifestyle issues'.

The following ten strategies demonstrate how to become a well-being company. As the ideas have been taken from North American literature they may not always be familiar to European work practices but nevertheless are worth serious consideration.

Strategy One – Proactive Health Promotion

Many companies mean by health promotion little more than disease treatment, problem solution, risk reduction and cost containment. These defensive steps are designed to prevent things getting worse but lack the proactive approach needed to create complete wellness. Strategy one requires a separation of defensive aspects from the more ambitious approach of active health promotion.

This requires every employee to be given a foundation knowledge base. The following perceptions and skills will be included in that base:

● a perception of health as a dynamic condition which can change for the better. It is not simply the absence of ill health. It is worth making the effort to achieve the difference

- an awareness of a personal wellness profile to include such things as body fat, cholesterol, resting heart rates, etc.
- an appreciation of developing a strong personal responsibility for wellness. This is essential for physical and psychological health status as well as other areas of life
- to recognize the values and limits of conventional medicine. The benefits of modern medicine are vast, but people can expect too much of it and too little of themselves
- a knowledge of group pressures and customs. Current standards or norms powerfully affect behaviour. A WBC should have norms which are consistent with wellness lifestyles
- a disciplined commitment to eat nutritious and healthy food which means the company must provide healthier options
- to understand stress management through training and the encouragement of management and colleagues. To deal with stress in a creative and constructive manner
- an enthusiasm to pursue personal standards of excellence in physical fitness
- to provide acceptance and opportunities for spiritual fitness. This could encompass a belief system in the form of organized religion or a philosophy based on personal experience.
- an explicit policy to provide support for a written personal 'business plan for wellness'. Such plans would be modified and updated and could be included in the assessment process. Company resources will need to support personal goals (e.g. special leave, assignments, training, etc.)

Strategy Two – Cost Reduction

The benefits of a WBC should not only be personal but also financial. The company should be examining such aspects as lower insurance premiums, reduced need for private medical insurance, switching from expensive illness costs to investing in preventative medicine. Health economies should be examined and linked to improved profitability or reduced wages costs due to less absenteeism.

Strategy Three – Systematic Programming

Avoid confusion over wellness. Employees fail to see the link between *ad hoc* activities such as aerobic dance, stress counselling, blood cholesterol measurement, etc. Continue to provide choices but encourage a wellness framework so staff can appreciate the total picture. Encourage inventiveness linked to cohesion.

Strategy Four – Poor Health Habits

Identify company practices and policies which reinforce mediocre or poor health habits. Once these are identified and understood use support teams to make wellness behaviour the more acceptable option. It should not be difficult to take the healthy option.

Strategy Five – Management Support

Convince the senior management that WBC is the platform for success. Without their support it will lack credibility, vitality and have little prospect of full implementation. Inactive support will rarely achieve a healthy workforce dedicated to personal and organizational excellence.

Strategy Six – Developing the Goal

A written description of the overall WBC goal must be produced with the active involvement of representatives throughout the company. The plan should have three parts: (1) getting started (2) the next five years and (3) beyond attaining WBC status. All employees should have the opportunity to contribute to the plans.

Strategy Seven – Facility Provision

Provision of facilities or gaining access to them is symbolic of the company's wellness programme. It will assist employees to pursue their fitness goals. Most companies or organizations have a large capital expenditure and some of this should be used to keep staff in good working order. For some companies memberships of local facilities may be the solution but active participation in the wellness programme would be the requirement of membership.

Strategy Eight – Wellness Graduation

Encourage each employee to strive to become a 'wellness graduate'. A 'wellness graduate' signifies a commitment to personal and organizational excellence beyond the level of 'good enough'. Decisions on reaching this status is personal not externally judged. In the WBC environment most people will have graduated. Qualities associated with a 'wellness graduate' are:

- comfortable with risks
- tolerant of uncertainty
- committed to excellence
- clarity of purpose
- high energy levels
- a balanced lifestyle
- committed to solutions not excuses
- oriented to action
- open to change
- dedicated to high physical condition
- optimism, confidence and being alert
- skilled in communication and leadership, resolving conflicts and team building, motivation and consolidation

WBC employees could not possibly achieve all these aspirations consistently. What is needed is a respect and appreciation for these qualities. If a person considers that these qualities are worthy, feasible and consistent with a wellness lifestyle then he/she is effectively a 'wellness graduate'.

Strategy Nine – Steady Progress

Becoming a WBC is not instantaneous. It is important to recognize that a solid base of achievement will come with incremental progression. Start with establishing the ethic of a WBC by convincing the workforce of the economic and social logic of this approach. A community which recognizes that caring for each other is valid will continue to succeed. Once the ethic is appreciated and accepted then the planning, execution, evaluation and modification can follow. Keep WBC in perspective. Although important, it is not the only or even main company motive. A positive association between the WBC approach and other company motives such as profitability will be essential. Recognize the risks of the WBC approach. Doing nothing and mediocrity are both inherently safe. However such a strategy is transient and doing nothing will soon generate other risks. The WBC approach needs cooperation, courage and commitment.

Strategy Ten – Reward Wellness

Appoint and promote those with a commitment to personal excellence. The goals and purposes of WBC will not survive without the right people in the organization. Qualifications for a job in a WBC is broader than elsewhere. This will be controversial and clearly is situational dependent. However *all other things being equal* a WBC will not hesitate to appoint people who will fit in with the new found ethos of the organization. It would be ridiculous to suggest that staff who have been relentlessly committed to self-destruction for decades can be converted on the basis of a few speeches, free T-shirts and the other paraphernalia of some styles of health promotion. This does not stop positive reinforcement being given selectivity to those who support the company policy. I have no hesitation in selecting non-smoking staff and students to my department. I believe the well-being of all is consistent with that policy.

7.4   Resources

The resources for becoming a health company include:

- local and regional health promotion units
- documentation and visual aids
- further and higher education institutes
- local authority provision
- sponsorship

Local and Regional Health Promotion Units

Most local or regional health authorities have some form of health promotion unit or the equivalent. Staff from these may be willing to become involved in workplace health promotion. They may charge a fee, especially if linked to a hospital with trust status. However they do have their own resource base which they are often willing to lend or hire. Most will be very keen to give advice and provide contacts with other professionals to provide assistance.

Documentation and Visual Aids

The main sources of documentation (often free) are the Health Education Authority (HEA), the Health and Safety Executive (HSE) and the British Heart Foundation (BHF).

The addresses of these organizations and other useful sources of documentation and visual aids are found in Appendix 7.

The range of pamphlets available include such titles as:

- Exercise. Why Bother? (HEA)
- Five steps to successful health and safety management (HSE)
- Five steps to risk assessment (HSE)
- 101 tips to safer business (HSE)
- Action on health at work (HEA)
- Working for a healthier future (HEA)
- Action on stress at work (HEA)
- Heart information series (BHF)
- Exercise for life (BHF)

It is also possible to get wallcharts, videofilms and other visual media from the above organizations. Many professional journals such as Occupational Health Review carry regular articles on aspects of health promotion at work.

Further and Higher Education Institutes

Colleges of further education, colleges of higher education and universities often have departments concerned with aspects of health promotion. They operate under different names such as health sciences, public health, physical education and movement studies. Many will have staff concerned with health, even if not specifically concerned with the workplace. Some of these departments may have research interests in health promotion at work and therefore have students who will be available to assist. Others may have students they wish to place for work experience and can spend some time in a company examining aspects of health promotion or provision. Some institutes may also hire facilities when not used by students.

Local Authority Provision

Every local authority has a department of sport and recreation responsible for providing facilities and services for the community. Some have expanded into health and fitness profiling. Contact with local authorities may reveal that they are prepared to work closer with industry. Examples may be the provision of facilities at off-peak times at reduced cost, organization of events and exercise testing.

Sponsorship

Some companies may find others willing to sponsor certain sectors of health provision such as games kit, special events or printing. Pharmaceutical or instrument companies may lend specialist equipment for a limited period of time in the anticipation of an eventual sale. More commonly a company will be asked to sponsor an activity associated with health promotion. This can provide a very positive message of support to the local community and raise the profile of a company in an area which is becoming of much more value to the whole population.

7.5   Company Size and Structure

The size of the company does make a difference to the approach that can be taken, although the planning principles described in section 7.1 are all relevant. A company of say 50 employees is unlikely to have its own occupational health department but may still have a company ethos which is concerned with a healthy workplace. Similarly it is unlikely that a small business will have the resources to provide an on-site exercise facility so may need to look elsewhere.

Small Businesses

A minimum objective for small businesses is to develop awareness of health promotion resources and the risks to personal health. Subsidized membership of local health-promoting facilities is a practical step. Fitness evaluation following by introductions to local community facilities is a way to become involved. Local professionals could be invited to the premises to talk to staff. Reference could be made to other examples at similar sized companies. The local chamber of commerce may well be interested in giving support. With small companies it will be necessary to network with others to maximise benefits. A group occupational health service could be supported by a range of companies. An excellent idea from the CBI was to establish 'occupational health surgeries' based on industrial estates, business parks or small towns. Access to facilities available in large companies could also be considered.

Many small businesses might consider employing a health and safety consultancy. An excellent booklet is available from the Health and Safety Executive entitled *Selecting a health and safety consultancy*. It has sections on:

- why health and safety is important to business
- when to use a consultancy
- what can a consultancy do?
- how to choose the right consultancy
- how do you judge performance?
- after the consultancy has gone
- the legal position

Larger companies have the benefits of economies of scale but cannot always take actions as quickly as smaller companies. Normally occupational health staff will be available for health promotion initiatives. It is critical to involve management, unions and all sectors of the workforce in planning. If it is possible to provide an exclusive exercise facility, it is important to plan for peak participation of 9–11 square metres per person. Two-thirds of the space should be allocated for group exercise and one-third for showers and changing rooms. Successful fitness programmes in large firms have 35–60 per cent employee participation. About 40 per cent will use an exercise facility on the busiest days with 60 per cent of daily use occurring during a two hour peak period. Thus participation at peak hours could be as high as 24 per cent of the workforce.

Large Educational Institutions

Most universities and colleges have recreation, occupational health and student health services. They also have suitable rooms and halls for promotional activities and counselling services. They should have expertise in a whole range of health-promotion activities and be more conducive to receiving health messages as they operate within an educational environment. Contact with relevant professional groups is the starting point and from this a health-promotion coordinator should be appointed. A team to plan and coordinate action can be formed which will represent personnel, welfare, safety, the students union, the chaplaincy and health and safety staff. The customers will need to be consulted to establish the need. As the educational standard will be high it means that surveys, computer packages and questionnaires may be easier to administer. Most institutions will be able to assist with generating new resources. Students may be available to assist the programme either as part of their courses or in a voluntary capacity.

Public Sector Organizations

As an example of a public sector organization, the NHS will be considered. This section is based on the action pack *Health at work in the NHS* which is fully acknowledged.

Health at work in the NHS plans to:

- 'introduce a systematic health-workplace programme throughout the NHS, incorporating health and safety issues, occupational health issues and health promotion'
- 'engage all NHS staff in health education and health promotion'

It will achieve this by building on existing activities and schemes and by developing long-term strategies related to the needs of the employees. Unit managers will be expected to demonstrate their involvement. It has an action programme summarized as follows:

- awareness-raising and provision of healthy living information to all staff
- establish a comprehensive smoking policy
- provide healthy food options
- promote sensible drinking and support for problem drinkers
- introduce physical-activity programmes
- identify and reduce sources of stress
- encourage positive attitudes to sexual issues including HIV/Aids policies
- provide health checks
- ensure products and practices are environmentally sound

- review health, hygiene and safety practices
- manage and monitor positive health practices
- design a training strategy to support health initiatives and reinforce health-promoting behaviour

This overall policy for the NHS is exemplary in principle. The practice will depend on the operational units which will range from large teaching hospitals to a small residential unit or health centre. Already some examples of good practice are evident but the eventual success will depend on the commitment of key staff and the finances made available.

7.6   Case Studies

In this section a selection of case studies will illustrate how individual companies or organizations have attempted to become healthier. As many of the strategies and initiatives will be similar, the bullet points will attempt to highlight special features of each case. When an organization is named, it must be emphasized that the bullet points will not represent *all* activities being undertaken.

A General Hospital

- review of all contracts to ensure specifications covering health and safety issues are included
- comprehensive HIV/Aids and sexual-health programme
- prohibition of sale of tobacco products on hospital premises
- food policy ensures healthy choices are available on all shifts
- lower-cost, low-alcohol and alcohol-free choices in staff social clubs
- best-practice advice for manual tasks given by occupational health department
- counselling for bereavement, workplace stress and organizational change
- robust evaluation for all staff health initiatives

A Health Centre

- health information displayed prominently and regularly updated
- health-at-work issues included in staff meetings
- flexible working hours to meet staff needs

- semi-skimmed milk and mineral water available with other beverages
- promotion of infectious-control procedures
- sponsored 'Walk to Work' week organized

A Residential Unit (NHS)

- subsidized membership of local health and fitness club
- exercise classes for staff and residents
- caterers contracts specify healthy food choices and nutritional needs
- safe-lifting and relaxation training
- regular events like health fairs
- environmentally-friendly materials and cleaning fluids encouraged
- free access to local music college concerts
- cycle storage and trim trails in grounds
- provision of special leave and counselling away from the workplace

Health Authority HQ

- positive health messages regularly conveyed to staff
- in-house magazine promotes positive health
- health information pack used in induction process for new staff
- price incentives for healthy food choices
- all-staff health group to develop health initiatives
- health-screening appointments attending during paid time
- poster displays recommending the use of stairs rather than lifts

National Westminster Bank

- five-yearly lifestyle health screening for over 40s
- women are taught breast self-examination
- men are taught testicular self-examination
- prevention of post-traumatic stress disorder using self-help groups immediately following bank raids
- telephone helpline for confidential counselling service
- quantity and quality audit by occupational health staff
- manual handling and display screen EC directives acted upon
- nationwide coordinated health-promotion programme planned
- analysis of causes of sickness and absence

Somerset Health Authority

- lifestyle activities, especially CHD, breast cancer, HIV/Aids and back care
- developing service for small businesses based on business parks or trading estates by using health visitors
- promoting health at work through a holistic approach
- promotion of the Heartbeat Award

Rowntree Mackintosh

- established 'whole body health' policy
- screening programme conducted by occupational health nurses
- immediate counselling sessions to discuss particular problems
- Weight Watchers involved at York plant with 50 per cent cost borne by company
- fitness centre built which is staffed by physiotherapists

Shell Expro

- Lifestyle programme allows contractors, employees and their families to take part in a number of activities to increase health and safety awareness
- aim is to encourage each individual to assume responsibility for their own family's lifestyle and safety
- free fitness testing, home-safety checks and driving instruction
- incentives to encourage continued participation, e.g. trip to Tokyo for winner of 'Safedrive' competition

Cheshire Constabulary

- medical screening and fitness testing for pre-employment and over 40s on a regular basis
- training in stress management and recognition
- self-referral confidential counselling
- now has lowest sickness absence and ill-health retirement of any North West force

Mobil Oil Company

- production of a lifestyle assessment programme (LAP)
- LAP addresses social and workplace health through a holistic approach
- LAP offered to young employees to encourage early lifestyle changes
- LAP presented attractively and informatively
- production of 'Passport to Health' filofax
- widespread company locations required production of Mobil *Health Matters* magazine
- occupational health staff proficient in desk-top publishing and graphics packages to produce in-house health-promotion material

Wicks and Wilson's Smoking Ban

- decided not to employ new staff who smoked at work
- staff newsletter indicated plans for a 'no smoking' company
- gradual process over four to five years
- concern over liability re passive smoking
- payment for medical help in smoking cessation
- claim for constructive dismissal before an industrial tribunal by an ex employee failed
- clear ruling over smoking inside and outside premises required

Midland Bank Wales

- full-scale review of company's cover from private medical insurer
- used consultancy Well Welsh to provide positive lifestyle messages to all employees over 35
- personal charts and regional profile established

Birmingham City Council

- target for blue collar absenteeism down to five per cent of days worked; white collar to three per cent
- reduce everything to small units where the manager is personally in touch
- every absence, even for one day, must generate a management response
- if someone is ill the management must at least enquire about their health

- aim to make people loyal to their team

Johnson and Johnson

- 'Live for life' programme since 1979
- significant reductions in absenteeism due to sickness
- good evidence that health initiatives have resulted in a major reduction in risk factors

Blue Cross and Blue Shield

- 'stay alive and well' programme since 1978
- by 1986, 2100 out of 2500 employees have participated in the programme
- lifestyle changes, monitored over a five-year period, appeared to be permanent

IBM United Kingdom

- good safety record linked to company's highly formalized management system
- employer-sponsored health-screening scheme for the benefit of all the company's employees
- operated by an outside contractor (BUPA)
- individuals have the primary responsibility for their personal health
- cholesterol levels were identified as too high across the whole company
- programme probably saved lives – two staff underwent cardiac by-pass surgery within a few days of participating in screening
- several mini gymnasia were constructed
- graduate nurse and nutritionist employed to introduce aspects of health education
- nutrition policy drafted with standards to be achieved by contract caterers

Polaroid

- groundwork based on series of 'health weeks'
- 87 per cent of workforce had a full health screening

- individual results sent to employee's GP
- high-fibre and low-fat meals added to canteen options
- food colour-coded for healthiness
- dietary advice intervention caused significant drop in cholesterol levels
- improvements largely maintained after several months
- cost of screening procedures and results achieved could be reproduced elsewhere at £15 per person for similar size organization
- second phase is community-based
- urban aid and Scottish HE Group have funded community phase

Barclays Bank

- sponsored 'Breath of life' campaign which offers free basic first aid training in several vital life preservation techniques
- sponsored 'Inspire a child for life' campaign which encourages children aged three to 15 to be aware of their bodies as part of drug education
- ban on smoking in all premises nationwide

Ecover

- produces a range of environmentally-friendly liquid soaps
- factory costs were twice normal but built to protect the environment
- wooden structure is from sustainable forest; rubber matting is recyclable; bricks from coal slag heaps; polycarbonate windows not glass
- better worker environment has given lower staff turnover
- travel allowance is three times higher for cyclist than those who drive
- big-engined cars get no allowance

Hillingdon Hospital NHS Trust

- routine tests for legionnella – staff advised and responsibilities clarified by managers
- every effort made to match jobs to employees, e.g. staff with diabetes or epilepsy are rostered on day shifts if possible
- health and safety issues described at staff induction course
- free monthly chiropody clinic for staff
- alcohol consumption forbidden

- stress-management workshops planned
- range of services may be purchased on a contract basis by outside companies from occupational health

Wandsworth Borough Council

- structured approach to monitoring sick-leave absence. Trigger points correspond to a specific review procedure
- computerized records enable fast response
- training and target setting for managers were identified as key areas for action

Michelin Tyre PLC

- line managers given designated responsibilities for dealing with unacceptable absence
- management action needed on performance reviews, face-to-face counselling and monitoring of absence patterns
- flow chart used for management action on problematic attendance
- attendance-related sick pay entitlement introduced

CT Bowring

- health poster displays changed weekly
- external health professionals give a monthly talk
- active participation in national health promotion days (e.g. Drink-wise)
- smoking-cessation support group established
- Flora's 'Health heart risk assessment computer' used for eight weeks annually
- open-door policy for blood pressure checks and counselling
- demonstration that a low-cost project can still be valuable

Granada (UK) Rental and Retail Limited

- section on lifting in health and safety guide
- induction training covers lifting demonstration
- all employees receive training on avoiding back problems
- alterations made as a result of back problems to work patterns and seating

- provision of two person lifts on larger equipment, trolleys and posture chairs

Halton Health Authority

- written policy and guidelines on lifting
- training period on manual handling of loads, working posture and avoiding back problems
- screening of all staff following an accident or complaint
- alterations made to employees clothing as a result of back problems
- nurses uniforms assessed on a two-year basis to ensure adequate freedom of movement

8

'Look After Your Heart' Workplace Initiatives

8.1 Introduction

The Look After Your Heart (LAYH) programme is jointly funded by the Department of Health and the Health Education Authority. As its name implies it is concerned with action to prevent CHD in England. LAYH provides information for the public to act upon CHD. It does this by utilizing existing opportunities concentrating on *The Health of the Nation* targets to reduce CHD and stroke.

LAYH is involved in a range of local projects. Some of these are long-term projects which include work with ethnic minority groups, community development and local media. Each health region was also supported by providing funds for smaller projects.

There are also national promotional activities sponsored by LAYH. In 1992 there was an 'Enjoy Healthy Eating' campaign throughout the month of September. This encourages people to eat more high-fibre starchy foods. The approach was to influence people by the distribution of over five million leaflets through local health promotion units, through members of the Good Trade Association and in conjunction with 10 of the largest food retail outlets.

Physical fitness is also an important component of the LAYH programme. It was the theme of an 'LAYH Take Part' event held in Birmingham in 1992.

One of its most successful initiatives has been the LAYH Workplace programme. This now promotes the full range of the HEA's activities including advice on smoking, alcohol and Aids/HIV in addition to its CHD prevention work. The LAYH Workplace programme had 653 employers (almost four million employees) by January 1st 1992 and by the end of the year the number of employers had risen to 835. These include local companies, national companies, government departments, local authorities, regional and district health authorities, family health service authorities and police authorities.

Another scheme within LAYH is the Heartbeat Awards. These are given to catering establishments that can demonstrate healthy food choices, smoke-free areas and food hygiene training for staff. The HEA is developing national initiatives with larger catering organizations. However the majority of the scheme is locally based. Awards are implemented by local teams comprising environmental health officers, health promotion officers and dieticians.

8.2   The LAYH Workplace Project

The normal starting point is that the HEA contacts employers through mailings, through occupational health departments, at exhibitions and conferences. Senior management are invited to make a commitment to the LAYH project and they will receive encouragement to become active. The efforts of the organization are monitored regularly.

The key action is to sign the LAYH charter. The basis of this is an agreement to adopt at least three of the ten points listed opposite:

Having undertaken to implement three of the above points, the others should be addressed later. All organizations are supported and encouraged by a core team of HEA Workplace officers. There are also 14 regional LAYH Workplace officers based within regional health authorities.

All organizations identify a named contact for daily matters and long-term planning. The person identified will normally need clerical or secretarial support to administer the programme successfully. Allocation of staff time has to be considered carefully to anticipate a successful outcome.

Having appointed a suitable coordinator it is recommended that a steering group is established. This will identify objectives, plan and supervise the workplace initiatives. The steering group would be expected to provide information on CHD prevention, to change attitudes and behaviour by workplace interventions and to develop health promotion policies and practices.

The objectives of the proposed programme would involve senior management. It should be decided which topic areas to undertake first

The LAYH 10-point plan

Employers are encouraged to:

- Provide staff with information about LAYH and healthy living

- Provide more smoke-free areas and develop a smoking policy

- Provide and promote healthy choices of food and develop a food policy

- Introduce physical activity programmes

- Promote sensible drinking and develop an alcohol policy

- Identify sources of stress and improve support for employees

- Increase opportunities for all staff to have health checks and follow up

- Use LAYH: LAY Workplace services as appropriate to help put across health messages

- Adopt management practices to provide staff with a healthy working environment

- Explore with the HEA opportunities to promote health products and services

Source: Health Education Authority

and which to cover later. Some existing activities may be consistent with the LAYH project. The depth of each project must be decided as must be the number of employees to be targeted. Finally a budget must be allocated consistent with the proposals of the steering group.

The LAYH Workplace project at a national level is evaluated regularly. One such evaluation involved analysing responses to a questionnaire sent to 469 organizations. In addition to receiving information about the project, LAYH workplace officers acted upon any issue highlighted in the responses as part of their follow-up visits to companies.

The outcome of the evaluation is summarized below by a series of bullet points for each of the most common activities undertaken. All percentage figures are based on those who responded.

Information about LAYH and Healthy Living

- most popular activity – 92 per cent involvement
- noticeboards mainly used
- leaflet distribution common – often with wage packet
- often supplied as part of induction procedure
- exhibitions and displays more common in health and local authorities
- messages conveyed by media or 'by word of mouth'
- screening and medicals show biggest difference between public and private sector
- in private sector, the medical is a powerful medium of communication
- in public sector, occupational health is used more commonly and less proactively

Nutrition and Healthy Eating

- main activity is provision of health food choices in staff canteens (69 per cent)
- dishes labelled, with health authority commonly using the 'traffic light' system
- some consider vegetarian choices a priority, but possible confusion over low-fat options
- promotion is less popular than provision
- public sector more concerned with policy
- private sector used more informal methods

In-house Newspapers

- 67 per cent used this approach to promote healthy messages
- some have a regular health section or feature articles in company magazines
- special events are promoted in this way
- large companies have articles written by their chief medical officer
- little difference between public and private sectors

Smoking

- 65 per cent involved in development of no-smoking policies
- wide variation in policies
- decisions reflect the consensus of opinion
- implementation was cited as a problem

Health and Fitness Screening

- 63 per cent of employers involved
- great variation on the type and the staff offered checks
- most claim that available on demand from occupational health staff
- evidence of discrimination (age, seniority, risk)
- more advice required in this area especially to ensure *all* staff benefit
- cost and site dispersal noted as constraints

Promotion of Physical Activity

- 53 per cent are promoting physical activity
- wide range recorded from in-house gymnasia and subsidized memberships to information on local facilities
- lunch hour or immediately after work is most popular time
- no difference in public and private sector
- increasing interest in this area, especially the provision of facilities and other opportunities

Stress Management

- 32 per cent involved in programmes on stress management
- courses and counselling most common
- provided preferentially to managers, but some companies plan to 'cascade down' to junior staff
- some offer special classes such as post-trauma counselling
- private companies tend to provide for senior staff whereas public sector tend to offer stress counselling for all staff on request
- low interest may be related to problem considered to be too complex

Alcohol Policies

- Only 27 per cent worked in this area

- emphasis varies from 'sensible drinking' to total ban
- few employers aim to raise levels of awareness

8.3   The Heartbeat Award

The Heartbeat Award as stated earlier is to encourage caterers to offer healthy choices, environment and standards. The award of a certificate informs the customer that at least one third of dishes on the menu are healthy choices; the seating area is non-smoking; food-handling staff have received training in hygiene. A booklet produced by the HEA and called *A guide to the heartbeat award* gives information on:

- healthy food choices
- fat
- fibre-rich starchy foods
- sugar
- salt
- marketing healthy eating
- introducing your new menu selection
- setting up a non-smoking area
- guidance on standards of hygiene
- useful addresses for further information

Within these sections it explains the place of the various foods within menus and during cooking and preparation.

For companies who wish to become involved in a healthier workplace this serves as an ideal model initiative for those who have canteens or restaurants. A further publication from the HEA called *Managing the heartbeat award* recognized the concerns and circumstances of local communities. It shows how the Heartbeat Award can be managed and operates by collaborative working groups in each local area. The booklet gives advice on the following topics:

- setting up a local group
- forming a consortium
- gaining approval from local or health authorities
- planning a strategy for implementing and administering the award
- monitoring and evaluating Heartbeat Award activity
- obtaining resource material
- using the media

It is not essential to extend the scheme beyond the company's own catering premises and the merits of doing so would need to be considered carefully. It will often depend on the extent to which a company is confident to operate independently or would welcome the resources available from further afield.

8.4 Resources

Support for the LAYH Workplace project is often provided by the regional health authority. Mersey Regional Health Authority has established a communication network for all signatories and produces a regular newsletter. In addition the authority holds regular meetings to discuss how organizations can take their LAYH activities forward. One-day training workshops covering issues such as implementing a smoking policy and developing stress management programmes are also offered to suit demand.

The topics covered in the newsletter include:

- promoting special events
- book reviews
- action pack reviews
- video reviews
- reporting recent signatories
- advertising educational and activity courses and conferences
- health messages
- offers of assistance
- information on provision of conference notes
- access to training materials
- useful phone numbers
- illustrative figures, graphs and photographs
- updates on research and occupational health
- facts and figures

The main source of resource material for the LAYH workplace project is the Health Education Authority. This includes display packs, training resources, acetates, merchandise and other publicity materials. The Look After Your Heart/Look After Yourself consortium can also provide tutors for national exhibitions, small exhibitions, seminars, workshops and workplace programmes. The fees are dependent on the physical and human resources required.

A number of leaflets produced to a high standard are available as workplace action plans. These include clear guidelines on sensible drinking, healthy eating, physical activities and stress. They differ in content but provide direct and realistic suggestions. The LAYH wallcharts and accompanying documentation are colourful and effective. One example is the 'S factor' fitness chart which illustrates a range of activities for suppleness, strength and stamina. An accompanying personal physical activity and exercise record card is useful to guide the participant to record the essential information for each exercise session.

Other pamphlets from the HEA include a series more closely linked to the Heartbeat Award. Topics include fat, sugar, fruit and vegetables, starch and fibre, and healthy eating. They all contain clear information and practical suggestions.

Many larger companies produce their own resources using either 'cut and paste', photocopying, offset litho or desk-top publishing. Some incorporate national or company logos and others will have special initiatives printed in colour to improve impact. An example of this is a scheme devised at the Speke (Liverpool) factory of Glaxo. This scheme gives exercise points for a variety of activities. Rather like air miles the exercise points accumulate and when specified worldwide destinations have been reached the participant is awarded a prize such as a sports towel or sports bag. Each 'tour' must include a fitness assessment which is arranged with the occupational health centre.

A variety of additional resources which could contribute to the LAYH Workplace project are available either freely or for a small charge from the addresses given in Appendix 7. The coordinator of the scheme within the company or organization would be advised to start by contacting the regional organizer who is likely to have reasonable stocks.

8.5   Case Studies

Case studies provide a valuable insight into the way different companies approach the LAYH Workplace project. A number of the activities will be common, so to avoid repetition the following lists do not necessarily include all the initiatives specified by a given company or organization.

Glaxo Pharmaceuticals UK Ltd

- signed LAYH charter in 1988
- cholesterol screening with follow up advice
- staff identified prescriptive advice on weight loss and exercise
- healthy eating, no smoking, drinkwise campaigns
- smoking cessation classes including use of nicotine patches
- purchase of fitness-testing equipment with software support
- small fitness centre available
- weekly aerobic step classes offered
- subsidized use of local authority leisure centres
- 'health manager' medical check provides individual computer print-out
- statistical analysis of fitness results available

Urenco (Capenhurst) Limited

- annual medical includes vision screening
- audiometry screening every three years for employees working in designated noise areas
- 18 parameter blood test
- counselling offered to employees suffering from stress
- frequency of health-related medical surveillance varies with age. Greater frequency given in fifth decade as this is considered the best time for corrective action
- gamma GT measured to indicate liver damage
- all results compared with norms and a programme of exercise and diet produced when required

Cheshire County Council

- with Cheshire Constabulary were the first local authority and police force to sign LAYH campaign
- advice and alternative healthy diets promoted through 'Cheshire Restaurants' throughout the county
- targeting is related to the nature of work, e.g. full medicals for waste-disposal operatives and fitness testing for fire officers
- total ban on smoking within county council establishments from July 1994
- finance and management services published LAYH bulletins

- stress awareness and coping skills are taught through regular lectures to groups of employees throughout the county council
- medical unit provides post-trauma debriefing for police and social services
- personnel and occupational health policy published on Aids/HIV
- 14-point 'self-audit' approach for managers to assess accident risks at work
- a series of cards have been commissioned to give advice on appropriate workplace exercises

British Rail

- LAYH exhibitions used in strategy to reduce short-term absences by 25 per cent
- guarantee of help for alcohol problems providing it is declared before imminent disciplinary action
- revised alcohol policy explained to employees via a cascade briefing exercise which included a video
- response to manual handling directive was to produce a training package which would meet the regulations but also included a more scientific preparation for work
- warm-up exercises before starting work were accepted by staff
- 300 people die under trains annually. This, in addition to other traumas at work, justifies a policy on post-trauma action. Supervisory staff are trained in 'first aid' counselling with automatic referrals to occupational health the next day
- 850 staff questioned on which health-promotion activities they would prefer. The responses altered plans and should improve effectiveness
- one-to-one advice on diet, exercise and smoking, reduced blood pressure in an experimental group

Liverpool City Council

- 'health promotion in the workplace' pilot project examined intervention in two distinct groups of workers
- health-promotion activities reduced: absenteeism, alcohol consumption, body fat, blood pressure in older staff and body mass
- health-promotion activities increased aerobic capacity

- occupational health and lifestyle questionnaire found large discrepancies in different sectors of the workforce
- coordination between management, unions, health team and employees essential prior to and during health promotion
- geographical siting of health testing is critical. The ideal location is at the place of work

Wirral Metropolitan College

- 'mail order' services used to deliver health education resources to departments
- sub-groups organized with wide representation to consider the identified areas of: health, exercise and fitness; stress management; smoking; healthy eating
- the cost of health and fitness assessments was less for unwaged
- a number of approaches or models were recognized. These include the: health risk advice model; education/rational model; self improvement model; action for change model
- 'recognizes the value of incorporating the promotion of health and prevention of illness into its responsibilities as an employer'
- appointment of a health education coordinator
- designated some of the in-service training budget to health-related education
- 'opportunity for health relating education across all courses as a core entitlement and implicit in the curriculum'
- provision of in-service staff training in relation to drugs, stress and health issues
- using the computer network as a source of information to staff and students on health-related issues
- central catalogue of health-promoting resources
- an intention to dedicate a determinable amount of time each academic year for staff to enhance or develop their own health choices

The following case studies have been extracted from *Working for a healthier future* published by the Health Education Authority.

British Telecom PLC

- checks on blood pressure available to all employees over 40

- staff who attend for screening complete a health questionnaire to cover other risk factors
- LAYH logo overstamped on envelopes of 80 million telephone bills
- graphics packages about HEA literature available on Prestel to any BT employee

ICL

- touring stress-awareness display and counselling
- local community around some ICL sites have access to prevention services
- human 'MOTs' including urine and cholesterol analysis held regularly
- training of occupational health nurses as LAYH-LAY tutors
- sponsored slimming

Common features which are regularly reported by companies and organizations involved in the LAYH workplace project are:

- a determined and motivated coordinator
- the value of initially establishing staff needs
- the importance of planning, preparation, maintenance and evaluation
- the need to respect and work within the employment culture
- using sources of local expertise

In summary, the advantage of the LAYH Workplace project and Heartbeat Award is that a company or organization wishing to engage in health promotion can benefit immediately from the experiences of others.

The Health at Work support team (contact HEA) or the LAYH-LAY project centre in Canterbury (Christ Church College, Kent, CT1 1QU) will suggest promotional plans and policies for the needs of any company.

9

Specific Actions at Work

This chapter concentrates on aspects which have previously been considered in passing or not at all. It is intended to guide the reader into a few special activities which could help in establishing a healthier workplace. The justification is assumed, as by this stage in the book acceptance of the principles and the value of health at work is unlikely to change.

9.1 The Fitness Centre

It is recognized that not every organization can afford either the capital funds or the space for an in-house fitness centre. However it is surprising how unassigned or poorly-used space can be employed effectively. As working situations vary so dramatically it is not proposed to be prescriptive. Certain issues concerning the commissioning of a fitness centre will be reviewed and successful installations exemplified.

Key ingredients for any centre are:

- ease of accessibility
- a pleasant exercise area
- adequate shower and changing facilities

Some of the issues to consider before embarking on the fitness centre are:

- likely demand

- recurrent funding
- level of direct supervision
- type of conditioning to be offered

The latter issue will largely determine the equipment to be installed. Most fitness facilities concentrate on aerobic fitness, but strength development, relaxation, testing and injury treatment would all be examples of how a centre could be oriented. Ideally most fitness centres would wish to be sufficiently flexible to offer a variety of fitness components. With ample space this is easy but with the normal constraints of British business these decisions become more important.

A large open space is ideal for an exercise class such as aerobics and is very efficient for the times it is used. However group sessions will only take up a proportion of the day and the remaining time it could remain dormant. The introduction of stationary equipment reduces the problem of dormancy because it will be used by individuals when it suits them best. However the better quality exercise machines can be large and expensive.

The following secondary considerations will apply once the fundamental decision to proceed has been made:

- quality of decor and flooring
- heating and ventilation
- need for a sound system
- scheduling of use
- user priority ranking
- charging structure (if any)

If the centre is newly built then some of the issues are automatically resolved. A portakabin is a very acceptable compromise for a small fitness facility and can easily accommodate adequate exercise machines for a small or mid-sized company. Security needs to be considered for a non-brick building, but it also provides the advantage of the possibility of expansion.

Many exercise facilities are converted basements. A false ceiling makes such a space more attractive but may detract from the feeling of spaciousness. Instead of hiding pipework it may be better to paint it a bright colour and make it into a feature.

Although scheduling of use may be considered an issue of more concern once established, it is important to recognize that women often lack opportunities to exercise compared with men. This is associated with having children to look after, lack of support and a lack of enthusiasm for exercise. Additionally certain religious groups forbid women to be seen by men wearing the type of clothing appropriate for exercise. There may be a case for a special consideration of the needs of women and minority groups in scheduling the exercise sessions.

The specific equipment to be installed in such a facility may be guided by the following aspects:

- it must be varied
- it must be robust and reliable
- it should be relatively maintenance-free
- ideally it should provide feedback to the user
- it should look attractive
- it should suit all levels of fitness, size and age
- it should be supported with clear instructions for use
- it should have associated information on warm up, cool down and exercise planning

Issues of cost-effectiveness have been omitted from the above list because they are dependent on the policy of the centre.

Many companies will provide free advice on establishing a fitness centre. They will naturally recommend their own products but should give information on previous customers so it will be easy to obtain an independent view. The *Which?* report regularly publishes features on exercise equipment. One disadvantage in mixing exercise equipment from different companies is the difficulty of linking them electronically. Initially, for example, it may be the intention for them to operate as stand-alone units without a fee structure. However, to organize a central electronic card reader which deducts units from a card based on usage time requires all the machines to be linked.

The popular types of equipment for aerobic exercise are the cycle ergometer, the electronic treadmill, the stepper and the rowing machine. It is worth investing in an electromagnetically-braked cycle ergometer as mechanically-braked models need regular calibration. Experience has shown that once you provide more than one of each of these units the ratio of five cycle ergometers : three steppers : two treadmills : one rowing machine is optimal. This does not take into account special interest groups (e.g. oarsmen) or heavily-used facilities where clients will simply take the first available exercise machine irrespective of type. Much of the modern aerobic exercise equipment has electronic control to set a variable exercise programme. The equipment will often estimate distance and energy expenditure and will certainly measure elapsed time. Some will alter the intensity of the exercise depending on the heart rate response measured simultaneously. There are regular sport and recreation exhibitions which will demonstrate all this equipment and give the opportunity for detailed analysis.

A facility which is concentrating more on strength training should also be guided by the principles listed above. Free weights are popular with the purist, the bodybuilder or the competitive weight lifter. However for a workplace provision, individual weight stacks, 'multi-gyms' or modular electro-mechanical systems are more suitable. This is mainly because they are inherently safer, especially those working on an isokinetic system which prevents muscle overload.

A key feature is to ensure that as many muscle groups as possible are exercised, usually on a circuit principle, and that the user alternates different muscle groups (e.g. arms, legs, abdominals, back, chest) as (s)he moves around the circuit. Ideally a supervisor should be available to advise on aspects of weight training but a more likely scenario is the occasional session from a professional health worker. If this is so, then it is strongly recommended that introductory sessions are organized before staff use the facility. This will reduce injuries caused by inexperience.

Once again advice can be sought from weight training equipment manufacturers who will advise on type and layout consistent with the space and funds available. If a company or organization prefers independent advice, university departments of movement science and physical education will offer this on a consultancy basis.

The third major type of fitness centre is one that provides limited exercising equipment, but sufficient space for group exercise. With the current interest in aerobics, step aerobics, rope skipping, boxercise, yoga, tai chi, martial arts, relaxation classes and other group activities this may be a viable option for some companies. These types of activities are best taught to groups for reasons of safety and motivation. This means that well-qualified and sympathetic staff are required at least on a sessional basis. A small room is of limited value but a medium-sized room can be made to appear quite large by covering a main wall with mirrors. Equipment storage (mats, steps) has to be considered as does performing rights for music. In many cases the provision of the facility will be the catalyst for outside staff to offer to run classes on a commercial basis or internal staff to become suitably trained.

9.2 Exercising in the Office

The most common reason for lack of exercise is 'lack of time'. Those committed to exercise will simply find the time, as evidenced by all recent US presidents. There is some evidence that the long-accepted recommendation of 20–30 minutes of reasonably intense activity, three times a week could be substituted with short bursts of activity. These five minute exercise sessions, achieved fairly regularly throughout the day, may cumulate to have the same effect. The practicality of short exercise sessions is another issue and is very much dependent on the lifestyle and commitment of the person involved. Parking the car five minutes walk away from work with a brisk walk to and from the office would be a good start. The regular use of stairs in place of the lift, especially if the stairs are climbed continuously at a good pace, will soon show an improvement of aerobic capacity.

The key is accepting exercise, at whatever level, as part of the normal workplace culture. There was a time when exercisers such as joggers were considered cranks. Not any more because jogging has become an acceptable part of our culture. The same could apply in the office. Those companies that have introduced formal exercise breaks would initially have met with resistance. Yet if delivered sensitively, and making the allowance for the wide range of individual differences, the benefits soon become recognized and the activity is accepted.

There will still be many people who prefer not to engage in any form of formal or informal exercise session, either alone or in groups, but still accept the need to exercise. Perhaps such people recognize that the body is a machine which deteriorates through lack of use. They wish to prevent premature ageing and degeneration of joints and muscles. The answer is to engage in some form of light exercise daily which will improve posture, flexibility and muscle power. Exercise at work or in the office will help an individual relax and cope better with stress. Even fairly brief, regular periods of physical activity at work will help maintain metabolic levels and assist in weight control.

Even finding small ways to improve physical condition can help:

- avoid slouching; stand and sit erect with shoulders held back, but relaxed
- stretch the whole body and breathe deeply every hour
- enjoy a brisk walk at lunchtime
- every time the telephone rings, pull in the stomach and hold it while talking
- smile; it is a good exercise for the face and will set a pleasant tone for greeting and meetings.

For typists or those that write a lot, alternately clench the fist and stretch out all the fingers. As a separate exercise, gently pull the fingers back. Relax the hands and arms by shaking them loosely at the sides of the body.

The following individual exercises can be undertaken in the privacy of an office, working in small groups or as part of an organized exercise break. In most cases staff will probably start by doing them privately but find others wishing to join in.

1. **Pedalling on the spot** (*Stimulates circulation, tones calves and thighs*)
   Keep the legs moving continuously in a pedalling motion by rolling the feet up high on the toes. Relax the arms and swing them in the opposite direction to the feet.

2. **Head semi-circles** (*To release tension in neck and upper back muscles*)
   Let the head fall gently forward and to the right side in a smooth motion. Then focus the eyes. Continue by relaxing the head down and across to the other side. Keep the chin in contact with your upper chest.

3. Side leans (*Increases flexibility and helps firm the waist and upper trunk*)
While standing, lean as far as comfortable to each side, reaching
down the leg with the hand.

4. Trunk twist (*To improve hip flexibility*)
With the arms relaxed and the feet apart, slowly twist around each

side and back, following the leading hand with the eyes. Avoid violent twisting.

5. **Desk push-ups** (*Tones arms and improves upper body strength*)
From the front rest position (see diagram), bend the arms, lowering the body to the desk and then back up. Keep the body straight and make sure that the desk will not move.

6. **Stretch arm to leg** (*Improves flexibility in legs and lower back*)
Sitting, extend one leg and slowly reach forward with the opposite arm, trying to touch the toes. Repeat on the other side.

7. **Shoulder exercises** (*Reduces muscle tension in neck and shoulders*)
Alternately shrug each shoulder as high as possible and then relax it. Lift both shoulders and roll them backwards. This exercise can be performed either sitting or standing.

8. Knee to nose (*For lower back and abdominals; it promotes relaxation*)
Seated, pull one knee up towards the chest, then try to touch the knee with the head. Movements should be slow and smooth.

9. Flutter kick and ankle circles (*For abdominals, legs and ankles*)
Sit at a desk, back pushed into the back of the chair. Lift both legs

and gently flutter kick. Relax with the feet on the floor. Now raise each leg one at a time and circle the foot from the ankle.

10. Leg and arm swings (*Firms the legs and relaxes the shoulders*)
Touch the back of the chair with one hand for balance. Swing the outside arm and inside leg back and forward in opposite directions. Repeat on the other side.

11. Shoulder stretch (*Relaxes shoulders*)
Reach back over the right shoulder with the right hand while bending the left arm up the back. Try to touch hands. Relax by dropping the arms to the sides. Alternate arms.

12. Deep breathing (*General relaxation*)
Sit in a chair with the arms relaxed. Inhale slowly as you 'sit tall', tightening your muscles and pulling the shoulders back. Exhale completely as you slump forward, relaxing the whole body.

Remember:

- these exercises can be performed regularly throughout the day, but
- start slowly with a few repetitions
- build up the number over time
- never strain
- avoid any that aggravate an injury
- if any exercise causes back pain, stop and seek further advice.

9.3   Health Promotion Initiatives

One of the more authoritative sources on promoting health at a national level is *The Health of the Nation* strategy published by the HMSO. It takes a number of specific aspects and makes recommendations for each one from relevant organizations in the following list:

- Health Education Authority
- food producers, manufacturers and retailers
- caterers
- health and local authority services
- media and advertisers
- voluntary sector
- employers.

It can be seen that employers are recorded specifically in the list but all the above will impact on employees and should be seen as a total resource.

The Health of the Nation document examines how the above can contribute to:

- opportunities for promoting healthy living
- opportunities for reducing excessive and inappropriate consumption of alcohol
- suggestions for reducing cancer
- recommendations for reducing mental illness
- aspects of HIV/Aids and sexual health
- proposed legislation on accidents

Many of these aspects apply directly to the workplace but it needs the employer to take the initiative to implement them. There is clearly a re-orientation of government policy on healthcare towards primary prevention. There is little evidence, however, of vast amounts of government money supporting the policy. The expectation is that the current structures will act within existing finance but have, possibly for the first time, a substantial strategy to support action.

Employers are recommended to read the complete document but the following are some examples taken from it which illustrate government thinking:

- development of workplace alcohol policies
- referral of staff with alcohol problems for specialist advice
- maintaining the real level of taxation on tobacco products
- encouraging insurance companies to offer preferential rates to non-smokers
- introduction of employment no-smoking policies
- implementing prevention strategies at work
- new legislation for 'systematic assessment and management of health and safety risk by all employers'
- new legislation for manual handling
- campaign and special requirements for high-accident sectors such as agriculture, construction and the offshore oil and gas industry

Since *The Health of the Nation* was launched a number of these initiatives have been implemented or initiated. The strategy has without doubt focused thought and action on primary health care and the leads taken by employers such as the NHS can be followed by many others. The remaining part of this chapter will consider a series of specific initiatives from a wide variety of sources which any employer could reasonably consider introducing. Some relate to aspects mentioned previously but others are quite independent.

Back Schools

This can be offered to those already suffering from back pain or to those wishing to avoid back pain in the future by learning preventative approaches. Employers can either refer staff to a back school organized by a local hospital or establish one at work. Back schools:

- increase awareness of posture
- educate about the back, its limitations and capabilities
- provide a programme to strengthen the abdominals and back muscles and to mobilize the spine
- teach relaxation exercises
- educate on prevention and reduction of back pain
- inform about causes of back pain in the work setting

Special Classes

People are understandably very resistant to being in unfamiliar situations where they have any inadequacies exposed. Obese people are unlikely to join aerobics classes full of lithe individuals in brightly coloured lycra leotards. It is important to make people comfortable and for them to recognize that others about them have similar problems. Examples might include:

- 'over 45' women's exercise class
- a slimming group
- a walking club

Attention should not exclusively be given to the less healthy because the healthier sector of the workforce may equally wish to work in groups for reasons of motivation and improved performance. Thus jogging clubs, circuit training, squash leagues and other individual and team sports may need to be organized if not already part of the company's social and sporting activities.

Special Events

These can link in often with national events such as No Smoking Day and Drinkwise Day. Alternatively the company can organize its own special events to give a more local flavour. This would include such things as:

- weight loss contests
- mini marathons or company fun runs
- healthy eating weeks
- stop smoking month

Incentives such as certificates, awards or prizes will often make a difference to levels of compliance.

Another option is to participate as a company in local or regional activities. Many cities or towns run 'corporate cup' competitions over about 5k in distance. These are designed deliberately to encourage corporations to enter teams, often based on a variety of ages and both sexes. As part of the entry, training programmes are often provided. Being part of a large fun run with company sponsored kit, etc., can provide great interest and motivation for many who would not normally participate.

Knowledge

As people become more interested in health at work they will start to ask more questions and expect a greater level of understanding and knowledge. This is especially the case in areas where the health message is not always clear or is controversial. It may be appropriate to establish a small resource centre with key texts, references, videofilms, pamphlets, government legislation, etc. This need not be an expensive operation as many organizations concerned with health provide material free. This is especially so in the food industry with retailers supplying their customers with information on healthy eating. Tesco is a good example of a company which operates this policy. Many exercise equipment manufacturers have documents advising on fitness (e.g. Dynavit, Tunturi) and more general texts can be borrowed from libraries or bought direct from specialist booksellers (e.g. Sportspages, Charing Cross Road, London). For companies which do not have resident health specialists another option is to organize a health at work phoneline. The questions could then be answered by someone on a sessional basis or re-directed to a suitable person.

Special Medical Conditions

Chronic illness or disease such as diabetes and epilepsy should be no bar to most jobs yet their management may require special consideration. Certain individuals may be acting strangely for example falling asleep, lacking concentration, spending more time in the washroom or becoming obsessive. It is possible that such behaviours have a simple acute reason but may mean the employee is suffering from a medical condition. The employee may not wish to divulge his or her illness for fear of ridicule from colleagues or being made redundant.

An example of a relatively unknown condition, but one which is two to three times more common that epilepsy, is obsessive compulsion disorder (OCD). It can affect otherwise excellent workers who have obsessive habits such as arriving to work at precise times or being over-concerned about details. It may result in an inability to complete certain tasks which would be a disaster in an organization relying on tight deadlines. Constant worrying about hygiene is one manifestation of OCD and it may result in the sufferer washing his or her hands up to 20 times a day.

A neurological disorder often present in OCD sufferers is Tourette's syndrome. This cannot be disguised because the patient usually has facial and verbal tics, uncontrollable movements and may be prone to shouting obscenities. The stress of work will commonly cause an outburst. This condition may affect the sufferer's colleagues more than the patient, who although well aware of the problem can still work effectively. A degree of control can be achieved by behaviour therapy and drugs.

A rather rare condition, and one which is recognized less in the UK than abroad, is attention deficit disorder. It is the adult version of childhood hyperactivity. Sufferers are easily bored, inattentive, impulsive, impatient, prone to procrastination and mood swings. These characteristics in themselves are not occasionally uncommon but employees with attention deficit disorder have them permanently and at an intensity where work suffers. Job restructuring may be necessary to get the best out of such sufferers. Working independently, giving them a number of creative jobs with short deadlines is one option.

Narcolepsy is a condition which manifests itself as the sufferer falling into a deep sleep during the day. It can be related to an emotional response such as laughter when the sufferer starts to laugh then loses control of muscles and collapses. It can be managed quite successfully by allowing the sufferer to take a short (15–20 minute) sleep in the middle of the day or if an attack is imminent. Drug control is also effective.

An increasingly common condition is myalgic encephalomyelitis (ME), otherwise known as chronic fatigue syndrome or even 'yuppie flu'. It is characterized by extreme weakness and excessive tiredness. A previous viral infection may be the cause, complicated by insufficient time off work at the time. The employee should consider slow rehabilitation and part-time work to aid full recovery. The problem with many of these conditions with unspecified pathology is that the sufferers can be accused of malingering or even hysterics. This is often inconsistent with their normal approach to work because a high proportion of these sufferers are ambitious individuals.

More common chronic conditions are those of epilepsy, asthma and diabetes. Employers are often unsure how to cope with sufferers, even though the condition will usually be highly controlled. Epileptics are not dangerous or violent when having fits. The frequency, normal duration and predictability of the epileptic seizures should be known by an employee's manager. As the effect can be disturbing for colleagues, they should be informed if that is the wish of the sufferer.

Diabetics only become a problem at work if their normal metabolic management is upset. The most common symptom is fainting when blood sugar levels drop. Warning signs usually prevent this with an insulin-dependent diabetic eating something sweet. There are certain work situations when this is not feasible and it is then that problems can occur. Like epilepsy it is valuable for colleagues to be aware of the condition and action. The correct action is especially important as different types of diabetes need different responses with the wrong action possibly making things worse.

Asthma is a very common condition, apparently increasing and with well over ten per cent of school leavers now suffering from it. Although potentially serious, it is usually very well controlled and it is only in unusual environmental conditions that an asthma attack is likely to be triggered. As most asthma sufferers will be seen using their medication (e.g. inhalers), colleagues are more likely to be aware of the condition. Employers may need to provide adequate ventilation in work processes which could otherwise provoke an attack.

In summary, a caring employer needs to be especially aware of certain chronic conditions. Special work arrangements may be needed to gain the best from people who wish to be treated as normally as any other member of the workforce.

Physiotherapy

Physiotherapy has not yet been considered as part of the occupational health team but there may be a role for this specialism to play. The physiotherapist can give specific advice concerning the prevention of injuries associated with poor posture, badly-designed equipment and work practices, and manual lifting. The physiotherapist may also have relevant knowledge in the area of fitness appraisal and advice. The special skill of the physiotherapist, however, is in treatment. A high proportion of work-related injuries and illnesses will be musculoskeletal. This is the particular *forte* of the physiotherapist and could result in a more rapid return to work than using conventional procedures. The current NHS system tends to route people from a GP to a consultant and only then to a physiotherapist. This often takes a long time and the condition could be getting worse without positive treatment. A physiotherapist working for British Telecom estimates that the saving from sickness absence was at least five times the cost of providing the service. The level of the service will depend on the size of the organization. It could vary from a sessional service with a private physiotherapist providing all the equipment to an in-house facility staffed regularly. A compromise that has proved to be successful at the University of Liverpool is to offer an out-of-hours service (5.00pm–8.00pm, four nights a week) utilizing facilities normally used by occupational health. Although this example is not directly work-related because all the patients have sports injuries, the principle is very similar to a workplace initiative.

Self-screening Courses

Self-screening procedures can be organized and taught as a valuable health promotion initiative. There are a number of examples but the following will serve to illustrate the principle:

- testicular self-examination
- breast self-examination

- skin self-examination

People, often out of ignorance, fear and embarrassment, will delay taking action over early signs of cancer which could be life-saving. The main problem, however, is that many people are not confident in performing self-examination. Breast self-examination is an issue which is discussed openly in women's magazines, but testicular and skin self-examination is less commonly described. The objectives of offering self-screening courses are to:

- discuss the reasons for self-examination
- describe the methods
- identify the frequency of the disease and the examination
- understand the relevant anatomy
- define what action to take if an abnormality is found

It is accepted that delivery of such a course has additional problems compared with more acceptable health issues. The staff, time, location, style of communication and peer group influence will all need to be managed sensitively. There will be problems of false positive and false negative reporting which can cause additional concern. However, on balance the courses could be of great benefit to various sectors of the workforce. Targeting may be necessary with different age groups given priority dependent on the epidemiology of the condition. The availability of videofilm and other visual material makes such courses more viable as the incidence of these conditions is thankfully rare and the exact procedures for self-examination need to be taught very precisely.

Courses of this nature need a high degree of planning because of the content. Like all courses, evaluation is also important possibly even more so if the investment is greater than normal.

10

Keeping *Health at Work* on the Agenda

This final, short chapter is a plea for action. The issues have been debated and suggestions have been made, but until the executive decision is taken, nothing will have been achieved.

This country, along with many others, is working at sub-optimal efficiency. Life expectancy is lower than Greece, absenteeism from work is higher than ever before, costing £13 billion annually, and workers face a one in 16 risk of being exposed to an occupational accident.

It was embarrassing that until relatively recently the model for government targets on health was New Zealand – a country with a population the size of Birmingham! Within the last two years this has changed and there now is a clear preventative healthcare strategy. Strategies however do not produce results. Every place of employment needs to develop or maintain a culture change which promotes health and includes health issues on every agenda.

Investing in health promotion is effectively investing in human development. Human development is a process of enlarging people's choices. Nurturing health at work means an investment in employment policy. It requires social health equity. This dictates that all employees are treated fairly, have equal access and equal opportunities to participate in healthy practices. It requires a sustainable workplace environment. Health issues are both personal and physical. As budgets are prepared and business plans are formulated questions concerning safety, resources and quality of life need to be included in the overall equation.

Dr Kenneth Calman, the Chief Medical Officer as part of *The Health of the Nation* strategy issued the following challenge:

> I am issuing a challenge to every person in the country to take one small step to improve their own health.

He produced a list of suggestions as follows:

- take the stairs instead of the lift or escalator
- exercise – cycle, jog, swim or dance
- walk – don't ride. Get off one stop early and walk
- grill rather than fry your food
- cut the fat off meat
- change to skimmed or semi-skimmed milk
- eat your greens – make sure you have plenty of vegetables or salad every day
- watch how much you eat – think twice before seconds
- try fresh fruit instead of cake or biscuits
- have fish instead of meat once a week
- be drinkwise – have at least two alcohol-free days a week
- give up smoking or set a date to stop
- protect your child from smoke – particularly if you are pregnant
- fit a smoke alarm – it is only the price of a pint and two packets of cigarettes
- is your home safe from accidents? Check it tonight
- don't drink and drive
- always wear your seatbelt
- watch your speed and make sure your children know about road safety
- protect yourself and your children from the sun – use a sunscreen and wear a hat
- reduce your stress – take a ten-minute time-out every day

I am now issuing you, the reader, with a challenge.

> Take each of the above suggestions, one by one, and re-write them as specific actions for the workplace.

To assist you I will re-write the first suggestion.

Action: Place a well-designed poster next to every lift or escalator exhorting staff to choose the stairs in preference.

It is inadequate to undertake this challenge mentally; each action has to be written down and given to the person who will execute it. It is also unacceptable to state that any of the suggestions do not apply to the workplace. This indicates a lack of imagination or concern for your employees when away from work.

To return to Dr Calman's original challenge, I propose the following modification in the very real hope that you will respond.

I am issuing a challenge to every worker in the country to take one small step to improve their health in the place of work. Having taken that one small step, I challenge you to keep stepping.

Health matters at work and the consequence of many small steps will be a healthier, happier, more content and more productive workforce.

Appendix 1

The survey questionnaire is composed of four sections. The first three ask questions dealing with existing fitness, sports and recreation, and health education programmes, respectively. The last section requests information from all companies, regardless of whether any programmes currently exist.

If your office is part of a company that has other offices, PLEASE ANSWER ONLY FOR YOUR PARTICULAR LOCATION, whether it is the Head Office or a branch location.

Please check the ☐ appropriate response for each question. For many questions, more than one response may be applicable. If so, check all appropriate responses. Where numbers are required in a response, please zero fill, e.g. 0,9,9.

A. FITNESS PROGRAMS — ON-SITE OR AT LOCAL FACILITIES
(e.g. aerobics classes, exercise breaks, jogging)

1. Does your company offer Fitness programs, activities or services for its employees?
   001 ☑ NO   (If NO, skip to Section B last page)
   ☑ YES   (If YES, please answer the following questions)

2. Which of the following are available to your employees? (Please check all that apply)
   002 ☐ Aerobics or group fitness classes
   003 ☐ Exercise breaks
   004 ☐ Jogging or running opportunities
   005 ☐ Individual exercise programs (e.g. weight training, calisthenics)
   006 ☐ Fitness assessment and counselling
   007 ☐ Financial subsidy in local facilities (e.g. fitness club, YM/YWCA)
   008 ☐ Other (please specify) _____

3. For whom are these opportunities available? (Please check all that apply)
   009 ☐ All employees
   010 ☐ Senior management
   011 ☐ Salaried employees
   012 ☐ Hourly employees
   013 ☐ Other (please specify) _____

4. Where do they participate? (Please check all that apply)
   014 ☐ On-site facility
   015 ☐ YM/YWCA
   016 ☐ Commercial facility
   017 ☐ Community facility
   018 ☐ Other (please specify) _____

5. If ON-SITE, what facilities are provided? (If NOT ON-SITE, skip to question 7)
   019 ☐ Showers
   020 ☐ Change area
   021 ☐ Group exercise area
   022 ☐ Individual exercise area
   023 ☐ Jogging or running area
   024 ☐ Other (please specify) _____

6. If ON-SITE, what is the:
   Indoor size in square feet?   025 └┴┴┴┴┴┘
   Capital cost per square foot?   026 £└┴┴┘

7. Approximately what percentage of your employees participate in some part of the overall program?
   027 └┴┴┘ %

8. Approximately what percentage of overall program participants are:
   028 └┴┴┘ % full-time   030 └┴┴┘ % salaried   032 └┴┴┘ % white collar   034 └┴┴┘ % male
   029 └┴┴┘ % part-time   031 └┴┴┘ % hourly   033 └┴┴┘ % blue collar   035 └┴┴┘ % female

9. On a yearly estimate, what percentage of employees participate in supervised activities?
   (i.e. aerobics or group fitness classes, exercise breaks, jogging or running)
   Very frequently (daily)   036 └┴┴┘ %
   Frequently (2–4 days per week)   037 └┴┴┘ %
   Occasionally (less than 2 days per week)   038 └┴┴┘ %
   Infrequently (less than 1 day per week)   039 └┴┴┘ %
   040 ☐ Unable to estimate accurately

10. On a yearly estimate, what percentage of employees participate in unsupervised activities?
   (i.e. jogging or running, weight training, calisthenics)
   Very frequently (daily)   041 └┴┴┘ %
   Frequently (2–4 days per week)   042 └┴┴┘ %
   Occasionally (less than 2 days per week)   043 └┴┴┘ %
   Infrequently (less than 1 day per week)   044 └┴┴┘ %
   045 ☐ Unable to estimate accurately

11. At what times can employees participate? (Please check all that apply)
    046 ☐ Before work
    047 ☐ At lunch
    048 ☐ After work
    049 ☐ During working hours
    050 ☐ Evenings or weekends
    051 ☐ Other (please specify) _____

12. Who provides overall management or co-ordination for your Fitness programs? (Please check one)
    052 ① Employee Association
        ② Management
        ③ Employee/Management Committee
        ④ Union
        ⑤ Outside agency (e.g. YM/YWCA)
        ⑥ Contract Consultant
        ⑦ Other (please specify) _____

13. Who provides day-to-day leadership for your programs? (Please check one)
    053 ① Staff fitness co-ordinator
        ② Volunteer employees
        ③ Outside consultant or firm
        ④ Outside agency (e.g. YM/YWCA)
        ⑤ Other (please specify) _____

14. Where do fitness programs fit within your company structure? (Please check one)
    054 ① Personnel or Human Resources Department
        ② Medical Department
        ③ Administrative Services
        ④ Informal — interested employees
        ⑤ Other (please specify) _____

15. Who pays for your Fitness programs? (Please check one)
    055 ① Company entirely
        ② Employees entirely
        ③ Shared — company and employees, with company paying 056 └─┴─┘ %
                                   and employees paying 057 └─┴─┘ %

16. If employees pay, either entirely or in part, how much does each employee pay?
    058 £└─┴─┘ per month

17. What are the gross annual operating costs of your Fitness programs?
    059 £ └─┴─┴─┴─┴─┴─┴─┘

18. How long have your programs been operating?
    060 ☐ Less than 1 year, or 061 └─┴─┘ years

19. Does your company assess or evaluate the impact of these programs on: (Please check all that apply)
    062 ☐ Absenteeism   066 ☐ Health
    063 ☐ Staff turnover   067 ☐ Accidents
    064 ☐ Productivity   068 ☐ Other (please specify) _____
    065 ☐ Morale   069 ☐ No assessment made (Skip to question 21)

20. Is this assessment or evaluation done: (Please check one)
    070 ① Formally
        ② Informally
        ③ Both

21. What is the general opinion in your company about the value of your Employee Fitness program?
    (Please check one)
    071 ① Extremely positive; an indispensable part of our company working conditions
        ② Generally positive; as long as interest continues we will sustain the program
        ③ Neutral; we do not really have a strong feeling one way or the other
        ④ Somewhat negative; we are reviewing whether it is worth continuing
        ⑤ Extremely negative; it will probably be dropped

B. SPORTS AND RECREATION PROGRAMS (e.g. team or outdoor sports, golf tournaments)

1. Does your company offer Sports and Recreation programs for its employees?
   072 ① NO   (If NO, skip to Section C)
       ② YES   (If YES, please continue)

2. Which of the following are available? (Please check all that apply)
   073 ☐ Team sports (e.g. baseball, hockey)
   074 ☐ Individual sports (e.g. tennis, swimming)
   075 ☐ Recreational events (e.g. ski trips, golf tournaments)
   076 ☐ Other (please specify) _____

C. HEALTH EDUCATION AND LIFESTYLE PROGRAMS (e.g. stress management, retirement planning)

1. Does your company offer Health Education and Lifestyle programs for its employees?
   077 ① NO   (If NO, skip to Section D)
       ② YES   (If YES, please continue)

2. Which of the following are available? (Please check all that apply)
   078 ☐ Stress management   084 ☐ Alcohol education
   079 ☐ Retirement planning   085 ☐ Drug education
   080 ☐ Preventive back care   086 ☐ Health education
   081 ☐ Nutrition education   087 ☐ Occupational health and safety
   082 ☐ Weight control   088 ☐ Employee assistance
   083 ☐ Smoking cessation   089 ☐ Other (please specify) _____

D. GENERAL (Please answer all of the following questions)

1. In the future, is your company considering introducing:

   FITNESS PROGRAMS?   SPORTS AND REC. PROGRAMS?   HEALTH EDUCATION PROGRAMS?
   090 ① NO   091 ① NO   092 ① NO
       ② YES   ② YES   ② YES
       ③ Not applicable,   ③ Not applicable,   ③ Not applicable,
         programs exist   programs exist   programs exist

2. Approximately what percentage of your employees are:
   093 └┴┴┘ % full-time   095 └┴┴┘ % salaried 097 └┴┴┘ % blue collar   099 └┴┴┘ % male
   094 └┴┴┘ % part-time   096 └┴┴┘ % hourly   098 └┴┴┘ % white collar 100 └┴┴┘ % female

3. Does your company have unions?
   101 ① NO   (If NO, skip to question 5)
       ② YES

4. What percentage of your total workplace is unionized?   102 └┴┘ %

5. Is this the company's Head Office?
   103 ① NO
       ② YES
       ③ Not applicable, this is the company's only office (Skip to question 8)

6. How many locations does your company have in all, including Head Office and branch locations?
   104 └┴┴┘ locations

7. Approximately how many employees are at all OTHER locations?   105 └┴┴┴┴┘

8. What is your position with the company? 106 _____

9. Do you have any additional comments you feel would help us?
   _____
   _____
   _____
   _____
   _____

Appendix 2

The University of Liverpool

MANUAL HANDLING ASSESSMENT CHECKLIST

This checklist should be completed by Departmental Manual Handling Assessors who have read the Health and Safety Executive booklet 'Manual Handling — Guidance on Regulations'.

There is a flow chart for manual handling assessment on the back page.

Summary of Assessment

Department ....

Operations covered by this assessment ....

....

....

Location(s) ....

Personnel involved ....

Date of assessment ....

(Turn over before completing the summary)

Overall priority for remedial action (circle)   Nil / Low/ Med/ High

Remedial action to be taken ....

....

....

....

Date by which action to be taken ....

Date for reassessment ....

Assessors name ....   Signature ....

If the risk assessment (Section C) is Med or High, a copy of the full assessment should be given to the University Safety Adviser and to the individual(s) concerned.

Section A — *Preliminary:*

Q1   What weight is involved?

Q2   Frequency of operation?

Q3   Is the operation done by: Females? ☐   Males? ☐

Q4   Does it involve twisting?   YES ☐   NO ☐

(Consult the guidelines before answering the next question)

Q5   After allowing for posture, frequency, etc., what are the relevant guideline weight for this
      operation?
                                                                        Females   Males
                                                                         ☐   ☐

Q6   Can operations be avoided/ mechanised/ automated at reasonable cost?   YES ☐   NO ☐

      If 'Yes' complete Section D, proceed, and then check by reassessment that the result is
      satisfactory.

Q7   What is the weight handled (Q1) as a percentage of the guideline (Q5)?   Females   Males
                                                                                ☐   ☐

      If 50% or less you may go straight to Section C if you wish. Otherwise go to B.

Section C — *Overall assessment of risk:*

(In the absence of complicating factors, risk maybe related to the answer to Q7 as follows:
<100: insignificant; 100-150: low; 150-200: med; >200: high; but if any problems are identified in
Section B this may raise the risk rating).

Q: What is your overall assessment of the risk of injury? Females: Insignificant/ Low/ Med/ High
                                                            Males: Insignificant/ Low/ Med/ High

      If 'insignificant' the assessment need go no further. Otherwise go to D.

Section D — *Remedial action:*

Q: What remedial steps should be taken, in order of priority?
      i ....
      ii ....
      iii ....
      iv ....
      v ....

And Finally

— complete the SUMMARY overleaf
— compare it with your other manual handling assessments
— decide your priorities for action
— TAKEN ACTION ....AND CHECK THAT IT HAS THE DESIRED EFFECT

Section B — More detailed assessment, where necessary:

Questions to consider: (If the answer to a question is 'Yes' place a tick against it and then consider the level of risk)	Yes	Level of risk: (Tick as appropriate)			Possible remedial action: (Make rough notes in this column in preparation for completing Section D)
		Low	Med	High	
The tasks — do they involve:					
• holding loads away from trunk?					
• twisting?					
• stooping?					
• reaching upwards?					
• large vertical movement?					
• long carrying distances?					
• strenuous pushing or pulling?					
• unpredictable movement of loads?					
• repetitive handling?					
• insufficient rest or recovery?					
• a workrate imposed by a process?					
The loads — are they:					
• heavy?					
• bulky/unwieldy?					
• difficult to grasp?					
• unstable/unpredictable?					
• intrinsically harmful (eg sharp/hot?)					
The working environment — are there:					
• constraints on posture?					
• poor floors?					
• variations in levels?					
• hot/cold/humid conditions?					
• strong air movements?					
• poor lighting conditions?					
Individual capability — does the job:					
• require unusual capability?					
• hazard those with a health problem?					
• hazard those who are pregnant?					
• call for special information/training?					
Other factors — .					
Is movement or posture hindered by clothing or personal protective equipment?					

Deciding the level of risk will inevitably call for judgement. The HSE guidelines may provide a useful yardstick.

When you have completed Section B go to Section C

Appendix 3

BODY COMPOSITION

Description

The old method of weighing someone on a scale and looking up an ideal weight from a chart, is not adequate for today's informed health fitness client. Athletes, weight loss clients, and health promotion groups require a percent body fat determination that is specific to the individual and not a recommendation based on "average."

The skinfold method of determining percent of body fat is widely used and scientifically accepted. If carefully done, this calculation is very accurate. Other methods may be utilized such as bio-electrical impedance. An omhs value or known percent fat may be entered.

Features

※ Three different skinfold testing methods are supported; a seven-site and two three-site methods. The seven skinfold site method provides very accurate results and includes the following:

Chest	Subscapular
Triceps	Abdomen
Axilary	Thigh
Suprailium	

※ The first three-site method takes measurements from the upper, middle, and lower body as shown below:

MEN	WOMEN
Chest	Triceps
Abdomen	Suprailiac (waist)
Thigh	Thigh

An alternate method with three skinfold sites using upper and mid-body measurements is available for occasions when subjects are not in running shorts.

※ A four page report is generated. The first page documents all measurements and presents the individual's current percent body fat, how many pounds of fat he is carrying (a great motivator), and the lean body mass. The computer calculates an ideal weight based on desired body fat. Recommended percent body fat standards for various ages are shown for comparison.

The second page computes the individual's RMR (resting metabolic rate), the energy expenditure from activity, and projects total energy needs. From this information a program is suggested for weight loss when indicated, or a third page gives guidelines for exercise to change body composition. The last page provides nutritional guidelines for weight loss.

A training video for correctly taking skinfold measurements is available to accompany this program. It is loaned for ten days at no charge, or can be purchased for use in skinfold testing training programs. Skinfold calipers are also available for purchase.

※ This program is highly popular at running clinics, weight control programs, nutrition classes, and health fairs. It serves as an excellent motivator for achieving ideal body weight, and is much more accurate and practical than trying to suggest ideal weights from a scale alone.

※ Program includes information on how to take the measurements.

※ A group statistical summary allows you to develop your own database, do research on any group, and demonstrate change over time.

Scientific Basis

The multiple regression equations used in calculating percent body fat were developed by Drs. Jackson and Pollock.

To order call 1-800-533-9355

Appendix 4

POLICY ON ALCOHOL

Alcohol Policy

A working party set up in 1989 by the Health and Safety Committee and Student Health and Welfare Group has reviewed the University's position on alcohol consumption. It endorses the view of the medical profession that consumption affects work performance and can affect health adversely, and that alcohol dependency is an illness amenable to treatment. The Working Party concluded that early diagnosis is crucial for the successful treatment of alcohol dependency, and that staff with an alcohol dependency problem are more likely to be persuaded to obtain treatment, and indeed problems of alcohol dependency avoided, if the University has a clear policy which is well publicised and commands general support amongst staff.

As an employer the University considers that alcohol should never affect work performance. It is also concerned that it should be seen to be setting a good example. To this end a number of guidelines are set down.

The University also wants to speed up the process by which those with problems get help. The second part of the policy therefore sets our the responsibilities of those who might be concerned and suggest various ways in which help can be obtained. The policy is set in the context of problems as they are presently seen; the policy will be monitored and changes may be recommended as circumstances change.

Guidelines

The best example of alcohol impairing performance is the effect on driving. It is now accepted, however, that even moderate consumption slows down reaction and impairs judgement; regular consumption over a long period damages the liver and aggravates other [disease] conditions. The following guidelines are intended to apply equally to all staff and not only those who might e.g. create hazards or who deal with the public.

1. Staff should not consume alcohol at work and when working, should never be affected by the consumption of alcohol.

2. Whenever the University provides or sells alcohol there should be available a range of non-alcoholic drinks. Wherever possible, opportunities should be taken to promote the benefits of substituting non-alcoholic for alcoholic beverages.

3. When, for social reasons, free alcoholic drinks are made available e.g. retirements, they should be served in moderation and consideration should be made in the arrangements for those who have to return to work or to drive home.

How to help

Alcohol dependency is recognised as an illness that can be successfully treated, particularly if it is diagnosed at an early stage. Statistics suggest that one per cent. of all employees are likely to be dependent on alcohol and that sufferers are more likely to be amongst white collar occupations than has been previously acknowledged. The experience of those in the University who deal with such problems suggests that we are not untypical. When cases have come to light it has been clear that those close to the sufferer have known about the situation and that diagnosis and treatment could have been given earlier. For the guidance of all who might be concerned, the following items set out what ought to be done where it is clear that a member of staff is behaving unusually and a problem is strongly suspected.

1. The Occupational Health Physician will provide advice and information in the strictest confidence to any University employee who has a problem. The Occupational Health Physician will provide names of outside agencies and others who can provide expert professional assistance. Staff should note that their own GP can also provide such assistance, if preferred.

2. Any staff member who believes a colleague to have a drinking problem should encourage him/her to seek help from the Occupational Health Physician or his/her GP.

3. If the problems persist, and start to affect work or working relationships or present a safety hazard, then the Head of Department should be advised of these problems. It is recognised that staff members may be reluctant to do this, but it does not help a colleague with a drinking problem to allow this to be left unattended and to worsen, so becoming more difficult to deal with.

4. Where a Head of Department is aware of a member of his/her staff who has a drinking problem, then the Head of Department should discuss the problem in confidence with the member of staff, and urge him/her to seek medical help, making it clear to the member of staff that the University has not been approached formally at this stage.

5. The University accepts that absence for medical help or treatment will be treated as sick leave with all the corresponding benefits and entitlements. Staffing Services can advise on such matters.

6. Where the behaviour has become unacceptable, then the Head of Department should advise the member that Staffing Services may have to be informed, and should again urge the individual to seek medical help from the Occupational Physician or his/her GP. If the head of Department does decide to inform Staffing Services, then he/she should inform the member of staff of this.

7. Staffing Services will make every effort to resolve the problems without disciplinary procedures.

8. In the event of misconduct or unacceptable behaviour, the University has the right to initiate the appropriate disciplinary procedures. However,

   (i) a drinking problem and refusal to undergo treatment are not themselves matters for disciplinary action or any other penalties, except in so far as they give rise to adverse performance or behaviour at work;

   (ii) where discussions have been held in accordance with paras. 5, 6 and 7, and in these discussions the possibility of disciplinary action has been put to the individual, then these shall not constitute formal warnings for the purpose of disciplinary procedures.

The policy applies to all staff regardless of status or occupation. Where senior staff are involved either a Dean, the Director of Staffing Services or a Pro-Vice-Chancellor can be approached to make arrangements as appropriate under e.g. 3 or 4 above.

Overall responsibility for monitoring the development of the policy will be with the Safety Committee in consultation with the Health and Welfare Group, and consideration will be given to the need for a broadly-based advisory group to support the operation of the policy in the longer term.

Appendix 5

UNIVERSITY POLICY ON DRUG ABUSE

Introduction

The term 'drug abuse' refers to the use of illegal drugs and the abuse of prescribed drugs and substances which can harm the individual (both physically and mentally) and through the individual's actions, other people and the environment.

As an employer, the University has to consider its responsibilities under health and safety legislation and under the Misuse of Drugs Act 1971. Drug abuse can impair work performance, cause relationships to deteriorate, lead to health problems including dependency and cause danger to others.

As part of its overall concern for health problems and welfare, the University has therefore adopted a policy which aims to ensure that drug abuse can be identified and the necessary help given. The University is, therefore, prepared to assist any employee who has a problem related to drug abuse.

1. The University has made available in this document, guidance on the effects of drug abuse including understanding drug abuse and the problems and risks arising from abuse.

2. A person who has a problem related to drug abuse might voluntarily seek advice and guidance and treatment if necessary. Such advice may be obtained from the University's Student Health Service, Occupational Health or the Counselling Service who will arrange, in confidence, for the employee to seek treatment.

   Any staff member who believes a colleague to have a drug problem should encourage him/her to seek help in confidence from any of the Services listed above.

3. Alternatively, The Merseyside Drug Training and Information Centre, 27 Hope Street, Liverpool L1 9BQ, telephone number: 709-3511, will help anyone concerned about drug abuse (whether friend, family or user) to find an appropriate form of help.

4. If during treatment an employee is unable to attend work, confidentiality will be maintained, he/she will be considered to be on normal sick leave and the rules of the Sick Pay Scheme will apply.

5. If an employee is absent for an extended period or where there are grounds to expect that the absence will be prolonged, or where there are regular periods of absence, the University will seek medical advice as to the likelihood of the employee being able to continue/resume duties.

6. Efforts will be made to ensure that an employee returns to the same job after treatment. Where there is no reasonable prospect of an employee being able to continue/resume duties, and where accordingly the employee is declared medically unfit to carry out the duties, an offer of suitable alternative employment will be made if this is possible. Where it is not possible to offer a suitable alternative post, the employee's employment will be terminated on the grounds of ill health.

UNIVERSITY POLICY ON DRUG ABUSE
(continued)

7. In the event of misconduct or unacceptable behaviour, the University has the right to initiate the appropriate disciplinary procedures. No disciplinary action will be taken against an employee unless treatment is refused, and if subsequent work performance is not satisfactorily maintained. If there are instances of gross misconduct the employee will be dismissed following normal procedures.

8. A relapse during or after completion of treatment will be considered in the light of the circumstances involved.

9. This policy applies to all staff regardless of status or occupation. It will be monitored and reviewed by the Health and Welfare Group.

Appendix 6

PREVENTION OF INFECTION IN EVERYDAY LIFE		OCCUPATIONAL PREVENTION OF INFECTION		RIGHTS OF INDIVIDUALS	
No risk and low risk	• Social proximity to HIV carrier or AIDS sufferer is not a risk. There is no evidence of any risk in working or living alongside HIV carriers, as air-borne droplet infection does not appear to occur. Normal hygienic practices are sufficient protection. Practices such as sharing items like razors or toothbrushes should be avoided not only on account of AIDS but to guard against other more infectious diseases such as Hepatitis B. • Guidelines on preventive personal and domestic hygiene are contained in Appendix I.	**Occupational prevention of infection**	• The main risk is from blood-to-blood transfer. • Codes of Practice have been drawn up and issued to staff involved in cleaning, catering and gardening. • Codes for laboratory workers have been strengthened where necessary and must be rigorously observed at all times, for the various health risks laboratory work presents. • Work with unscreened blood is not permitted except under carefully-controlled conditions. • Further information and guidance can be obtained from the Safety Adviser.	**Employment rights**	• Disclosure of HIV status is not required from any employers or applicants for employment, and employment rights are in no way affected by it. However, those working in the medical field are subject to particular obligations (see below)*.
High risk activities	• The greatest risks of HIV infection exist in unprotected vaginal intercourse and in anal intercourse, in sharing hypodermic needles and in transfusion with infected blood. • Guidelines on safer sexual activity are contained in Appendix II. • The Liverpool Syringe Exchange Scheme (see Appendix III) aims to reduce the risk of infection through shared hypodermic needles. • In some countries blood for transfusion is not screened for the presence of HIV and medical equipment may not always be adequately sterilised.	**Guidelines for First Aiders**	• Revised guidelines have been drawn up for First Aiders. Resusciaide Packs are supplied in all First Aid Boxes and must also be taken on field trips. Guidelines and packs are available from the University Safety Officer, Bedford House.	**Admission of students**	• Disclosure of HIV status is not required from applicants for admission as students, and if volunteered, such information will be disregarded for admissions purposes.
		Advice of the General Medical and Dental Councils	• Within the Medical Faculty the staff and students of Medicine, Dentistry and Nursing should take careful note of the advice from the General Medical and Dental Councils, and must ensure that they adhere to such advice rigorously.	**Agencies for referral**	• Any member of the University who is worried about his/her HIV status is encouraged to seek assistance within the University, by consulting the Occupational Health Service or Student Health Service as appropriate, where they will be treated in strictest confidence. The University's Health Services may refer individuals to outside agencies for further assistance and support as necessary. A list of such agencies is given at Appendix III for any members who may wish to use them for themselves or for someone else.
Overseas travel	• The prevalence of HIV is higher in some areas of the world than others and travellers are advised to seek advice from the University's Occupational Health Service, Student Health Service or the Tropical School clinic. Travellers packs' of sterile syringes and needles may also be obtained and may be useful. Some countries have imposed restrictions on foreign visitors who are HIV positive. Advice to intending travellers is contained in booklets published by the DHSS.	**Needlestick**	• If anyone is stabbed or scratched by a discarded needle or anything suspected of being contaminated with blood, the offending item should be retained (handle with care) for testing. The risk of HIV infection by this route is low; a bigger risk is hepatitis B, for which the vaccine can be given if necessary. Anyone stabbed or scratched in this way should contact Student Health or Occupational Health for advice, or out of hours, the Medical Micro-biology Department in the Royal Liverpool University Hospital which has a 24 hour call-out system 051—706 - 4412 during office hours, 051—706 - 2000 outside office hours.	**Financial arrangements**	• It is in the best interests of any employee who may have a terminal illness to seek professional financial advice as to their best course of action. The Assistant Director of Finance (Superannuation) can be consulted in confidence.
				Medical staff and students	• Medical, Dental and Nursing staff have a moral obligation, if they know or suspect that they are HIV positive, to take expert advice, including how they may need to limit their activities. Professional bodies have issued guidance on this. Clinical students should also be aware of this and should also take expert advice, in confidence, if they suspect they are HIV positive.

Appendix 7

Other Sources of Helpful Information

Health Education Authority
Health Promotion Information Centre
Hamilton House
Mabledon Place
London WC1H 9TX
Tel: 071 413 1994/1995

Health at Work Business Unit
Christchurch College
Canterbury
Kent CT1 1QU
Tel: 0227 455564

Department of Heath
Wellington House
133–135 Waterloo Road
London SE1 1UG
Tel: 071 972 2000

Department of Employment
Caxton House
Tothill Street
London SW1H 9NE
Tel: 071 273 3000

Advisory, Conciliatory and Arbitration Service (ACAS)
Clifton House
83–117 Euston Road
London NW1 2RB
Tel: 071 388 5100

Health and Safety Executive
Library and Information Services
Baynards House
1 Chepstow Place
Westbourne Grove
London W2 4TY

Health and Safety Executive
Library and Information Services
Broad Lane
Sheffield S3 7HQ

British Heart Foundation
14 Fitzhardinge Street
London W1H 4DH
Tel: 071 935 0185

Institute of Occupational Safety and Health
222 Uppingham Road
Leicester LE5 0QG
Tel: 0533 768424

Institute of Personnel Management
IPM House
35 Camp Road
Wimbledon
London SW19
Tel: 081 946 9100

Trades Union Congress
Congress House
Great Russell Street
London WC1B 3LS
Tel: 071 636 4030

QUIT
102 Gloucester Place
London W1H 3DA
Tel: 071 487 3000

ASH
109 Gloucester Place
London W1H 3PH
Tel: 071 935 3519

CPG (Coronary Prevention Group)
102 Gloucester Place
London W1H 3DA
Tel: 071 935 2889

Faculty of Occupational Medicine
6 St Andrews Place
London NW1 4LE
Tel: 071 487 3414

Index

absence 6, 8, 55, 138, 185, 190–91, 206– 8, 211, 222, 241
absenteeism 1, 3, 5, 7–8, 11, 15–17, 19– 20, 56–7, 73, 98, 169, 186, 192, 195, 197, 208–9, 222, 243
accident(s)(al) 5, 15, 29–31, 37, 45, 49, 51, 53, 57, 76, 78–9, 87, 114, 129, 133–4, 136, 144, 151, 162, 169, 183, 192, 212, 222, 236, 243–4
action 243
action list 177
active 46, 198
active pursuits 14
activity(ies) 35–6, 49, 88, 115, 155, 184
advocacy 27
aerobic capacity 120, 123–4, 222, 229
aerobic fitness 36, 226
aerobic power 22
aerobic(s) 46, 59, 226, 228
aggression 162, 184
aggressive 163–4
Aids/HIV 29, 64, 107, 109, 134–7, 190, 193, 204–5, 207, 213, 222, 236
air traffic controllers 6
air-conditioned 96–7
airline pilots 6
alcohol 4–6, 22, 32–3, 43, 47–8, 51, 62, 93, 107, 116, 122, 129, 132, 153, 161– 2, 173, 189–90, 194, 205, 210, 213, 215, 217, 222, 236, 244
alcohol consumption 51, 151–2, 222, 236
alcohol misuse 8
alcohol policy 129–34, 222, 236
alcoholism 20, 29–30, 107

Allied Dunbar 29, 34, 36–7, 110
alternative(s) 178, 182
ambitious 168
ambulance 14–15, 20, 127, 135, 148, 182
American College of Sports Medicine 124, 126
angina 36, 152
anxiety 53, 93, 115, 128, 140–41, 183–5
anxious 161, 185
arousal 157
arteriosclerosis 115
arthritis 25
Arthur Anderson 7
asbestos 109
assumptions 168
asthma 31–2, 39, 42, 64, 71, 97, 109, 240
asthmatics 24, 94
attention deficit disorder 239
attitude 167, 214
audiometry 102, 221
audit 67, 83, 86–7, 90, 94
Audit Commission 1
autogenic training 174
autonomy 164

back 47, 59–60, 62–3, 79, 90, 125, 127, 142, 148, 194, 207, 237
back injuries 20
back pain 15, 17, 56, 80, 144–8, 150, 235, 237
back problems 4, 45, 107, 211–12
backache 11
behaviour(al) 146, 161–2, 164, 180–81, 190, 197–8, 214
beliefs 167

bending 45
bias 57
biodegradable 68
blood 134–6, 240
blood pressure 34, 39–40, 46, 49–51, 64, 76,
    111–12, 115–16, 121–3, 126, 152, 162, 165,
    169, 188, 211, 222–3
blood test 221
body fat 22, 36
body mass index (BMI) 50, 118, 122, 154
body mass 154, 222
body size 40
body weight 37
bonuses 7
British Heart Foundation 10, 201
British Rail 222
British Telecom PLC 223
building sickness score 96
BUPA 189
burn-out 163
bus conductors 5

Camden 1, 7, 100
Canada Life 19
cancer(s) 29–32, 51–3, 64, 71, 75, 91–2, 107–9,
    114, 116, 129, 162, 188, 207, 236, 241
canteen 44
car exhaust 95
cardiac rehabilitation 12, 128
cardiovascular 123, 126, 152, 161
cardiovascular disease(s) 29, 93
carpal tunnel syndrome 138–9, 143
case study(ies) 205
CHD 114–18, 129, 207, 213–14
chemical 133
Cheshire County Coucil 221
cholesterol 24, 34, 46, 49–50, 64, 108, 112–16,
    120–23, 188, 195, 197–8, 209–10, 221, 224
cholesterol screening 195
chronic fatigue syndrome 9, 240
churches 25
circadian rhythms 93–4
circulatory disease(s) 33, 42
Civil Service 2
coal miners 2
commitment 191–2, 196, 200, 229
communication 38, 76, 149, 170–71, 173, 178,
    186, 216, 242
community 25–6, 53
community support 23
company 11
compensation 10

compliance 12, 77–8, 94, 195, 238
computer 142
computer screens 142–3
Confederation for British Industry(ies)(CBI)
    1, 189–90, 203
confidence 178
confidentiality 183
construction 2, 6, 36–8, 61, 148
consultancy 203
consultation 192
contaminants 71
control 164, 180
coping 158, 164, 172, 186, 222
coronary artery disease 11
coronary risk 109
corporate cup 238
corporate image 17
corporate philosophy 26
corrosive 70
COSHH 71
cost effectiveness 10–11, 227
cost reduction 197
cost-beneft 13
counselling 131, 135, 140, 155, 172–3, 183,
    185–9, 193, 195, 197, 203, 205–7, 211, 217,
    221–2, 224
culture 12, 23, 36, 56, 67, 84, 171, 224, 229,
    243

dead time 12
deadline(s) 182
death 159
defensive driving 151, 190
delegate 177, 182
demography(ic) 12, 23
depression 4, 40, 53, 91, 93, 114, 146, 161,
    183–4
design 88
diabetes 64, 108, 112, 117, 152–3, 162, 210,
    239–40
diet 12, 33, 40, 47, 50, 107, 115–16, 118, 155,
    183, 221–2
diet counselling 194
disability 21, 23
disadvantaged groups 23
discomfort 88
display panel 106
diurnal rhythms 153
divorce 4, 41
Dow Chemical Company 76–7
drainers 167

drinking 5, 110, 130–31, 204, 215, 218, 220, 238, 244
driver stress 151
driving 133, 150–51
driving aggression 151
drug abuse 29, 107, 129, 136
drug dependence 9, 25
drug(s) 4, 39, 53, 62, 64, 109, 115, 132–4, 140, 143, 152, 162, 189–90, 210, 223, 239–40
Du Pont 77
dust 45, 70, 84

EC 166, 206
economic climate 9
economic development 20, 25
economic implications 106
economic regeneration 13
education 25, 67, 97, 150
elderly 42
electrocardiogram 111
electromagnetic fields (EMFs) 91–2
emissions 68–9
emotional 25, 40, 94, 161, 240
employment 2
endurance 123, 125
energy 155–6, 158, 199, 228
environment(s) 4, 15, 24–6, 29, 45, 67–9, 78, 86–7, 95–6, 98, 102, 134, 141, 146, 148–50, 155, 158, 160, 163–4, 174, 178, 186, 210, 215, 243
environmental 45, 68, 70, 75, 90, 95, 97, 101, 106, 108–9, 157, 170, 204, 206, 240
epilepsy 152–3, 239–40
equal opportunities 27
equity 243
ergometer 27
ergonomic(s) 86–7, 89–90, 100, 140–42, 144–5, 149–50
error(s) 19, 88
ethical decisions 11
ethinic 13
Europe 3, 11
evaluation 195, 199, 218, 242
executive 11, 189
exercise equipment 227
exercise facility 12, 202, 217, 227
exercise prescription 12, 128
exercise(s) 12, 13, 19, 24, 33, 35–7, 43, 46–7, 59–60, 63–4, 66, 110, 113, 115, 117, 122, 125, 128, 142, 149, 155, 172–4, 183–4, 190, 193–4, 201–2, 206, 220–23, 225–30, 235, 237, 244

exhaustion 158, 164–5, 169
exposure 70–71, 86, 92
eye strain 45

facility(ies) 198, 201–2, 225–6, 228–9
fairness in trading 26
familial hypercholesterolaemia 115
fat(s) 33–4, 37, 40, 50, 113–14, 118–19, 121–2, 125, 154–5, 197, 210, 216, 218, 220, 222, 244
fatigue 19, 93, 150–51, 153
fatty acids 50
fear(s) 181
FHSA 101
fibre 24, 40, 118, 155, 210, 213, 218, 220
fight or flight 184
financial status 14
fire 20, 44, 77–8, 106, 127, 182, 221
firemen 1
first aid 44, 77, 98–9
fishermen 5
fitness 12, 18–22, 34, 36–7, 56, 59–60, 62–3, 79, 98, 106–7, 110–11, 120–27, 149, 151–2, 193, 195, 197–8, 203, 207, 213, 220–21, 223, 225, 227, 238, 241, 246
fitness centre 225–8
fitness promotion 13
fitness screening 217
flexibility 22, 34, 125, 229, 231–2
food 3
Futrex 123

gardening 46
general household survey 30
general practitioner 33
geriatric care 21
glare 83
Glaxo Pharmaceuticals UK Ltd 114–15, 220–21
goals 176, 198, 200
government xii

hand-arm vibration syndrome (HAVS) 143
hazard(s) 78, 100–2, 106, 170, 185
hazardous substances 70, 72
headache 96
health 13
health and fitness 18, 20, 46–7, 56, 64, 111, 202, 206, 223
health and lifestyle 65
health and safety 6, 44–5, 55, 60, 78–9, 98, 100, 102, 129, 136–7, 144, 189–90, 201, 203–5, 207, 210–11, 236

health audit 55–7, 59, 66, 72
health authority 27, 206, 214, 216, 218–19
health behaviour 12
health benefits 35, 37
health care 11, 23
health checks 188–9
health education 120, 209, 223, 246
health insurance 105
health intervention 11
health options 120
health policy 112
health promotion 12, 18, 20, 24–6, 57, 61, 63,
    65–6, 98–9, 107, 110, 112, 189, 191–2,
    194–6, 200–6, 208, 213–14, 222–4, 235,
    241, 243
health screening 105–7, 109–10, 112, 193,
    209, 217
health service 3, 6, 18–19, 21, 26–7
health status 17, 110
Health and Safety Commission 38
Health and Safety Executive (HSE) 49, 77,
    79–80, 82–3, 87, 97, 104, 137–8, 144, 148,
    190, 201, 203, 251
Health Education Authority (HEA) 20,
    129–31, 136–7, 157, 170, 189, 193, 201,
    213–15, 218–19, 223–4, 235
Health of the Nation 48, 50, 235–6, 244
Health Promotion Research Trust 29, 37,
    145, 151
healthy eating 156
hearing 85, 102–3, 106–7, 111, 185
hearing protection 85
hearing tests 108, 185
heart attack 10, 115, 117, 121
heart disease(s) 4, 9–10, 16, 20, 30–32, 34–5,
    38, 49, 53, 112–13, 117, 121–2, 128, 141,
    152, 162–4, 186
heart rate 124–6, 197, 228
Heartbeat Award 218, 224
heat 91
heating 95, 226
heavy engineering 2
hepatitis B 135
hoists 148
holiday 165–6, 177
housewives 10
housework 46
humidity 84, 91, 97
hygiene 84
hypertension 4, 129, 165
hypnotherapy 75

ICL 224
illness 159
illumination 84, 91
imbalance 157, 185
incentives 3
Industrial Society 2, 7–8, 60, 130, 133, 136
industry 25
inequity 23
injury(ies) 4–5, 15, 17, 19, 22, 24, 33, 37, 45,
    76, 78–9, 87–8, 98, 100, 142, 144–5, 148,
    151, 159, 226, 228, 235, 241
Institute of Personnel Management (IPM)
    190
insurance 10, 18, 148
insurance premiums 22
intensity 89, 171
interaction 187
internal focus 167
irrational beliefs 167, 168

Japanese 7–8, 61, 171
joints 229

keep-fit 43
Kelloggs 71–2, 74, 188–90

landfill 68–9
large companies 3
legislation 24
lesiure 14, 24–5, 163, 175
Lever Brothers 68
life events 41, 159
life expectancy 243
lifestyle 18, 20–23, 37, 56, 58–62, 109–10,
    120, 150, 164–6, 169, 176, 188, 195–6, 199,
    206–9, 223, 229
lifting 44, 80, 149, 206, 211–12
lifting aids 148
lighting 45, 67, 77, 79–80, 84, 87, 93, 96, 164
litigation 139
liver cirrhosis 5–6
Liverpool 100
Liverpool City Council 222
local authority(ies) 214, 216, 221, 235
local community 23, 26–7
local council 25
local economy 27
London and Manchester Group 74
Look After Your Heart Workplace Project
    213–15, 219–20, 224
Look After Your Heart (LAYH) 48, 157,
    213–15, 224

lung function 123

maintenance 224, 227
management 159–60, 170–72, 178–9, 181–5,
   187, 192–3, 196–8, 201, 203, 207, 209, 211,
   214–15, 217, 219, 223, 236, 239
managers 189, 208, 210, 217, 222, 240
manual 8, 57, 79, 140, 175
manual handling 79, 89, 144–3, 147–9, 190,
   206, 212, 222, 236, 241, 251
manual workers 33, 38–9, 55, 186
manufacturing 130, 141
medical insurance 66
meditation 174–5
memory 134
mental disorders 33
mental health 41
mental tasks 26
mental(ly) 40–42, 52, 161, 133, 146, 158, 162,
   236
milk 47
mission statement 169, 192
mobility 22, 150
monitoring 218
mood 16
moral 169
morale 17
mortality 38–9, 42, 54, 92, 93, 108, 129
motivation 17, 76, 164, 193–5, 199, 228,
   237–8
muscle function 139
muscle(s) 158, 174, 228–9, 232, 237, 240
muscular strength 22
musculature 163
musculo-skeletal 33, 185, 241
myalgic encephalomyelitis (ME) 9, 39, 240
myocardial infarction 128, 152

narcolepsy 239
national health service (NHS) 10, 73, 112,
   236, 241
needs assessment 193
Netherlands 3
neurotic disorders 8
noise 44–5, 85–6, 91, 100, 102–3, 164, 174
nuclear family 166
nurses 144, 147, 185, 209, 212
nutrition(-ous) 33, 47, 60, 62, 64, 122, 154,
   193–4, 197, 206, 209, 216

obese 36, 40, 50, 117, 153, 155, 237
obesity 29, 39, 51, 66, 107, 113, 116–17, 154

observational audit 67
obsessive compulsion disorder (OCD) 239
occupational health 62–3, 66–7, 97–8, 100,
   102, 112, 131, 137, 144, 155–7, 189–90,
   192, 202–4, 206–8, 211, 214, 216–17,
   219–20, 222–4, 241
occupational hygiene 72
office 229
officers 5
OSI screentest 164
overweight 40
oxygen consumption 123, 124

pain 139–40
passive smoking 48, 56, 72, 74, 208
peer group 183, 242
performance 19
personal action 24
personal choice 24
personality(ies) 133, 141, 143, 145, 162–3,
   166, 172, 178
philosophical 169
physical 161–2, 184, 197, 199
physical activity 22, 34, 204, 215, 209, 217,
   220
physical training 22
physiotheraphy 98, 140, 144–5, 147, 207, 241
police 1, 2, 20, 127, 182, 214, 221–2
policy(ies) 56, 57, 73, 188, 198, 209, 214–15
pollutants 84–5, 96, 164
Post Office workers 1
posture 88, 90, 125, 140–41, 144–6, 149, 175,
   212, 229, 237, 241
power 229
praise 178
pregnancy(ies) 4, 53, 159
premature death(s) 10, 31, 35
preventable diseases 23
preventative medicine 21, 154
prevention 98, 237
primary health care 20, 236
priorities 176
private screening 110
private sector 3, 7, 216
problem drinkers 4
Proctor and Gamble 69
production 16, 21
productivity 9, 13, 15–20, 55, 94, 169
professional 204
promotion 191, 217
protection 86
protective clothing 67

protective equipment 78
psychological 89, 95, 106, 140–41, 143, 146–7, 187, 197
psychology 145
public attitude 13
public health 26, 105
public sector 11, 216
publicans 5–6, 107

quality of life 14–15, 22, 55, 243

radiators 167
recommended levels (alcohol) 33
recreation 12, 59, 65, 173, 175, 202–3, 246
recreational 13–14, 19, 55, 140–41, 155, 166, 172
recreational activities 94
recycle 60, 210
redundancy 9
reflective time 177
rehabilitation 98, 111, 127, 186, 240
relationship(s) 160, 166, 173, 179–80, 195
relaxation 150, 172–4, 184–6, 194, 206, 226, 228, 230–31, 233–4, 237
repetitive strain injury (RSI) 88–9, 102, 104, 138, 141, 143–4
resources 200, 219, 243
respiratory problems 43
responsible(-ility) 178, 183
rest 88, 140
retirement 10–11, 169, 187, 207
risk(s) 89, 91, 107, 113, 115–17, 120–22, 128, 141, 149, 196, 198, 200–1, 217, 224

Safacare 98, 100
safety 26, 37, 45, 67, 75–7, 90, 99, 107, 150, 204, 207, 228, 243
safety officers 44
salt 116, 128
screening 61, 111–12, 120, 132, 135, 188–9, 206–7, 210, 212, 216, 224, 241–2
self-certification 1, 4
self-confidence 181
self-image 16
self-perceived fitness 45
Self-reported Health 39
self-respect 178
Selye, Hans 158
sensible limit (alcohol) 32–3
Shell Oil UK 75–6, 97, 188
shiftwork 93, 110, 164
ship's officers 6

sick building syndrome 80, 95–7
sickness 1, 7, 30, 55–7, 73, 138, 192, 195, 206–7, 209, 211, 241
skin 71
sleep apnoea 153
sleep(ing) 39, 133, 161, 173–4, 240
small companies 3
smoking 12, 21–2, 32–3, 40, 42–3, 48–50, 52, 59–60, 62, 64, 66, 72–3, 109–10, 112, 116, 121–2, 161, 200, 208, 210, 213–15, 217–19, 221–3, 236, 238, 244
smoking cessation 12, 75, 191, 193–4, 211
smoking policy 3, 73–4, 189, 204, 217–19, 236
social factors 187, 243
social pressures 42
social pursuits 180
social responsibility 24
social support 25, 179
socialization 16
socio-economic 41
sodium 51
solvents 70
special events 238
spiritual beliefs 169, 175
sport(s) 36, 43, 47, 59–61, 65, 155, 173, 202, 228, 246
sporting 61, 194, 237
stereo systems 152
stimulation 159–60
strength 19, 36–7, 79, 87, 122–3, 125, 127, 141, 150, 220, 226, 228, 232
strengthen 150
stress 4, 15, 17, 23, 26, 41, 45–7, 60, 62, 64, 88, 90, 100, 103, 107, 110, 112, 117, 122, 141, 145–7, 151–3, 157–60, 162, 164–6, 168, 170–72, 175–6, 178–88, 190, 194, 197, 201, 204–5, 207, 211, 215, 217, 219–24, 229, 239, 244
stress reduction 180
stress-related 15
stretch(ing) 141–2, 184, 230
strikes 5, 112
stroke(s) 31, 34, 36, 49, 116, 213
students 10
substances 101
suicide(s) 29–31, 49, 52–3, 91, 114, 136
support 24–5
survey(s) 78, 193
symptoms 160

target(s) 8, 243
task 88

team building 180
teamwork 17, 179
teenagers 32
telephone operators 187
temperature 77, 84, 95–6
tension 158, 174, 232
Tesco 148, 238
testing 193, 207
time 162–3, 172–3, 177, 184
time management 176
tinnitus 185
tobacco 22
Tourette's syndrome 239
tourism 13
trade unions 44, 48, 56, 58, 66, 98, 101–2,
    104, 131–2, 144, 192, 196
training 20, 26–7, 76, 78, 87, 97, 117, 124–5,
    127, 131–3, 142, 144–5, 148–51, 160,
    170–72, 180, 182–3, 190–92, 194–5, 197, 204,
    206–7, 210–12, 214, 219, 222–3, 228, 238
tranquillizers 133
treatment 106, 132, 144
triglycerides 114, 123
twisting 141
type A behaviour 162–4, 172
type B behaviour 162

UK 18, 20–21, 34, 60, 66, 71, 75, 129–30,
    133, 136, 154, 171, 239
UK companies 8, 118
UML Ltd 115
unemployment 26, 164
United Biscuits (UK) Ltd 28, 120

university department(s) 228
University of Liverpool 80, 104, 128, 134,
    136, 180, 241, 251
Urenco (Capenhurst) Limited 221
USA 18, 21, 95, 166, 171, 186, 196, 229

VDU(s) 80, 142, 190, 195
ventilation 67, 71, 77, 84–5, 95–7, 226, 240
vision 83–4, 107–8, 188
vision screening 221

waist to hips ratio 118
weight 40, 59–60, 62, 64, 67, 188, 194, 221
weight control 154, 229
weight reduction 155
weight training 228
well-being 196
wellness 17, 20, 196–200
Wellsource 125–6
Wirral Metropolitan College 223
work capacity 18
work-related upper-limb disorders
    (WRULD) 88–9, 138–43
workaholic(s) 162, 171, 185
worker satisfaction 18
working life lost 31
workstation 88, 90, 141, 149
World Health Organization 48, 92

Xerox 17

yuppie flu 9, 240